1981

BENJAMIN TOMPSON
Colonial Bard

BENJAMIN TOMPSON

Colonial Bard

A Critical Edition

Peter White

The Pennsylvania State University Press

University Park and London

Publication of this book has been assisted by a grant
from the National Endowment for the Humanities.

CENTER FOR
SCHOLARLY EDITIONS
AN APPROVED EDITION
MODERN LANGUAGE
ASSOCIATION OF AMERICA

Library of Congress Cataloging in Publication Data
Tompson, Benjamin, 1642–1714
    Benjamin Tompson, colonial bard.
    Includes bibliography and index.
    I. White, Peter, 1947– II. Title.
PS850.T45A6 1979   811′.1   79-21367
ISBN 0-271-00250-6

For my mother and father

Contents

Preface

The appearance of a critical edition of Benjamin Tompson's poetry approximately three hundred years after the publication of his most recognized work, *New Englands Crisis*, is more than mere chronological coincidence. Over the last twenty years, the growth of colonial American literary studies has been, if not a flowering, at least a progression toward full maturity. Original, energetic, and meticulous scholarship across the country has given Puritan cultural studies the respectability I think it deserves through more careful editorial, textual, bibliographical, and critical work. From the very beginning of this project it seemed that an edition of Tompson's poetry could measurably assist both students and scholars in their efforts to think and write perceptively about the American experience and the Puritan mind. In fact, it seemed incredible to me that while the pioneers in our field regularly included Tompson in their anthologies, or made reference to him in their intellectual histories, no one had attempted to replace Howard Judson Hall's collection with a text employing more modern editorial methods and standards, even in light of the increasing demand for more and better classroom material.

The exciting thing about Tompson's poetry is that it not only meets the growing demand but pays the reader extra dividends: here are poems enough to substantiate further that not all Puritans were sober, rigid, mean-spirited, and narrow-minded sectarians. We can argue more convincingly that the Puritans, like people in any age, could laugh at themselves, could extend heartfelt compassion and affection for one another, could fear that God had abandoned them in time of war, and that they could find the means to construct an entire mythological framework in an effort to understand and shape their past creatively. We discover as well from reading Tompson that, besides the "Day of Doom," Puritans admired, read, and used the ideas of Augustine, Origen, Basil, Jerome, and Ambrose, the "pagan" writers, Homer and Virgil, and that long before Emerson they considered natural facts signs of spiritual truths.

My hope is that this edition belatedly bestows upon William Tompson, an insanely zealous minister victimized by the pressures of the wilderness, and Benjamin Tompson, the discouraged schoolteacher turned spokesman for his colony, some of the recognition they so earnestly sought. In their lives and work, we have a microcosmic model of American frontier, intellectual, and artistic life. In the career of the father we see the archetypally tragic encounter between European intellectualism and the satanic forces of the American forests. Massachusetts Bay becomes a Heart of Darkness for William Tompson. The son, in turn orphaned, adopted, and educated, rejected a ministerial commitment to alternately mock and mourn the breakdown of The Dream, while he simultaneously sought preferment from aristocratic Bostonians like Increase Mather, or more powerful Englishmen like Sir Edmund Andros. Ultimately the son comes dangerously close to despair himself; the life of the artist in America is a bubble, a flash, a blaze, a rush, and a trap. His own success and that of his family are paradoxically the source of his pride and the origin of his discontent.

I would like to thank the librarians and curators who made Tompson's poetry available to me: John D. Cushing of The Massachusetts Historical Society; Irene Norton of The Essex Institute; Marte Shaw and Michael Winship of The Houghton Library; H. Hobart Holly of The Quincy Historical Society; Carey S. Bliss and Daniel H. Woodward of The Henry E. Huntington Library; Samuel Hough and Thomas R. Adams of The John Carter Brown Library; Ruth M. Blair of The Connecticut Historical Society; Christina M. Hanson of Yale University Library; Robert St. George of The Museum of Fine Arts, Boston; Cynthia English of The Boston Atheneaum; and the staff of the manuscripts division of the New York Public Library and the Boston Public Library.

I also wish to thank Professor Ives Goddard of Harvard for supplying me with information about American Indian Pidgin English; Ralph Newel Thompson for his family genealogy and history; Joseph McCarthy of The Pennsylvania State University and Columbia University and Warren Smith of the University of New Mexico for their translations of the Latin and Greek portions of this edition; and Ilene Glenn and Penelope Katson for conscientious and efficient typing.

As I began assembling, editing, and annotating Tompson's poetry, I soon realized that aspects of the project would require experience and critical perspectives beyond my own. I wish, therefore, to thank these individuals, who through the example of their own research or through critical reading of the manuscript have guided, corrected, or encouraged my work: C. Conrad Cherry of the Department of Religious Studies at The Pennsylvania State University; Roy Harvey Pearce of the University of California, San Diego; and Brom Weber of the University of California, Davis. Norman Grabo of Texas A & M University conducted an examination of this volume on behalf of the MLA Committee on Scholarly Editions. Professors Grabo and George Arms, of the University of New Mexico, were particularly helpful in their corrections or suggestions for sound editorial methodology. I am similarly indebted to other colleagues at the University of New Mexico for textual proofreading and advice: Professors Robert and Esther Fleming, Linda Dowling, Carolyn Seidel, Mary Bess Whidden, Sam Girgus, Hamlin Hill, Patricia Smith, and Leon Howard. I wish also to thank John M. Pickering and Carole Schwager of The Pennsylvania State University Press for their encouragement throughout this endeavor.

For Professor Harrison T. Meserole, under whom this edition was originally written, I have a professional respect and personal affection that is shared with his other students and colleagues across the country.

Since 1975 Mary Ann, my wife, has given me her intellectual, moral, and financial support; I deeply appreciate her help.

This edition was supported by two grants from the Nation Endowment for the Humanities: a summer stipend for independent research and a publications grant. The University of Mexico Research Allocations Committee also provided financial support.

CHAPTER I

William Tompson:
First-Generation American Puritan

No matter what one chooses to label the predominant form of government in seventeenth-century America—federalism, theocracy, oligarchy, democracy—it is clear that certain families achieved aristocratic status in colonial history. For their intellectual superiority and ministerial stubbornness, the Mathers were both revered and despised; for their missionary zeal and philosophical sophistication, the Mayhews were congratulated; and for their continued political, military, and scientific successes, the Winthrops were practically adored.[1] Generation after generation these families rose to the top of their small, but expanding, colonial world. Historical societies and local antiquarians, sometimes motivated by family pride and New England patriotism, have devoted years to the gathering of their papers, letters, legal documents, commonplace books, and diaries, examining even the most insignificant matters.[2] But on a plane just below the aristocratic actions of these early American Brahmins, there is yet an unexplored world of exciting social and literary accomplishment. Along with the excitement of such discoveries, there is a touch of tragedy—the pathos of unrealized hopes. The wilderness, or the frontier, does not always function as the grand equalizer: rather, it provides an environment in which some may excel and others may be brutally beaten. Some families, like the family of William Tompson, spent a great deal of time battling insanity, war, epidemical waste, and constant unemployment. Under these circumstances it is a wonder that they produced anything at all.

None of the leaders of the Pilgrim and Puritan exodus ever claimed that establishing a Holy Commonwealth would be easy. We have given the Bradfords, Winthrops, Cottons, and Mathers so much attention because they fully articulated the tragic and majestic potentiality of their experiment in the New World. Moreover, their delineations of the condition for survival have given the modern historian a framework for understanding and evaluating the response of the rank and file. One of William Bradford's major purposes in "Of Plimouth Plantation" was to explain to

1

future generations, in concrete yet moving simplicity, the trials that faced the common man:

> But here I cannot but stay and make a pause, and stand half amazed at this poor people's present condition; and so I think will the reader, too, when he well considers the same. Being thus passed the vast ocean, and a sea of troubles before in their preparation (as may be remembered by that which went before), they had now no friends to welcome them nor inns to entertain or refresh their weatherbeaten bodies; no houses or much less towns to repair to, to seek for succour.
>
> What could now sustain them but the Spirit of God and His grace? May not and ought not the children of these fathers rightly say: "Our fathers were Englishmen which came over this great ocean, and were ready to perish in this wilderness; but they cried unto the Lord, and He heard their voice and looked on their adversity," etc.[3]

Against overwhelming odds, "soul-amazing" difficulties, the Pilgrims embarked on their desperate journey. Call it what we will—a reluctant voyage, an exile, an errand, a forced Separatism—it was nevertheless a movement from home to a strange and possibly alien land.

By 1630 when John Winthrop, the American Moses, led his people into Massachusetts Bay, the Puritan folk had developed a more complex image of their mission in history and their place in the New World. Perry Miller argues in "Errand Into The Wilderness" that Winthrop's covenanted generation "could see in the pattern of history that their errand was not a mere scouting expedition: it was an essential maneuver in the drama of Christendom . . . ; the puritans were performing a job not so much for Jehovah as for history."[4] If Bradford's "Of Plimouth Plantation" represents the prologue to this drama, then Winthrop's "A Modell of Christian Charity" stands as its first heroic monologue:

> . . . wee shall finde that the God of Israell is among us, when tenn of us shall be able to resist a thousand of our enemies, when hee shall make us a prayse and glory, that men shall say of succeeding plantacions: the lord make it like that of New England: for wee must Consider that wee shall be as a Citty upon a Hill, the eies of all people are uppon us; so that if wee shall deal falsely with our god in this worke wee have undertaken and soe cause him to withdrawe his present help from us, wee shall be made a story and a by-word through the world, wee shall open the mouthes of enemies to speake evill of the wayes of god and all professours for Gods sake; we shall shame the faces of many of gods wourthy servants, and cause theire prayers to be turned into Cursses upon us till wee be consumed out of the good land whether wee are goeing: . . .[5]

Aboard the flagship *Arabella*, Winthrop spelled out for his people the glories of success and the hazards of failure: he was, in effect, daring them to control their own destinies. The stakes were high, Winthrop said, and if they lost, they lost everything. Unlike the Pilgrims, the Puritans were not leaping into the void, but they were purposefully stepping into the spotlight where the eyes of God were on every actor in this serious play. That common men would even entertain such a large gamble is convincing evidence of their heroic temperament.

C. Conrad Cherry has argued that the founders of the Holy Commonwealth were inclined to ascribe a variety of motives to their actions.[6] As they looked at their position in time and their stake in American space, they discovered a tension between the promise of God's Plantation and the threat of the demonic wilderness, as well as a tension between New England's distinctive (elect) status and God's larger plan of salvation. Many of the clerical leaders of the first generation claimed ambiguity of place as a religious asset; it allowed them to use a symbolic and typological approach to history and to see a multiplicity of reasons for removing to the New Israel. The founders, therefore, developed a shifting but analytical perception of the possible consequences of their holy experiment, "prayse and glory" or "Cursses and shame." The uncertainty and the apparent anxiety reflected in their formal and informal statements do not reveal a failure of nerve; they are, rather, candid acknowledgments of the possible dangers and rewards.

As one of the more enthusiastic Puritans of the first generation, William Tompson must have experienced the full force of the tension between promise and threat. In 1636 when he left Winwick Parish in his native Lancashire, he struck out for Agamenticus (York), Maine, one of the most forbidding and desolate areas in New England.[7] Tompson, who had graduated as Nowell Scholar from Brasenose College, Oxford, on 28 February 1621/22,[8] could only have been appalled by the primitive condition of the people, both native and European, in this Christian outpost. We have no record of Tompson's private thoughts as he carried his wife and three young children across the ocean and through the wilderness to Maine, but we can assume the trials of their life were extreme. At least one public account verifies this. *New England's First Fruits*, written just six years after Tompson's emigration, describes, in the typical imagery of light and dark, the transition from forest to Plantation effected by Tompson and other missionaries:

> Let us here give a touch also of what God hath done and is further about to doe, to divers Plantations of the English, which before that time that God sent light into our coasts, were almost as darke and rude as the Indians themselves.
> 1. First at *Agamenticus* (a Plantation out of our jurisdiction) to which one of our Preachers [Tompson] comming and labouring amongst them, was a meanes under God, not only to sparkle heavenly knowledge, and worke conviction and reformation in divers of them, but conversion also to Christ in some of them, that blesse God to this day, that ever he came thither.[9]

In the fourth volume of the *Winthrop Papers*, collected and edited by the Massachusetts Historical Society, there appears one of the most interesting letters in colonial American correspondence. Dated May 1638, this rather lengthy letter from William Tompson to "the noble governor of Metachasets Baye Mr. John Winthroppe" concerns Tompson's present condition and his hopes for the future of New England.[10] By 1638 Tompson was clearly dissatisfied with what he called the lack of "church discipline" at Agamenticus and with his own spiritual progress. Apparently, Governor Winthrop had written a testimonial letter to the people of New England, recommending that Tompson be allowed to carry the word of God into the wilderness. Tompson worried that Winthrop's "conceites were stronge of mee, that carried you to wryte so farre in the behalf of a poore ignorante, stonieharted, faithlesse almost, fruitlesse creature, unfitte for anie thinge almost, especially unfitte for so great a busienesse as to carrie Chrysts name, to a sorte of poore creatures, that have a longe tyme sette in darkenesse and in the region and shaddowe of death: yet if you have sayd anie thinge of mee, I hope you neede not bee ashamed: . . ."[11]

Although the self-deprecation of these statements reflects conventionalized modesty and the typical respect shown to the Governor, later admissions are more forthright appeals for financial, political, and spiritual favors. Tompson asks Winthrop to confer with Mr. Mavericke about property rights and discipline, for as Tompson says,

> I came not out of England, for love of discipline, that I mighte live in churches, rightly gathered and instituted; to live out of the churches: or to live longe where their must not bee church discipline: Though I love Accomenticus dearely, and hope well of divers of them, and I perceive god is goinge on, yet I will not staye amongst them, without wee maye have libertie to all gods ordinances: . . .[12]

Having summoned all his courage to make several requests of the Governor and, in fact, threatening to leave if not assisted, Tompson next presents one of the clearest and most concise typological explanations of the Congregational errand into the wilderness:

> Though wee bee lyke the men of Gilead, on the other syde Jordan, yet wee will either have a patterne of your altars, and your churches, or truly wee will god willinge come over Jordan againe: for your god shall bee our god, and your meanes and manner of worshippe will wee use. it is not twentie leagues of by water shall hinder us god willinge, from you: oh blesse god for his goodnesse to you, rejoyce in your priviliges. oh what people lyke unto you, to whom the lord is so neere, that hath such blessed conduite pypes? ordinances? wee mourne for our absence from the house of god: Though as Nehemiah about the buildinge of the wall: wee about buildinge god a house, wee though poore brethern. . . .[13]

William Tompson's communication to the Governor contains that ambiguous combination of anxiety and bravado, of uncertainty and determination—the tension between promise and threat so frequently displayed by first-generation Puritan leaders. Tompson concludes by asking the Governor to remember him to the Reverend Mr. Cotton, "though of little acq[uaintance] and I confesse my faulte, that I asked not his iudgment, and tooke no more solomne leave when I wente to Acc[omenticus]. . . ."[14] In the spring, one year later, Tompson abandoned the outpost at Agamenticus for another unsettled area, this time south of Boston.

On 24 September 1639, three years after he arrived in Agamenticus, William Tompson was installed at the First Church of Braintree, now Quincy, Massachusetts.[15] He must have known that Braintree had been the nesting grounds for two of the most troublesome groups in New England's early history. First, Thomas Morton, who always signed himself "of Clifford's Inn, Gent.," established a settlement at Mount Wollaston, called Pasonagessit by the Indians and Merry Mount by Morton. Beginning in 1625, Morton waged psychological and social war with William Bradford's Plymouth Colony, located only a few miles to the south. Tradition has it that Morton constantly ridiculed the Pilgrims, frolicked with the Indians, traded guns and liquor to them for furs, and finally, in 1627, set up a Maypole to celebrate the traditional English folkfestival of Spring. Of course this infuriated Bradford, who immediately sent Captain Miles Standish (Morton called him Captain Shrimp) to seek out and destroy the enemy. Morton reports in the *New English Canaan* that

> Now Captain Shrimp, the first captain in the land (as he supposed) . . . takes eight persons more to him, and (like the nine Worthies of New Canaan) they embark with this preparation against Ma-re Mount, where this monster of a man (as their phrase was) had his den; the whole number (had the rest not been from home, being but seven) would have given Captain Shrimp (a quondam drummer) such a welcome as would have made him wish for a drum as big as Diogenes' tub, that he might have crept into it out of sight.[16]

Technically, the battle between Bradford's colony and Morton's was over, but Morton himself continued to plague the Pilgrims until his death in 1646.

Thomas Morton's house at Merry Mount was burned to the ground in December 1630, and its occupants were driven away.[17] But as the little village of Boston expanded into a larger New England town, the inhabitants began to consider resettling and repopulating the Mount. This time, however, measures would be taken to insure the development of a Christian community. In May 1634, the General Court ordered that

"Boston shall have convenient enlargement at Mount Wollaston."[18] William Coddington, Edmund Quincy, and, ironically, John Wilson and William Hutchinson were granted parcels of Morton's land. Two years later the General Court would meet to consider the fate of Anne Hutchinson, William Hutchinson's wife and John Wilson's greatest antagonist. It is ironic, too, that Anne Hutchinson was a legal and spiritual relative of John Wheelwright, Mount Wollaston's first minister and an outspoken Antinomian. Thomas Morton may have been banished from the Mount, but his spirit of dissent lived on.

Essentially, the Antinomian Crisis of 1636-1638 was a fierce and desperate struggle for power in the fledgling colony.[19] Anne Hutchinson, inspired by her own interpretation of the doctrine of grace, argued that the regenerate are capable of receiving direct and immediate revelations from God. Thus the justified of the New Israel owed no allegiance to the established civil or ecclesiastical authority. Those ministers, like John Wilson, who preached a Covenant of Works rather than a Covenant of Grace, were among the unregenerate and unconverted. Such an accusation, coupled with her increasing and dangerous popularity, made Anne Hutchinson a serious threat to order and stability.

Because Anne Hutchinson and her Bostonian devotees wanted to hear the Word from one of their own mind, they attempted to install the Reverend John Wheelwright as a teacher in the Boston Church. Winthrop and Wilson vigorously opposed the appointment, and even John Cotton, a minister whom the Hutchinsonians considered a model Christian, rejected the proposal. Cotton said he "could not consent . . . calling in one whose spirit they knew not, and one who seemed to dissent in judgment; . . . seeing he was apt to raise doubtful disputations. . . ."[20] Wheelwright's ordination was prevented at the First Church, but he was allowed to preach to a group of "Farmers" at Mount Wollaston.[21]

Cotton's original opinion of Wheelwright was an accurate one. On 19 January 1636/37, a fast day was appointed to bring about reconciliation in the Church of Boston. But, somewhat foolishly, Cotton allowed Wheelwright to deliver what has been described as the most incendiary and seditious sermon in New England's history. D.M. Wilson, Quincy's premier historian, says that "no other sermon ever preached on this continent has ever had such a remarkable effect. Immediately it arrayed 'legalists' in open and concerted hostility against 'antinomians,' and brought the colony to the very verge of ruin."[22] Wheelwright's harangue only served to bring about his own ruin; when the General Court met in March of that year, Wheelwright was judged guilty of "sedition" and "contempt," crimes for which, the following November, he was banished from the colony.[23] Once again, the poor "Farmers" of Mount Wollaston were left without spiritual direction.

Fortunately, the General Court and the directors of the Massachusetts Bay Company persisted in their determination to settle the Mount Wollaston outpost. Perhaps it was through the assistance or urging of John Wilson, an old friend, that William Tompson accepted the call to Mount Wollaston. Located only nine miles from Boston, the Mount offered Tompson accessibility to education, commerce, and social contact. Whatever his motives, Tompson was ordained Pastor of the First Church of Mount Wollaston on 24 September 1639.[24] D.M. Wilson conjectures that Tompson was selected for this position because he was a comparatively recent arrival in the colony and shared none of the bitterness toward the Antinomian faction harbored by other Bostonian clergy.[25] Henry Flynt was ordained teacher of the church on 13 March 1640, after he agreed to end his defense of Wheelwright.[26] The incorporation of the town of Braintree was accomplished in May 1640,[27] when the General Court acceded to the petition of the inhabitants; in effect, the government officially sanctioned the work of Tompson and Flynt.

New England's historians, especially contemporary historians like John Winthrop, made a great deal of Tompson's role in procuring social solidarity and orthodoxy for Braintree. Winthrop called Tompson a "very gracious, sincere man," a "very holy man, who had been an instrument of much good at Acomenticus. . . . "[28] Edward Johnson, in his *Wonder-Working Providence of Sion's Saviour*, recounts the actual events leading to the settlement of Braintree and concludes that the "people are purged by their industry from the soure leven of these sinful opinions that began to spread. The Reverend Mr. Tompson is a man abounding in zeal for the propagation of the Gospel, and of an ardent affection; insomuch that he is apt to forget himself in things that concern his own good."[29] Johnson goes on to memorialize Flynt and Tompson in verse: "With two fold cord doth Flint and Tompson draw / In Christ's yoke, his fallow ground to break, / Wounding men's hearts with his most righteous Law. . . . "[30]

More than most of his contemporaries, Tompson was a man fired with the missionary spirit. He seems to have dashed furiously from one assignment to another from 1642 until 1648. Although the records and details of his accomplishments are fragmentary, it is clear that he was not only willing but eager to spread the Word among his colonial brethren, the English, and the American Indians.

In 1642, according to John Winthrop, Mr. Bennet arrived from Virginia with a petition from the elders of Norfolk County, "bewailing their sad condition for the want of the means of salvation, and earnestly entreating a supply of faithful ministers, whom . . . they might call to office."[31] The elders of the Boston Church met and decided that, with the permission of the local congregations, Thomas James, John Knowles, and William Tompson would begin their mission on 7 October 1642. After a harrowing eleven-week journey down the coast, through Hellgate, and past the Dutch at Long Island, Tompson arrived to "advance the Kingdom of Christ." Winthrop says that Tompson, "being a very melancholic man and of a crazy body, he found his health so repaired, and his spirit so enlarged, etc., as he had not been in the like condition since he came to New England."[32] The Virginia Assembly and Governor Sir William Berkeley did not experience this spiritual enlargement; they promptly ordered all nonconformists to depart the colony. Before his expulsion, Tompson did manage to convert Daniel Gookin, who eventually became one of New England's foremost missionaries to the Indians. So ardent was Tompson that, after being expelled from Virginia, he and Gookin ventured into Maryland and held meetings in private homes of that Catholic colony.[33] But neither Gookin's conversion nor missionary success in Maryland proved compensation to Tompson when he discovered that his wife, Abigail, had died on 10 July 1643, and that his children were scattered throughout the Bay Colony. Tompson and Gookin returned to Boston in 1644.

One would expect such events to be followed by a period of inactivity or more sedate endeavors, yet 1644 appears to mark the beginning of Tompson's most feverish period. In collaboration with Richard Mather, Tompson's schoolmate at Brasenose College, Oxford, and former neighbor from Lancashire, he published in London *A Modest and Brotherly Answer to Mr. Charles Herle his Book, against the Independency of Churches*.[34] The Boston Town Records for 1644 indicate that Tompson and Henry Flynt were granted (perhaps as compensation for their scholarship) a "parcell of marish" and "two Hillucks of upland" in Braintree.[35] The following year Tompson and Richard Mather again collaborated on a long, consolatory address (284 pages) to their warring countrymen in Lancashire who were, as Tompson and Mather believed, engaged in open combat with forces of the Antichrist. That same year Tompson readied himself for war with homegrown Antichristian beasts, the Narragansets. According to Edward Johnson, who loved nothing better than a good Christian fight, the Commissioners "raised an Army of horse and foot out of the Colonies . . . ; the reverend Mr. Tompson, one of the elders of the Church at Braintree was to accompany them, and to preach the Word of God unto them, during this time of war. . . ."[36]

Immediately following his expedition among the Narragansets, Tompson left his second wife, Anna Crosbie, widow of Simon Crosbie of Cambridge, for another sally into Maryland. While records indicate that many were impressed with his preaching, Lord Baltimore, acting on an unofficial report, ordered colonial authorities to conduct an investigation into Tompson's character and conduct. The provincial assembly of

Maryland subsequently wrote to Lord Baltimore exonerating Tompson. Perhaps disheartened by these events, Tompson returned to Braintree in 1648, just in time to attend the final sessions of the Cambridge Synod.[37]

In the spring of 1646, when an English Presbyterian victory seemed imminent, the General Court of Massachusetts summoned representative ministers to Cambridge for their second major synod. There is some evidence that Tompson attended the first synod called in 1637 to grapple with the Antinomian heresy, but clearly, as a newcomer, he played an insignificant role.[38] By 1648, however, Tompson was a more mature and recognized clergyman, but ironically it was as the result of a completely spontaneous and instinctive reaction that Tompson assured himself a place in history. For nearly two years the Cambridge Synod had dragged on, hopelessly deadlocked over questions of infant baptism, grace, the covenant, Congregationalism, and internal strife, but in one of the final sessions held on 15 August 1648,

> It fell out, about the midst of [Mr. Allen's] sermon, there came a snake into the seat, where many of the elders sate behind the preacher. It came in at the door where people stood thick upon the stairs. Divers of the elders shifted from it, but Mr. Thomson, one of the elders of Braintree, (a man of much faith,) trode upon the head of it, and so held it with his foot and staff with a small pair of grains, until it was killed. This being so remarkable, and nothing falling out but by divine providence, it is out of doubt, the Lord discovered somewhat of his mind in it. The serpent is the devil; the synod, the representative of the churches of Christ in New England. The devil had formerly and lately attempted their disturbance and dissolution; but their faith in the seed of the woman overcame him and crushed his head. . . . So they ended in less than fourteen days.[39]

In the view of many of the Puritan folk present at the synod that day, Tompson had instinctively accomplished what the greatest minds in the colony were unable to do in two years of bitter debate. Charles Feidelson uses this incident in *Symbolism and American Literature* to demonstrate how the Puritan mind "unites the objectivity of history with the meaningfulness of Scripture. . . . The destruction of the serpent was a symbolic act, grounded in biblical speech and the heroic dreams of the New England theocracy."[40] Acting out his heroic part publicly must have been very satisfying to Tompson; little did he know, however, that his duel with the serpent would soon be staged in the private theater of his mind.

During the period 1648 to 1661, there was a rather sudden decline in Tompson's visibility and productivity. When John Wheelwright deserted his flock in Exeter, New Hampshire, in 1648, Tompson was offered thirty pounds a year, the profits of the town sawmill, and the use of Wheelwright's house and land to accept a call from that northern community.[41] Speculation leads one to believe that Tompson's religious opinions were similar to Wheelwright's, since he had been considered a suitable successor in both Massachusetts and New Hampshire. Furthermore, if Tompson was present at the Synod of 1637, he may have impressed Wheelwright's congregation by treating their pastor in a more benevolent fashion than others, such as the contentious John Wilson. In any case, Tompson refused the liberal offer from New Hampshire; possibly, he had already committed himself to missionary work among the American Indians on Cape Cod and Martha's Vineyard.

The first mention of Tompson's work among the Indians does not appear in colonial records until September 1657, but the records do indicate that he had been engaged in that service for some time.[42] That year the Missionary Corporation, otherwise known as the Society for the Propagation of the Gospel, submitted to the Massachusetts Bay Commissioners a list of their expenses and employees. While John Eliot and the Mayhew family were the most prominent members of the Corporation, Messrs. Pierson, Bourne, Blinman, Leveridge, Newman, and Tompson carried on the daily work of teaching, writing, and interpreting religious and secular material. In Connecticut, one William Tompson, Jr. (A.B. Harvard, 1653), labored among the Pequots at Mystic and Pawkatuck, but recent scholarship has called into doubt his previously supposed relationship to William Tompson, Sr.[43] In 1659 the records show William Tompson, Sr., still employed with Folger, Mayhew, and Eliot, but in 1661 diarist John Hull penned the following ominous note:

> 27th of 12th [1660/61]. It being a public fast in most churches, Mr. William Thomson, pastor of the church of Brantrey, being solicited earnestly by the people—Mr. Henry Flint, their other teaching elder, being sick—to preach, did hearken; though before this, through deep melancholy, had wholly neglected all public exercises, and, of late, family worship as to his own performance, calling himself a reprobate, yet now doth preach again: but, since this, his must be a mournful estate, constantly [half a line illegible].[44]

Tompson responded to the invitation to deliver a fast-day sermon not only because it was an honor, but because it was yet another opportunity to be of service to the church and the colony. And it was probably this opportunity which bolstered his confidence enough to enable him to continue his missionary work for three more years. In 1664, however, Robert Boyle, the President of the Missionary Society, reported to the Bay Commissioners that Tompson could no longer go on.[45] Now in the throes of what Cotton Mather called a "*Balneum diaboli*," Tompson had lost control of his mental and physical health. Moreover, the Dorchester Town Records provide evidence that Tompson was in financial trouble and in need of relief from neighboring communities.[46] He had remarried in 1647 and had one child by Anna Crosbie, his second wife, and when he became so disabled that he could not perform his ministerial office, Braintree apparently discontinued his yearly salary. If such was not the case, one wonders what Tompson did with his handsome salary of 55 pounds per year.

At such a historical distance from the seventeenth century, speculations over the cause of Tompson's insanity must be guarded and cautious. Of course, even this brief outline of his life makes it obvious that he had to come to grips with a number of crises, including the death of his wife in his absence and the dispersal of his four children. Tompson's nomadic wanderings, from Maine to Virginia and back and forth from Boston to Martha's Vineyard, could clearly have affected his physical health. Coincidentally, but perhaps significantly, William Tompson, Jr., disappeared into Virginia in 1664, the year of his father's greatest mental instability.[47]

Poets and historians of the seventeenth century, discovering a providential pattern in Tompson's life, focused on his combat with the serpent first enraged at the Cambridge Synod. Samuel Danforth, clerk of the Roxbury Court, felt that Tompson "had been held under the power of melancholy for the space of 8 years. During which time He had diverse lucid intervales, & sweet revivings...."[48] Danforth, obviously moved by Tompson's death, wrote two anagrams: "now i am past ill" and "now i am slipt home." In the first anagram Tompson describes his struggle and God's victory:

> Lo, now all evill things are past and gone,
> Terror, black Coller & strangullion;
> My pains are Curd, no greif doth me anoy,
> My sorrows are all turned into joy.
> No fiend of hell shall hence forth me asay,
> My fears are heald, my teares are wipt away....[49]

Even the contentious, stiff-necked John Wilson, one of Braintree's first landholders and an eminent Bostonian divine, wrote two anagrams on Tompson: "most holy paule mine" and "Lo my i[j]onah slumpt." Wilson compares Tompson's temptations and trials to those of Jonah, Job, Mary Magdalen ("with seven foul fiends posest"), and Paul. In Wilson's anagram Tompson says,

> So he was pleased to visit me
>   With trials more than many:
> Not onely persecutions
>   Of proud malignant foos
> But he hath let the devill loose
>   Me strongly to oppose,

11

[A]s he did paule with buffeting
[Tha]t he was black and blew,
[So th]at he was at his wits end
[And kne]w not what to do.[50]

Samuel Torrey tried to console the family by positing that Tompson's existence was a living death, and by death Tompson was "deliverd from y^t living grave. . . . But yet we cannot Chuse but sigh to se / A saint to make a Dark Catastrophe."[51] All the theological reconciliations in the world, however, are not enough to mitigate the tragic aspects of Tompson's sickness and death.

As a renowned clergyman, philosopher, historian, and member of the Royal Society, Cotton Mather felt qualified to diagnose Tompson's malady as a severe case of hellish indigestion. Indeed, Mather reckoned that

> There are many men who, in the very constitution of their *bodies*, do afford a *bed* wherein busy and bloody *devils* have a sort of lodging provided for them. The *mass of blood* in them, is disordered with some fiery *acid*, and their *brains* or *bowels* have some juices or ferments or vapours about them, which are most unhappy *engines* for *devils* to work upon their souls withal. The vitiated humours, in many persons, yield the *steams* whereinto Satan does insinuate himself, till he has gained a sort of possession in them, or at least an opportunity to shoot into the mind as many *fiery darts* as may cause a sad life unto them; yea, tis well if *self-murder* be not the sad end unto which these hurried people are thus precipitated.[52]

According to Mather, because Satan was irritated by Tompson's evangelical labors, he declared a fiendish crusade upon him, infecting both body and soul. But Satan is at liberty to "sift" holy men only for a time; his assaults may grow furious during this season of temptation, but extraordinary prayer and ardent supplication soon overcome the Evil One. Finally, says Mather, "by praying always, without fainting, without ceasing, they saw the devil at length flee from him, and God himself draw near unto him, with unutterable joy. The end of that man is peace!"[53]

While William Tompson's end may have been peaceful, the death of one of the venerable fathers—those heroic saints who founded the Commonwealth and subdued the wilderness—was an alarming symbol of cosmic disorder to the sons, the second and third generations. As the first generation passed away, the remaining sons feared Divine displeasure, and felt unprepared, ill-equipped, and unworthy to pick up the reins. Edward Taylor, a major seventeenth-century American poet, summarizes the apprehension and feeling of inadequacy occasioned by the death of John Allen and other colonial prophets, including Tompson:

How are our Spirituall Gamesters slipt away?
Crossing their Hilts, & leaving of their play?
Leaving the ring to us who'de need before
We take up hilts, ye Fencing Schoole implore.
Are Norton, Newman, Stone, Thompson gone hence?
Gray, Wilson, Shepherd, Flint, & Mitchell since?
Eliot, two Mather's Fathers first, then th'Son,
Is Buncker's Woodward's Rainer's hourglass run?
With Davenport's, Sim's, Wareham's? Who are gone?
That Allen now is Called hence? Shall none
Be left behinde to tell's the Quondam Glory
Of this Plantation? What a bleeding Story
Doth this present us with? Mine eyes boile ore
Thy gellid teares into this Urn therefore,
Wherein their Noble ashes are, & know yee
ALL ENd in ALLEN, by a Paragoge.[54]

Notes

1. See, for example, Robert Middlekauf, *The Mathers: Three Generations of Puritan Intellectuals, 1596-1728* (New York: Oxford University Press, 1971); Kenneth Murdock, *Increase Mather: The Foremost American Puritan* (Cambridge: Harvard University Press, 1925); Mason I. Lowance, Jr., *Increase Mather* (New York: Twayne Publishers, 1974); Barrett Wendell, *Cotton Mather: The Puritan Priest* (1891; rpt. New York: Harcourt, Brace, and World, 1965); Edmund S. Morgan, *The Puritan Dilemma: The Story of John Winthrop* (Boston: Little, Brown and Company, 1958); Darrett B. Rutman, *Winthrop's Boston* (Chapel Hill: University of North Carolina Press, 1965); Robert C. Black, III, *The Younger John Winthrop* (New York: Columbia University Press, 1966); Charles W. Akers, *Called Unto Liberty: The Life of Jonathan Mayhew* (Cambridge: Harvard University Press, 1964); Charles Edward Banks, *The History of Martha's Vineyard*, 3 vols. (Edgartown, Mass.: Dukes County Historical Society, 1966).

2. I am thinking particularly of *The New England Historical and Genealogical Register; The Transactions and Proceedings of the American Antiquarian Society; The Proceedings and Collections of the Massachusetts Historical Society; The Publications of the Colonial Society of Massachusetts; and The Publications of the Prince Society.* These represent only the most well-known Massachusetts organizations, but one might also include numerous local clubs and historical groups throughout New England. Anyone who has done work in American culture owes a debt of gratitude to these societies for preserving and publishing valuable historical and literary information, regardless of their motives.

3. William Bradford, "Of Plimouth Plantation," in Samuel Eliot Morison, ed., *Of Plymouth Plantation, 1620-1647* (New York: Alfred A. Knopf, 1976), pp. 61-63.

4. Perry Miller, "Errand Into The Wilderness," in *Errand Into The Wilderness* (New York: Harper and Row, 1956), p. 11.

5. John Winthrop, "A Modell of Christian Charity," in Steward Mitchell, ed., *The Winthrop Papers (1623-1630)* 5 vols. (Boston: Merrymount Press, 1929-1955), II, 294-295.

6. C. Conrad Cherry, "New England as Symbol: Ambiguity in the Puritan Vision," *Soundings: An Interdisciplinary Journal*," 58 (1975), 348-362. Cherry modifies and corrects the historical interpretations of Perry Miller *(Errand Into The Wilderness)* and Robert

Middlekauf *(The Mathers)*, who are inclined to see the Puritan experiment conducted by the first generation as either wholly an errand (Miller) or an exile (Middlekauf).

7. The primary evidence for Tompson's presence in Maine is found in John Winthrop, *The History of New England, 1630–1649*, ed. J.K. Hosmer, 2 vols. (1908; rpt. New York: Barnes and Noble, 1959), I, 325; William Hubbard, *History of New England* (1680; rpt. Boston: Little, Brown and Company, 1848), pp. 276, 410, 411; "New England's First Fruits," ed. Samuel Eliot Morison, *The Founding of Harvard College* (Cambridge: Harvard University Press, 1935), Appendix D, p. 429.

8. Morison, *The Founding of Harvard College*, p. 402. Kenneth B. Murdock, ed., *Handkerchiefs from Paul* (Cambridge: Harvard University Press, 1927), p. xxvii, says that Tompson left the university without a degree.

9. Morison, *The Founding of Harvard College*, Appendix D, p. 429.

10. Allyn Bailey Forbes, ed., *The Winthrop Papers: 1638-1644* (Boston: Merrymount Press, 1944), IV, 31.

11. Ibid., p. 32.

12. Ibid., p. 33.

13. Ibid., pp. 33–34.

14. Ibid., p. 34.

15. *The New England Historical and Genealogical Register*, hereafter cited as *NEHGR*, 15 (1861), 112–116. Winthrop, *The History of New England*, I, 325, gives the date as 19 September 1639, and Ralph Thompson, "Some Descendants of Rev. William Tompson First Pastor of Braintree, Mass.," unpublished typescript in possession of Quincy Historical Society, identifies the date as 19 November 1639. I am indebted to Ralph Newell Thompson, whose thirty-page genealogy of the Tompson family provided me with information to help establish a corrected version of Tompson's background, education at Oxford, direct descendants, and experiences in Maryland. Mr. Thompson has written a thorough and accurate history.

16. Thomas Morton, *New English Canaan or New Canaan* (Amsterdam: Jacob Frederick, 1637), p. 141.

17. Charles F. Adams, *Three Episodes of Massachusetts History*, 3 vols. (Boston: Houghton Mifflin, 1894), I, 363.

18. Ibid., p. 365.

19. The literature on the Antinomian Crisis is massive, but all relevant primary material has been recently and expertly edited by David D. Hall, ed., *The Antinomian Controversy, 1636–38: A Documentary History* (Middletown, Conn.: Wesleyan University Press, 1968). See also Chapter 10, "Seventeenth-Century Nihilism," in Edmund S. Morgan, *The Puritan Dilemma;* and Charles Francis Adams, *Three Episodes of Massachusetts History*, for classic interpretations.

20. D. M. Wilson, ed., *The "Chappel of Ease" and Church of Statesmen* (Cambridge, Mass.: John Wilson and Son, 1890), p. 16. Of the primary sources for information about Wheelwright and the ecclesiastical controversy in Boston and Mount Wollaston, see Thomas Lechford, *Plain Dealing* (London, 1642), ed. J. Hammond Trumbull (Boston: J.K. Wiggin and Wm. Parsons Lunt, 1867). See page 41 for reference to Tompson's role in establishing the Braintree Church.

21. Winthrop, *The History of New England*, I, 254, 239–241. See also David D. Hall, p. 152.

22. Wilson, p. 19. See Perry Miller, *From Colony to Province* (Cambridge: Harvard University Press, 1962), pp. 60–61, for more on Wheelwright's Fast-Day Sermon.

23. David D. Hall, p. 152.

24. See note 10 above.

25. Wilson, p. 35.

26. Ibid., p. 36.

27. Ibid., p. 37; and Adams, II, 589.

28. Winthrop, *The History of New England*, I, 315, 325.

29. Edward Johnson, *Wonder-Working Providence of Sion's Saviour In New England* (1654), Facsimile Reproductions (New York: Scholars' Facsimiles & Reprints, 1974), pp. 161–162.

30. Ibid., p. 162, ll. 1–3.

31. Winthrop, *The History of New England*, II, 73.

32. Ibid., p. 94.

33. Ralph Newell Thompson, MS, Quincy Historical Society.

34. Richard Mather and William Tompson published two works in collaboration: *A Modest and Brotherly Answer to Mr. Charles Herle his Book, against the Independency of Churches* . . . By Richard Mather Teacher of the Church at Dorchester, and William Tompson Pastor of the Church at Braintree in New England (London: Henry Overton, 1644), (Sabin, 46781); *An Heart-Melting Exhortation, Together with a Cordiall Consolation, Presented in a Letter from New-England, to their dear Countreymen of Lancashire: Which may as well concern all others in these suffering times.* By Richard Mather Teacher of the Church at Dorchester, and William Tompson Pastor of the Church at Braintry in New-England (London: J. Rothwell, 1650), (Sabin, 46780). The second work was written in 1645.

35. *Second Report of the Record Commissioners of the City of Boston* (Boston: Richwell and Churchill, City Printers, 1877), II, 80.

36. Johnson, p. 198.

37. Ibid.

38. Ibid., p. 117.

39. Winthrop, *The History of New England*, II, 347–348.

40. Charles Feidelson, Jr., *Symbolism and American Literature*, Phoenix Books (Chicago: University of Chicago Press, 1952), pp. 77–78.

41. Wilson, p. 39.

42. Joseph B. Felt, *The Ecclesiastical History of New England; Comprising Not Only Religious, But Also Moral, And Other Relations*, 2 vols. (Boston: Congregational Library Association and The Congregational Board of Publication, 1855), II, 162.

43. Ibid., pp. 193–194. Almost every printed account of the Tompsons lists William Tompson, Jr. (A.B. Harvard 1653), as the eldest son of William Tompson of Braintree. However, Waldo C. Sprague, one of New England's foremost genealogists, died before publishing his massive collection entitled "Genealogy of the Families of Braintree, Mass. 1640–1850, including the modern towns of Randolph, and Holbrook and the city of Quincy after their separation from Braintree, 1792–93." On card 5081, Quincy Historical Society, Sprague says, "He William did not have a son Rev. William Tompson of Springfield and Connecticut as stated in the Register vol. 15, and elsewhere." Working independently, Ralph Newell Thompson assembled a family genealogy which agrees with Sprague and also corrects the *NEHGR*, 15, entry on the Tompsons.

44. *The Diary of John Hull*, in *Transactions and Collections of the American Antiquarian Society*, 3 (1857), 200. See Hull's *Diary*, p. 223, for an account of Tompson's death.

45. Felt, II, 342.

46. *City of Boston: Fourth Report of the Record Commissioners* (Boston: Richwell and Churchill, City Printers, 1880), IV, 141.

47. Felt, II, 332.

48. *A Report of the Boston Record Commissioners, Containing the Roxbury Land and Church Records* (Boston: Rockwell and Churchill, City Printers, 1884), VI, 205.

49. Samuel Danforth, "now i am past ill," in Kenneth B. Murdock, ed., *Handkerchiefs from Paul* (Cambridge: Harvard University Press, 1927), p. 19, ll. 3-8.

50. John Wilson, "most holy paule mine," in Murdock, p. 13, ll. 27-36.

51. Samuel Torrey, "Upon the Death of Mr. William Tompson, pastour of the Church in Braintry, who dyed 10th of the 10th month, Etati sue 68 1666," in Murdock, p. 18, ll. 23-24.

52. Cotton Mather, *Magnalia Christi Americana* (London, 1702), Bk. III, Ch. 27, 118-120; see also Nathaniel Morton, *New-Englands Memorial* (1669; rpt. Boston: The Club of Odd Volumes, 1903), p. 181.

53. Mather, Bk. III, Ch. 27, 119.

54. Edward Taylor, "An Elegy upon the Death of that Holy man of God Mr. John Allen, late Past. of the Church of Christ at Dedham, who departed this life 25th 6m 1671," in *The Publications of the Colonial Society of Massachusetts: Transactions 1937–1942*, 34 (1942), 528, ll. 49–64.

CHAPTER II

Benjamin Tompson: Colonial Bard

In attempting to define the psychological state of the second and third generations of American Puritans, Perry Miller looked beneath the formal rhetoric of the Jeremiad, the declarations of the Reforming Synod, and the confusion of the Half-Way Covenant. Miller discovered that the children of the mighty progenitors were faced with problems of personal identity:

> This sense of meaning having gone out of life, that all adventures are over, that no great days and no heroism lie ahead, is particularly galling when it falls upon the son whose father was once a public hero or the great lover. He has to put up with the daily routine without ever having known at first hand the thrill of danger or the ecstacy of passion. True, he has his own hardships—clearing rocky pastures, hauling in the cod during a storm, fighting Indians in a swamp—but what are these compared with the magnificence of leading an exodus of saints to found a city on a hill, for all the eyes of the world to behold? . . . He would be reduced to writing accounts of himself and scheming to get a publisher in London, in a desperate effort to tell a heedless world, "Look, I exist!"[1]

It may be, as Emory Elliott has argued in *Power and the Pulpit in Puritan New England*, that the sons labored under a mythology, and that the clerics of the 1660s used the pulpit to exaggerate for political purposes the religious fervor and heroic idealism of the founders. Perhaps, as Elliot's sources indicate, there never was a period of moral degeneracy, nor a decline in church membership.[2] In America, however, even as early as the seventeenth century, mythology helped to shape and determine the corporate and individual sense of self. Historians of the seventeenth century, like Cotton Mather, who was himself a third-generation American, saw the Great Migration of the 1630s within a mythological, or as Sacvan Bercovitch believes, an epic framework.[3] Whatever the motives, whatever the rhetorical tactic—allegory, typology, symbolism, metaphor, analogy—the past, the present, and the future are subject to imaginative interpretation. Personalities and events in this New World have their counterparts in Providential, Redemptive, biblical history. Thus the founders, those humble "servants of God," clasped the bible in one hand

and the Hebrew sword in the other, gathered tribes under them as did Abraham, or Moses, or Nehemiah, and flew across the "Bloudy Sea" to what Mather calls the "American Strand." Their sons, those who created and maintained the mythology, were left with the singularly anticlimactic tasks of mopping up the ancient battlefields, rooting out the last remnants of opposition, chastising stragglers, refurbishing citadels, and chanting the wonders of the past. While the patriarchs thought it sufficient to label themselves "saints," the sons had to declare more specific roles in the community; they had to choose occupations. Benjamin, the fourth and youngest son of William Tompson, declared himself a teacher, a physician, and a poet—three occupations particularly suited to the task of maintaining a civilized existence.

William Tompson brought his wife and three children—John, Elinor, and Samuel—from England to York (Agamenticus), Maine. But two more children—Joseph (b. 1 May 1640) and Benjamin (b. 14 July 1642)—were born to William and Abigail in Braintree, Massachusetts.[4] Benjamin, the subject of this study, was born three months before his father departed New England for Virginia.

In mid-winter, 1642–43, just about the time Tompson, Knowles, and James were receiving "slender entertainment" from the Dutch on Long Island, Abigail Tompson died of a cold taken while walking through the snow to public worship. Verses in the records of the first Roxbury Church, written by John Wilson soon after Abigail's death, represent her as saying to her husband: "Yea, if thou lovest Christ—as who doth more?— / Then do not thou my death too much deplore."[5] Wilson's anagram, "i am gone to all bliss," was copied by Joseph Tompson and sent to William in Maryland. In this manner he learned of the death of his wife and the dispersal of his children.

John Winthrop says in his *History of New England* that Abigail was a "godly young woman, and a comfortable help to him [William]" and that his children were "well disposed of among his godly friends."[6] At the age of six months, Benjamin was adopted by a neighboring family. When William Tompson returned from Virginia and Maryland in 1644, he seems not to have reclaimed his children, nor did he ever, even though he remarried in 1646. One can only assume that by 1646, when William was remarried and thus capable of caring for them, the children had become attached to their foster parents, or that these parents were unwilling to release the children.[7]

As could be expected, the colonial records provide little information on Benjamin Tompson's boyhood. It appears that Benjamin was adopted by the Thomas Blanchard family of Braintree and later Charlestown. The April 1863 *New England Historical and Genealogical Register* published "Abstracts of Early Wills" in which Blanchard entrusts "Benjamin

Tompson, unto and with my wife to provide for, and bring up in learning (at her owne pleasure) so as to fit him for the university, in case his parents please to leave him with her, and shee live to that time." Edward Collines and Joseph Hills took "in brief notes from Thomas Blanchards mouth the particulars expressed in this Will" on 22 May 1654.[8]

By 1654 Thomas and Mary Blanchard had amassed an estate valued at £562.09.08, as inventoried by Thomas Danforth, recorder of the Charlestown Court. Howard Judson Hall, an early editor of Tompson's poetry, scrutinized documents in the Middlesex County Archives and discovered that Blanchard was a "substantial but not a wealthy man . . . a generous and thrifty farmer whose home afforded abundant food and shelter, but lacked any luxury in furnishings or plate, and was negative in what we to-day call culture. The library consisted of '3 old bibles,' a 'new Covenant & psalme booke,' 'A law booke,' and 'Cooper on the Romans.' "[9] The Blanchards felt it an honor to afford Benjamin, the son of a former neighbor and eminent divine, a university education. Benjamin was twelve years old in the year of Blanchard's death, and it is possible that under John Morley, the Charlestown schoolmaster, Benjamin had proven himself worthy to carry on the intellectual tradition of his family.

Blanchard's deathbed wish was realized in 1662 when Benjamin graduated from Harvard College at the age of twenty, and, coincidentally, on the twentieth anniversary of the first Harvard Commencement. Among Tompson's immediate associates and classmates at Harvard were some of the most promising young men in the colony: James Noyes, one of the founders of Yale College; Simon Bradstreet, the son of the politician, Simon, and the poetess, Anne Bradstreet; Solomon Stoddard, the frontier revivalist and grandfather of Jonathan Edwards; and the three sons of College President Charles Chauncy.[10]

A second, and more important, historical coincidence marks the date of Benjamin Tompson's graduation. The year 1662 was one of the most hectic and frustrating years for the sons, the second generation. In that year Michael Wigglesworth, a major seventeenth-century American poet, penned the jeremiad poem, "God's Controversy with New England,"[11] in which he traced God's providential relationship with His New Israel. Wigglesworth, who calls himself "a lover of New England's Prosperity" (headnote), describes the catastrophic nature of the movement from plantation to declension to punishment, finally effected and manifested in "the time of the great drought Anno 1662" (headnote). The God of the Puritans kept His hand in affairs of men, marking, checking, judging, and punishing those backsliders who refused to live up to the letter and spirit of the conditions of the social covenant. Earthquakes, epidemics, floods, and droughts were interpreted as signs of

spiritual facts, as signs of God's divine displeasure. The second genera-
tion, after they had recognized the recent tendency toward what Wig-
glesworth calls a "Dead-heartedness" (l. 213) or "luke-warm Indiffer-
ency" (l. 212) in the children of the founders, formulated in 1662 the
ecclesiastical policy now called the Half-Way Covenant. In one particular
passage Wigglesworth demonstrates his own displeasure with the "self-
conceited, stiff, stout, stubborn Race" (l. 283) of children who refuse the
"saving experience" which would qualify them for church membership:
"Such is the Generation that succeeds / The men, whose eyes have seen
my [God's] great and awfull deeds" (ll. 327–328).

In addition to natural disaster, ecclesiastical compromise, and the re-
cent Restoration of the Stuarts, the Puritans faced another disappoint-
ment in 1662: this was one of the few years in the history of Harvard
College in which there were no candidates for the Master's degree, an
occasion surely taken as another indication of the lamentable spiritual
state of the colony. There is some reason to believe, however, that Benja-
min Tompson may have profited from this situation.

In December 1930, George Lyman Kittredge published a Latin Salu-
tatory Oration of 1662 in the *Transactions of the Colonial Society of
Massachusetts*.[12] Kittredge discovered this oration in the commonplace
book of Elnathan Chauncy, A.B. Harvard 1661, A.M. 1664. In attempt-
ing to identify the exact date and authorship of the oration, Kittredge
used both internal and external evidence. First, to determine the date, he
relied on a passage in the document itself: "Mother Academy has had a
miscarriage in the birth of Masters and has brought forth no Masters this
year . . . ; as to the candidates for the First Degree, we have presented to
you six."[13] The years 1662 and 1677 were then identified as the only
two years within Chauncy's lifetime in which there were six candidates
for the A.B. and none for the A.M. Kittridge ruled out 1677 because
Chauncy had been sixteen years out of college, and in August of that
year he had been in England, practicing medicine long enough to have
achieved a good reputation. Thus, the Latin Salutatory Oration was
probably delivered at the Commencement of 1662.

Kittredge also ruled out Chauncy as the author of the oration. Al-
though it is written in Chauncy's handwriting, there are errors in the
copy that prove it is not an autograph. While Kittredge believed that the
language of the oration showed a degree of sophistication above that of
an undergraduate, he speculated that "If the orator was a member of the
graduating class of 1662 and not a Tutor or a Fellow, I should be
tempted to identify him conjecturally with Benjamin Tompson, the 're-
nowned poet of New England' as his tombstone calls him. The oration is
clever enough to be Tompson's, and Tompson was clever enough to
compose it. His *New England's Crisis* (1676) contains at least one pas-

sage which seems akin in its wit and humor to some of the quips and cranks of our Salutatorian."[14] Kittredge said King Philip's speech in Tompson's mock-epic is in the spirit of the mock oration, but in his final analysis he doubted whether an undergraduate, even the satirical Tompson, could have delivered this address. Kittredge's scholarship was, of course, thorough and cautious; however, in 1930 he had only Hall's edition of Tompson's poetry to work with. Today, as a result of Harold Jantz's fine bibliographical research,[15] we have ten more Tompson poems to use in comparative analysis. These poems make a stronger case for Tompson's authorship of the oration. (Appendix C to this edition contains an English translation of the Latin oration.)

Other efforts to discover something of the Harvard years of Tompson have been disappointing. Many of the poets, politicians, and clergymen of the seventeenth century, according to the practice of the time, recorded biographical, academic, literary, and even "profane" information in commonplace books, journals, and diaries. A few of the Harvard commonplace books, such as Elnathan Chauncy's and Seaborn Cotton's, illustrate the Puritans' urbanity, aesthetic appreciation, and frivolity. Unfortunately, Benjamin Tompson's commonplace book is not extant. In fact, we have only five documents in Tompson's handwriting—three letters and two poems. It seems impossible that Tompson, the "renowned poet of New England" and one of the colonies' best Latin teachers, did not keep a Harvard commonplace book or a journal of some kind.

A second difficulty with the Harvard period of Tompson's life is the curious fact that he, John Norton (A.B. 1671) and Edward Taylor (A.B. 1671) were the only three poets during the administrations of Henry Dunster (1640–1654) and Charles Chauncy (1654–1672) who did not publish poems in the annual Harvard College Almanac. Samuel Eliot Morison calculated that this period of Harvard's history "sent forth a more abundant galaxy of poets, in proportion to her numbers, than any subsequent period of her history."[16] From 1658 to 1662, the years of Tompson's matriculation, almanac poems were contributed by such inferior poets as Zechariah Brigden (A.B. 1657), Samuel Cheever (A.B. 1659), and Nathaniel Chauncy (A.B. 1661). There are two reasons why Tompson may not have contributed: first, he may have disliked the spatial and aesthetic limitations of almanac verse; second, he may have quarreled with, or even been the victim of, the politically oriented method of producing the almanac, particularly the selecting of student "editors."

The only other source of information about a student's life at Harvard is *Chesholme's Steward's Book*, a running account of the College's charges and debts to students and fellows.[17] Once more, though, fate has determined that Tompson shall remain in obscurity. Pages 352 to 355, including most of Tompson's accounts, are missing. On page 356, half of which has been torn from the book, there are five entries entitled "Bingmain tomson is debitor." The account covers the period from May 1658 to May 1659. Of course Tompson was assessed the usual tuition fees, but it appears that he was, at least in that year, both mischievous and inordinately thirsty. On 7 May 1658, he was charged 2^d for "wryting his nam," and through the remainder of the year, he was billed for extra "sizinges," or pints of beer, and for "detrements," additions to the customary commons. But this scrap of budgetary information is hardly enough evidence upon which to base a sound estimation of young Tompson's character.

The years following Benjamin's graduation from Harvard were probably difficult for a man of his talents and training. His father, William, was by 1662 in the early stages of his final illness. On 24 July 1662, Joseph Tompson, one of Benjamin's older brothers, married Mary Bracket and settled in Billerica, Massachusetts, where he became a captain in the Artillery Company and a member of the General Court.[18] Benjamin, therefore, had to assume the responsibility of maintaining the family estate and caring for his half mother, Anna Crosbie Tompson, and his half sister, Anna, who was fourteen years old.

One can infer from colonial records that Benjamin did not have an easy time managing the affairs of the estate. In 1664 Elizabeth Harder of Braintree, a close friend of Samuel Tompson's (Benjamin's older brother, born in 1631), willed "unto Benjamin Thomson, 40ˢ, to be paid unto him within halfe a year after my Decease."[19] Elizabeth's wish that the money be quickly conveyed to Benjamin probably reflects her knowledge of the family's plight. In colonial America individual congregations felt obliged to support the ministry through even the most trying circumstances. If a community allowed one of its Patriarchs to die in poverty, shame and disgrace would have been its lot. Further, one town often came to the aid of respectable persons in another town. In 1665, for example, Richard Mather's congregation in Dorchester contributed to a relief fund for the Tompsons. Two years later, several months after William Tompson's death, the Selectmen of Dorchester resolved that

Wheras ther was Some time since a Contribution by the church and Towne for the reliefe of the Reverend Mr. Tomson of Brantry in the time of his weaknes, and the same Committed to the hands of Deacon Jn Capen of Dorchester, to be improved by him for the said Mr. Tomsons supply as he had need, and the said Mr. Tomson dying before the said Contribution was al disposed off, the Select men of Dorchester (conceaving it was a free gift for Mr. Tomson and therefore to shew oʳ further respect to Mr. Tomsons Relations) doe order that the said Deacon John Capen doe dispose of the remainder of the Contrebution as Followeth Viz one theird p[ts] to the widdow of Mr. Tomson and other two-third p[ts] to the Children of Mr. Tomson.[20]

Just as the ministers of a congregation felt ethically bound to provide religious solace to civilly banished members of the church, congregations and towns extended their generosity to clergymen throughout the colony. The ministry and the populace realized a dependence upon one another for survival in their "wilderness condition."

The year after William's death Benjamin was apparently free to pursue his own objectives, and like most young men, he found a job and a wife. But unlike the vast majority of his college classmates, Benjamin decided against accepting a call to the ministry. Either by temperament or by unavoidable separation from the university atmosphere, Benjamin preferred a more secular occupation.

Among the more disturbing ambiguities surrounding the life of Benjamin Tompson are the few brief indications that he was a minister who preached occasionally. Waldo C. Sprague, a dedicated genealogist, Ralph Newell Thompson, the family historian, and Fredrick L. Weis, founder of the Society of the Descendants of the Colonial Clergy, have advanced this information without identifying their sources or elaborating upon the circumstances.[21] It would seem that the Bay Colony was sufficiently secure by Tompson's post-Harvard years to consider lay or occasional preaching highly irregular and to discourage its practice. Yet Tompson's penchant for public performance—witness the salutatory oration and the Lord Bellamont greeting—coupled with his reputation for learning and the orthodoxy of his poetry lend some credence to acceptance of his occasional ministry. Benjamin Tompson was perhaps a much more talented man than our meager sources indicate; Cotton Mather not only lauds him as a poet and physician but as a mathematician.[22] In many instances his poetry reveals more than superficial acquaintance with alchemy, astronomy, geography, and related scientific endeavors. It was still possible in the mid-seventeenth century for a man to learn and occasionally practice several disciplines.

Available and appropriate full-time occupations were another matter for the educated colonist. If a graduate of Harvard did not choose to enter the religious life by accepting a call from an established congregation, he could either teach school or practice law or medicine. When Robert Woodmancy, master of the Boston Latin School, died on 13 August 1667, the town officials met to find a suitable replacement. Two weeks later the selectmen resolved that "Benj. Thompson being made choice of by the selectmen for to officiate in the place of the schole master for one yeare, Mr. Hull being appointed to agree for tearmes, what to allow him p. Annu."[23] It appears that the selectmen of Boston were prepared to offer Benjamin only a temporary appointment. Howard Judson Hall believed that "the influence of the Mather family helped to secure for the inexperienced young graduate of twenty-five this place as master of one of the leading schools of the colony."[24] Whatever the particulars of Tompson's contract, the wealthy and influential Bostonians were satisfied with his performance for at least three years. Benjamin's contract was probably renewed in the second year, because in 1668 Daniel Hinchman, Woodmancy's assistant since March 1666, was sent on an official expedition to lay out a town "about twelve miles westward from Marlborough, neare the road to Springfeild [sic]."[25] The court granted Hinchman 10 pounds in addition to his yearly salary as assistant to the schoolmaster, and Benjamin assumed full control of the Latin School.

The success of a teacher is often measured by the success of his students, and if that standard is applied to Tompson, he deserves a good deal of praise. During his tenure as master, Tompson had the unique pleasure of educating Cotton Mather from age five through nine. In 1702, when Cotton Mather's *Magnalia Christi Americana* went to press in London, it contained a biography of William Tompson and several of Benjamin Tompson's poems. Mather probably solicited the poems from Tompson out of respect for his former teacher. Samuel Mather wrote of his father's schooling: "His education was at the free School in Boston under the Care, first of Mr. BENJA THOMPSON, a Man of great Learning and Wit, who was well acquainted with Roman and Greek Writers, and a good Poet; last under the famous Mr. EZEKIEL CHEEVER, who was a very learned pious Man, and an excellent Schoolmaster. Under these two Masters he made a laudable Proficiency."[26]

Although Samuel Mather takes great pride in mentioning the famous schoolmaster Ezekiel Chevers, it is doubtful that Tompson felt such enthusiasm on 29 December 1670, when the Boston town officials decided to replace him with Chevers. Evidently this was a matter of colonial importance and great delicacy. One week before the actual decision was made, Governor Richard Bellingham, Major General John Leverett, magistrates Mayo, Allen, Oxenbridge, and Thatcher, and other worthies and selectmen of Boston met and "agreed that Mr. Ezachiell Chevers, Mr. Thomson, and Mr. Hinksman should be at the Govern[rs] house that day seaven-night to treat with them concerning the free schoole."[27] Accordingly, on 29 December, these same men "agreed and ordered that Mr. Ezechiell Cheevers should be called to, and installed in the Free schoole as head Master thereof, which he beinge then present, accepted of: likewise that Mr. Tompson should be invited to be an assistant to Mr. Cheevers in his work in the schoole, w[ch] Mr. Tompson beinge present, desired time to consider or to give his answer; . . ."[28] Hall believed, and I think quite

23

correctly, that this was an embarrassing arrangement which may have involved a breach of contract. On 3 January Tompson refused Boston's offer because he had accepted a call to teach at Charlestown, filling Chevers's former position. Tompson delivered the schoolhouse keys to the Governor on 6 January 1670/71. Five days later the court ordered that 10 pounds be taken out of the town treasury and given to Tompson in addition to his yearly salary. One might reasonably infer that the town officials used this "bonus" to ease its collective conscience.

Tompson taught in the Charlestown school from January 1670/71 to 7 November 1674, under the following contractual terms:

1. That he shall be paid thirty pounds per annum by the town, and receive twenty shillings a year from each particular scholar that he shall teach, to be paid by those who send children to him to school.
2. That he shall propose such youths as are capable of it for college, with learning answerable.
3. That he shall teach to read, write, and cipher.
4. That there shall be half a year's mutual notice by him and the town, before any change or remove on either side.[29]

As far as can be determined, the fourth clause is an unusual one in colonial teaching contracts; Tompson may have wanted to protect himself from the kind of treatment he had received at the Boston Latin School.

On 7 November 1674, the selectmen of Charlestown called Mr. Samuel Phipps to be the schoolmaster, but the records do not explain the reasons for this change.[30] Apparently Tompson continued to live in Charlestown until 1679 when he returned to teach in his native town of Braintree. The record book of the First Church of Charlestown, published in the *New England Historical and Genealogical Register*, tells us that Susanna Kirkland Tompson, Benjamin's wife, was admitted to full communion in the year 1677. Three of their children—Abigail (b. 1670), Susannah (b. 1673), and Anna (b. in Charlestown, 1676)—were baptized in this church on 10 June 1677.[31]

But what the now unemployed school teacher was doing in Charlestown between 1674 and 1678 remains uncertain. We do know, however, that Tompson was also a physician, and that he probably practiced medicine as a profession during King Philip's War of 1675–1676. On 22 September 1676, Samuel Sewall wrote in his Diary: "Spent the day from 9 in the M. with Mr. [Dr.] Brakenbury, Mr. Thomson, Butler, Hooper, Cragg, Pemberton, dissecting the middlemost of the Indian executed the day before. [Hooper] who, taking the heart in his hand, affirmed it to be the stomack. I spent 18s., 6d, in Ale, 6d in Madera Wine, and 6d I gave to the maid."[32] M. Halsey Thomas, editor of the 1973 edition of the diary, identifies Tompson among the participants in this "dissection, which was not an autopsy, but obviously performed from curiosity and for instruction."[33] Thomas also found this dissection to be one of the earliest in American history, perhaps preceded only by Giles Firmin's "anatomy" of 1674. Entries in diaries and court records indicate that Benjamin and his youngest son, Philip (b. 1687), attended cases together. Philip practiced medicine in Roxbury, where Benjamin spent the last years of his life. Howard Judson Hall believed that medicine increasingly occupied Tompson's attention as he advanced in years.[34]

There is another, more conjectural explanation for the four years (1674–1678) Tompson spent in Charlestown. During that period Tompson published *New Englands Crisis* (Boston, 1676), *Sad and Deplorable NEWES FROM NEW ENGLAND* (London, 1676), *New-Englands Tears* (London, 1676), an elegy on John Winthrop, Governor of Connecticut (Boston, 1676), and a poetic introduction to William Hubbard's *A Narrative of the Troubles with the Indians in New-England* (Boston, 1677). Now free of his responsibilities as schoolmaster, and perhaps only occasionally practicing medicine, Tompson apparently devoted a good deal of his time to writing public and publishable poetry. The poems of this period seem to have been deliberately aimed at attracting colonial and continental notice. Tompson consciously takes on the persona of the colonial bard, the public, representative voice. He may have attempted to supplement the income from his medical practice through this self-appointed position as poetic spokesman for the colonies. If his verses on New England's ancient glories and political worthies were favorably received, in either America or London, perhaps he could secure preferment from one of the more aristocratic families, such as the Winthrops. When Howard Judson Hall edited Tompson's poetry in 1924, he reasoned that Tompson

> could hardly have dreamed that his little excursion into poetry could bring him a living, for living by literature without patronage was unknown in his time even in London. In Boston there were no wealthy patrons who might come to his support, and there were no party factions in that theocratic, homogeneous commonwealth that might raise head and use Tompson's gift for satiric verse to their profit, even if the press had been free. . . . There were no noble lords in the little state who might venture to dispense private benefactions from the public treasury. . . .[35]

However, in 1924 Hall knew nothing of Tompson's relationship with the Davie family, especially Humphrey, the London merchant, and Edmund, the brilliant Harvard graduate. In the early 1940s Harold Jantz discovered two poems by Tompson in the commonplace book of Samuel Sewall, one an elegy on Edmund Davie and the other entitled "To my

Honored Patron HUMPHERY Davie."[36] Humphrey Davie was the sixth son of Sir John Davie of Creedy, England, who had been made a baronet on 9 September 1641. Humphrey, a successful merchant in both England and America, owned a considerable amount of land in Boston, Massachusetts, and Hartford, Connecticut. Humphrey Davie's eldest son, Edmund, graduated from Harvard in 1674 and probably received an M.D. from Padua University shortly thereafter. In 1707 Edmund's younger brother, John, became the fifth baronet of Creedy. Until 1943–1944, when Harold Jantz published *The First Century of New England Verse*, critics, genealogists, and antiquarians erroneously believed that Edmund was Humphrey Davie's younger brother. Through the discovery of Tompson's poems on the Davies, we have corrected the family relationships and have established the date of Edmund's death as February 1681/82.[37] More important, these two poems strongly suggest that Tompson had secured Humphrey's patronage as well as Edmund's friendship and respect. Although neither poem on the Davies describes the exact nature of Humphrey's patronage, both demonstrate Tompson's knowledge of their noble ancestry, civic achievements, and personal family affairs. In both poems Tompson assumes a self-deprecating, even subservient, stance to heighten the encomiastic effects; for example, he concludes "To my Honored Patron HUMPHERY Davie" with the Latin phrase "Amplitudini tua devinctus—Overwhelmed by your greatness." Thus, between 1674 and 1678, and for possibly a longer time, Tompson almost certainly received support from the Davie family; there is no other satisfactory way to explain how he could have supported a wife and three or four children.

According to the Records of the Suffolk County Court published in 1933 by the Colonial Society of Massachusetts, Tompson returned to Braintree sometime before 30 April 1678. On that date Tompson filed suit against three of his neighbors—Zacheus Curtis, Abraham Whitaker, and Samuel Simons.[38] From the records it appears that Tompson had purchased the Braintree estate of John Godfrey and was thus legally entitled to a total of 31 pounds owed to the previous proprietor. For reasons unknown, Tompson did not appear in court to press his suit against Whitaker, but he did win his cases against Curtis and Simons. Both debts were to be discharged before the end of the year. On 29 October 1678, Tompson signed the official Oath of Allegiance to Massachusetts Bay.[39] The fact that his name appears under the heading of "Brantery" residents may be taken as further evidence of his removal from Charlestown in 1678.

The following year Tompson finally secured more permanent employment as the master of the Braintree school, a position which he held for the next twenty years. Charles Francis Adams, one of the first historians to study the New England town as a social unit, meticulously investigated the official documents of Braintree, Massachusetts. He found that Benjamin Tompson was Braintree's first officially contracted schoolmaster and that he received for his services the rent of the town land (estimated at 15 pounds per year), an additional 15 pounds from the town treasury, and a half cord of wood from every child who attended the school. In 1700, twenty years after Tompson began teaching in Braintree, his salary remained at 30 pounds, but every student was then required to pay one shilling for each quarter of attendance. A year later Braintree officials voted to assess resident parents 5 shillings and nonresident parents 20 shillings. In 1701 Braintree required all inhabitants of the town to aid those families too poor to pay regular tuition. Although the town selectmen increased the school taxes and tuition, Tompson never received much more than 30 pounds per year for his services.[40]

This may explain why, in 1683, Tompson began writing letters to figures of colonial influence. First, he implored Increase Mather, William Tompson's lifelong friend from Lancashire, England, to assist him in obtaining a position in one of the new schools to be built in Boston. In this letter dated 9 November 1683, Tompson was moved to seek Mather's help, not so much out of "ambition of honor, as of a full imployment, and its comfortable attendants."[41]

But as nothing ever came of Tompson's efforts to relocate in Boston, he continued in Braintree as master of the grammar school. Tompson's original contract of 1679 with the town of Braintree guaranteed him "a piece of land to put a house on upon the common, . . . not exceeding an acre and a half or there-about; and, in case he leave the Town, the land to return to the Town, they paying for his building and fencing as it is then worth; but if he die in the Town's service, as Schoolmaster, the land to be his heirs' forever."[42] On 7 October 1679, seven months after Tompson signed the first contract, the Braintree selectmen voted "that the acre and a half of land formerly granted by the town conditionally . . . for the time of his abode, shall be to him and his heirs forever absolute."[43] Through the years, the town of Braintree promised Tompson a good deal of land, in fact several hundred acres if we can take Tompson's word for it. In 1688 Tompson wrote to Sir Edmund Andros, the English Governor of the Colony, claiming a legal right to "twenty acres of upland, . . . twelve Acres of Salt Marish, . . . Also one or two hundred Acres of Wilderness land. . . ."[44] In this letter Tompson was petitioning "for part of the lands to mee demised by the towne." One year later Tompson penned another letter, this one with a more insistent and irritated tone, in which he says to the unknown addressee, "I cannot unlesse I relinquish my imploy which is meane and Incoragements meaner, prosecute my petition as I ought to doe: But it would bee the highest incivility and ingratitude not to owne his Exc^lt Indulgency therein."[45] As a postscript to this letter, Tompson adds, "The petition I hereby intend is my last petition." In all probability the frustrated, underpaid schoolmaster did, indeed, drop the familiar pattern of conflict and reconciliation with the town of Braintree.

In 1690, perhaps to avoid prosecution and to keep Tompson in Braintree, the selectmen voted that he should have "ten pounds of country pay . . . at the country price, and all other pay accordingly. . . ."[46] Again on 2 March 1696, the town awarded Tompson 10 pounds in addition to his regular salary if he would acquit and fully discharge "the town of all former debts and arrearages to this day on that account. . . ."[47] Following Tompson's acceptance of this financial arrangement, the town demonstrated its gratitude by electing him town clerk, a position he held for several years.[48] However, these conciliatory measures were evidently superficial remedies. By 4 March 1699, the town of Braintree felt it necessary to appoint a committee empowered to "treat and make up the account with Mr. Benjamin Tompson, and to defend the town, if in case he prosecutes us in course of law."[49] Apparently, the town took this defensive posture because Tompson had either resigned or been released from his duties as schoolmaster, and the officials knew from experience that Tompson would demand full compensation. Braintree officials also knew, as the records of March indicate, that they were required by law to maintain a grammar school and a competent teacher; thus they voted to comply with the law and appoint a new master, Nathaniel Eells, a recent Harvard graduate. It was not until 29 July 1699 that Tompson and the town settled their difficulties. The insistent Tompson entered into the record the following statement: "Whereas—there had been an old reckoning upon ye account of my services for many years, which I have served them, that all may issue in love, and all other matters of differences ended, and all former accounts balanced, upon their clearing debt to Jonathan Hayward and Mr. Willard, in all being five pounds, I do forever acquit and discharge the town of Braintree from all dues and demands, this being a mutual and everlasting discharge."[50] Thus, for the second time in his career, Tompson released Braintree from "all former accounts."

From a brief entry in Waldo C. Sprague's unpublished history of Braintree families, I have been able to trace the outlines of Benjamin Tompson's personal affairs in the decade 1690–1700. Benjamin's first wife, Susanna Kirkland, died in 1693, leaving Tompson, now fifty-one years old and the father of eight children, a lonely and disgruntled Braintree schoolmaster. Sprague notes on card 5085 of his massive genealogy that Benjamin Tompson "married 2nd before 1698 Prudence Payson, widow of Samuel of Roxbury."[51] Further proof of this 13 December

1698 marriage is abundant, including detailed, cross-referenced entries in Clarence A. Torrey's "New England Marriages Prior to 1700" (Torrey also notes that Tompson registered in Boston, on 7 February 1695/96, his intention to marry Amy Bridges).[52]

Various family genealogies and vital records reveal that Prudence Payson had earlier married a ruffian-adventurer, William Lincoln of Lancaster and Roxbury. Lincoln died in Dedham in December 1675, as the result of wounds suffered in a fight with the Narragansets under Captain Johnson.[53] In 1657 William Lincoln had been sentenced in Ipswich court "for abusive carriage to Rebecca Blake to be whipped in Rebecca's presence."[54]

Prudence next married Samuel Payson of Roxbury, who died in 1697, officially leaving her fourteen acres in that town and property elsewhere.[55] The following months are marked by a series of rapid legal transactions: Tompson married Prudence Payson on 13 December 1698, in Dedham;[56] Prudence sold to Nathaniel and Jherabiah Butt "a certain Island commonly called or known by the name of the Moone" on 12 February 1698/99 for 115 pounds;[57] on 1 June 1699, Gabriel Bernon sold Prudence and Benjamin Tompson his mansion and two and one-half acres in Roxbury for 110 pounds.[58] The disgruntled schoolmaster, having profited from the marriage, was presumably comfortably settled in Roxbury by 1700.

During the next three or four years, Tompson taught at the free school in Roxbury. This school had been founded earlier in the seventeenth century by John Eliot, a Roxbury resident known as Apostle to the Indians. Cotton Mather said of Eliot, "God so blessed his endeavors, that Roxbury could not live quietly without a free school in the town. And the issue of it has been one thing that has almost made me put the title of *schola illustris* upon that little nursery; that is, that Roxbury has afforded more scholars first for the college and then for the public than any other town of its bigness, or if I mistake not twice its bigness, in New England."[59]

On 16 May 1704, the town of Braintree, perhaps with great reluctance, sent the "present selectmen to treat and agree with Mr. Benjamin Tompson" to return to Braintree as their schoolmaster. The officials voted to offer Tompson 30 pounds per year "during the time he performs the work until the present law referring to schools be repealed."[60] In other words, the town hired Tompson only to comply with the law. Hall believed that Tompson stayed on in Braintree until 1710 when old age forced him to return to Roxbury to live with his sons, Benjamin, a saddler, and Philip, a physician.[61] Most probably, however, Benjamin returned to Roxbury with Prudence, his second wife, and resettled at the Bernon mansion. Shortly after his last departure from Braintree, the town gave Benjamin Tompson's decrepit 20-by-16 foot schoolhouse "to Benjamin Webb for the securing of his hay till the first of May next. . . . ."[62]

Benjamin Tompson's successor as town clerk of Braintree was moved to make the following entry in the records: Mr. Tompson, a "Practitioner of Physick for about thirty years, during which time hee kept a Grammar School in Boston, Charlestowne, and Braintry, having left behind him a weary world, eight children, twenty-eight grand children deceased April 13th, 1714, and lieth buried in Roxbury, A[e]tatis su[a]e, 72."[63] As Hall pointed out, though, the diary of Samuel Sewall, Jr., and the Edward Tompson manuscript agree in placing the date of Tompson's death as 10 April 1714.[64] Possibly the Braintree records and Tompson's tombstone confused the date of his death with the date of his burial. Tompson's tombstone reads:

SUB SPE IMMORTALL, Y[e]
HERSE OF M[r] BENJ THOMPS[on]
LEARNED SCHOOLMASTER
& PHYSICIAN & Y[e]
RENOUNED POET OF N: ENGL:
OBIIT APRILIS 13. ANNO DOM
1714 & AETATIS SUAE 72
MORTUUS SED IMMORTALIS
HE THAT WOULD TRY
WHAT IS TRUE HAPPINE[ss] INDEED
MUST DIE

Four years after her husband's death, Prudence Tompson began disposing of her estate; from 1719 to 1722 she made five legal transactions through which she sold her home in Roxbury and land in Braintree.[65] Through the practice of gradual divestiture, surviving wives or husbands avoided the necessity of devising and registering a will, and, unfortunately, this seems to have been Prudence Tompson's intention. Careful scrutiny of the probate records in Suffolk County, where wills registered in much of the Boston area, including Roxbury, would be recorded during that period, has failed to produce any record for either Benjamin or Prudence Tompson. This loss is particularly frustrating because itemized wills frequently mentioned the deposition of libraries, journals, and other important papers or possessions. Surely the renowned poet of New England left in his family's care more than two poems in his own handwriting, and certainly a learned schoolmaster and physician kept some sort of record of his medical practice, spiritual condition, daily affairs, or intellectual stimulation. But the existing records provide no clues.

Quoting from an unidentified source, Charles Francis Adams said that

Tompson was known as "a character," was subject to "sullen fits," and was apt to be "full of matter."[66] Howard Judson Hall, Tompson's first editor, remarked, "To the curious searcher there is, perhaps, a hint of eccentricity, or moodiness, or even testiness of temper. . . ."[67] Finally, Harold Jantz concluded that Tompson was "talented, witty, facile, and perhaps a bit unstable and erratic, to judge from his verse and the few facts we know about his life."[68]

While it cannot be denied that Tompson was a rather contentious spirit, legal suits in the seventeenth century were relatively common. Anticipating the difficulties that would attend the settling of a wilderness, the founders of the Bay Colony had established a comprehensive legal system to insure peaceful and just settlement of land disputes, inheritance claims, and questions of civic welfare. Tompson threatened to prosecute only as a last resort, and frequently he quietly accepted a compromise offer. Moreover, there are lengthy periods when he appears to have been satisfied with his meager salary as the Braintree schoolmaster.

Tompson seems always to have been aware of the fact that his father was one of the colonies' most dedicated and respected ministers. As the son of a renowned clergyman who died in spiritual combat, Tompson felt entitled to special considerations, to the continued respect of his neighbors. Bitter circumstances had forced a promising young scholar to retreat from college to the confines of a rural outpost to care for his family and manage the household affairs. Anna, who was fourteen when Benjamin returned to Braintree, never forgot her brother's generous spirit. Sometime after 1714 Anna wrote an elegy on Benjamin, her surrogate father and friend. Joseph preserved this elegy in his journal "not for the poetry, but for the love and spirit of Christian spirit breathing in them."[69] Since this is the only extended characterization of the "Renouned Poet of N: Eng:[,]" it deserves to be quoted in its entirety:

Ah, my dear brother, tho your gone,
I do you often think upon,
Of your great kindness shown to me
In my greatest extremity.
You all ways had a friendly Care
Of what might be for my wellfare,
And often did me Councell giue
How i should walk and happi liue.
But now your gon, and left me hear,
A place of sorrow, Care & fear.
I hope that you'e attaind that rest
Where nothing there will you molest,
Where i do hope ere long to be,
Whers better times & Company.

Yow'ue left me caus of great Content:
Before your life was fully spent,
Many a time we walk't together
& with discorce haue pleasd each other
(Sum yt haue wondred how i could find
Discours with you to pleas your mind.)
But we must now discours no more,
As we weare ust to do before
And mourn as much as any among;
But time is short, & then ile sing another song.
Youe broght up many plants
That are plants of renown
And, now that you are taken henc,
Ad luster to your Crown,
To our dear father showd respect
And dutie to him neuer did neglect.
He to his friends was all ways kind—
On all ocations they did find
A reddy and comprizeing wit—
& all ways had [an] answer fit,
That sumtimes maizd the ignorant,
But pleasing to the wise,
That did his wit & learning highly prize
"Speak well of the liueing, don't reproach the dead,"
That was his Councell might in his lif be read;
Be not fond of liueing, yet prepared to dye,
Was his aduice to me in mine extremity.
Courtious to all, both high & low,
And due respect to all & euery one did show.
Thus we daily drop away & take out flight
Both from each others Company and sight.
Did we but realize what we daily see,
Other manner of persons we should be:
Not so Concernd for things thats here below,
Not knowing how soone we from henc must go.
Here we haue seen, with in a little space,
Chang upon Chang, & many run y^r Race,
Who, may be, thought but little of death or dyin[g],
Or litle minded how their time was flying.
O hapie they, that are prepard to dye,
And are Conuincd of this worlds uanity,
And haue made sure of a more hapi pl[ace]!
There soules are now in a most hapie c[ase.][70]

Tompson's poetry confirms Anna's view of her brother. Unless one holds that all satirists are by nature "unstable and erratic," there is no justification for Tompson's historical image. Certainly, he was a man who despised ignorance and mocked pretentiousness, but he was also a sympathetic and affectionate person. His elegies on leading colonial figures are filled with both respect for their accomplishments and grief at their loss. His domestic elegies are deliberately simple and straightforward consolations for the surviving members of the family.

Tompson saw himself as the colonial bard, the singer of the American past. He memorialized the Patriarchs and marveled at the "virgin simplicity" of the New World, but he also lamented the deplorable condition of the late seventeenth-century Bay Colony. Always looking at events from the larger perspective, always trying to achieve a balanced vision and tone, Tompson was an independent thinker, even though his poetry reflects a lifelong adherence to mainline Congregationalism—to The New England Way. He had a native American sense of humor, especially evident in his refusal to worship gratuitous aristocracy or in his reluctance to be victimized by the rabble. Through innumerable disasters—his father's insanity and death, Indian wars, his daughter's early death, and financial problems—Tompson kept his sense of humor and his religious commitment. There is nothing unstable or erratic about that.

Notes

1. Perry Miller, *Errand Into The Wilderness*, pp. 14–15.
2. Emory Elliott, *Power and the Pulpit in Puritan New England* (Princeton, N.J.: Princeton University Press, 1975), *passim*. Elliott relies upon Robert G. Pope, *The Half-Way Covenant* (Princeton, N.J.: Princeton University Press, 1969). For a more complete list of Elliott's sources on moral degeneracy in New England, see pages 4–6 of Elliott's Introduction.
3. Sacvan Bercovitch, "New England Epic: Cotton Mather's *Magnalia Christi Americana,*" *English Literary History*, 33 (1966), 337-350. See also Bercovitch's *The Puritan Origins of the American Self* (New Haven: Yale University Press, 1975), esp. p. 66.
4. *NEHGR*, 15 (1861), 112–116, lists the three English-born children as Helen, William, and Samuel. However, both Waldo C. Sprague and Ralph N. Thompson, working independently, list these: John, b. 1625, Winwick, Lancashire; Elinor, b. 1631, Winwick, Lancashire; Samuel, b. 1631, Winwick, Lancashire; Eliezur, baptised 21 October 1635, died in infancy. Waldo C. Sprague, "Genealogy of the Families of Braintree, Mass., 1640–1850, including the modern towns of Randolph, and Holbrook and the city of Quincy after their separation from Braintree, 1792–3," MS, Quincy Historical Society, card 5081; Ralph N. Thompson, "Some Descendants of Rev. William Tompson First Pastor of Braintree, Mass.," MS, Quincy Historical Society; Frederick L. Weis, *The Boston Transcript*, May 1932.
5. John Wilson, "Anagram made by mr John Wilson of Boston upon the Death of Mrs Abigaill Tompson, And sent to her husband in uirginia, while he was sent to preach the gospell yr," in Joseph Tompson's journal, edited by Kenneth Murdock, *Handkerchiefs from Paul* (Cambridge: Harvard University Press, 1927), pp. 7–9.

6. Winthrop, II, 94.

7. There is another reason why Tompson may not have claimed his children when he returned from Virginia: in the seventeenth century parents in both England and America frequently apprenticed their children to neighboring families. See Elliott for a discussion of this matter, especially its psychological consequences, pp. 174–76.

8. *NEHGR*, 17 (1863), 156.

9. *Benjamin Tompson...His Poems*, ed. Howard Judson Hall, (Boston: Houghton Mifflin, 1924), p. 8.

10. John Langdon Sibley, *Biographical Sketches of Graduates of Harvard University*, 17 vols. (Cambridge: Harvard University Press, 1873–1881), II, class of 1662, esp. pp. 103–111.

11. Michael Wigglesworth, "God's Controversy with New England," in Harrison T. Meserole, ed., *Seventeenth-Century American Poetry*, Anchor Seventeenth-Century Series (Garden City, N.Y.: Doubleday, 1968), pp. 42–54. References to Wigglesworth's poem are cited in the Meserole text by line numbers based upon the manuscript autograph in the Massachusetts Historical Society.

12. *Publications of the Colonial Society of Massachusetts: Transactions*, 28 (1930–33), 1–24. This publication hereafter cited as *PCSM-T*.

13. Ibid., p. 14.

14. Ibid., pp. 15–16.

15. Harold Jantz, *The First Century of New England Verse* (1943–44; rpt. New York: Russell and Russell, 1962), pp. 264–269.

16. Samuel Eliot Morison, *Harvard College in the Seventeenth Century*, 2 vols. (Cambridge: Harvard University Press, 1936), I, 132.

17. *Publications of the Colonial Society of Massachusetts: Collections*, 31 (1935), 266. This publication cited hereafter as *PCSM-C*. See also p. 240 for another entry relating to Benjamin Tompson.

18. *NEHGR*, 15 (1861), 112–116.

19. *NEHGR*, 13 (1859), 12.

20. *City of Boston: Fourth Report of the Record Commissioners*, IV, 141.

21. Sprague, card 5085; Ralph Thompson, MS, Quincy Historical Society; F.L. Weis, *The Boston Transcript*, May 1932.

22. Sprague, card 5081.

23. *PCSM-T*, 27 (1927–30), 136, but also see this publication, pp. 130–156, for a history of schoolmasters of Colonial Boston, with certain items corrected in *PCSM-T*, 32 (1933–37), 184–185.

24. Hall, p. 11.

25. *PCSM-T*, 27 (1927–30), 136.

26. Samuel Mather, *The Life of the Very Reverend and Learned Cotton Mather* (Boston, 1729), p. 4.

27. *A Report of the Record Commissioners of the City of Boston, Containing the Boston Records from 1660 to 1701* (Boston: Rockwell and Churchill, City Printers, 1881), VII, 57.

28. Ibid.

29. *The Memorial History of Boston, Including Suffolk County, Massachusetts: 1630–1880*, ed. Justin Winsor, 4 vols. (Boston: Ticknor and Co., 1880), IV, 258.

30. Ibid.

31. *NEHGR*, 23 (1869), 437; *NEHGR*, 26 (1872), 158.

32. *The Diary of Samuel Sewall, 1674–1729*, ed. M. Halsey Thomas, 2 vols. (New York: Farrar, Straus and Giroux, 1973), I, 23.

33. Ibid., note.

34. Hall, pp. 20 and 35, note 39.

35. Ibid., p. 14.

36. Jantz, pp. 267 and 157–167, for Jantz's edition of these poems.

37. W. Bruce Bannerman, ed., *The Registers of St. Martin Outwich, London*, in *The Publications of the Harleian Society* (London, 1905), 32, 105. Edmund was buried "in ye South Ile by ye Middle Pillar" on 23 February 1681/82.

38. *PCSM-C*, 30 (1933), 904–909.

39. Ibid., pp. 973–974.

40. Adams, *Three Episodes*, II, 764–782.

41. For a complete copy of Tompson's letter to Mather, see Appendix B to this edition.

42. Sibley, II, 105.

43. Ibid.

44. For a complete copy of Tompson's letter to Andros, see Appendix B to this edition.

45. For a complete copy of this letter, see Appendix B to this edition.

46. Sibley, II, 106–107.

47. Ibid.

48. Adams, *Three Episodes*, II, 772. Adams says that Tompson was the Braintree town clerk from 1690 until 1710, but Hall seems to think that Tompson held the position only several years after 1699. See Hall, p. 19. Tompson did spend 1700–1704 in Roxbury, but he could have traveled to Braintree for the town meetings.

49. Sibley, II, 107.

50. Ibid.

51. Sprague, card 5085.

52. Clarence Almon Torrey, "New England Marriages Prior to 1700," MS, bound 1962, New England Historical and Genealogical Society, Boston, XI, listed alphabetically.

53. Waldo Lincoln, "The Lincolns of New England," MS, 1926, Worcester, Mass., in possession of New England Historical and Genealogical Society, Boston, pp. 378–379.

54. Ibid., p. 379.

55. Ibid.

56. Torrey, XI, listed alphabetically.

57. Suffolk Deeds, Suffolk County Court House, Boston, XIX, fol. 80.

58. John Osborne Austin, *The Genealogical Dictionary of Rhode Island* (Albany, N.Y., 1887; rpt. Baltimore: Genealogical Publishing Co., 1969), p. 20.

59. Winsor, I, 420.

60. Sibley, II, 107–108.

61. Hall, p. 20.

62. Adams, II, 774.

63. Ibid., p. 772.

64. Hall, p. 2l.

65. Suffolk Deeds, XXXIII, 268; XXXV, 8; XXXVI, 94, 130, 194.

66. Adams, II, 771.

67. Hall, p. 21.

68. Jantz, p. 74. Jantz also includes this curious reference on p. 71: "To judge from a passage in Cotton Mather's unpublished diary for 1712, all was not well then with his old schoolmaster's religion, and this may help explain his lifelong failure to secure preferment." Mather's diary has since been published, and I can find no reference to Benjamin Tompson. See William R. Manierre, II, ed., *The Diary of Cotton Mather D.D., F.R.S. for the Year 1712* (Charlottesville: University Press of Virginia, 1964).

69. Joseph Tompson on Anna Hayden's elegy for Benjamin Tompson, quoted in Murdock, p. 22.

70. Anna Hayden, elegy on Benjamin Tompson in Joseph Tompson's Journal, ed. Murdock, pp. 20–22. This poem headnoted in Joseph Tompson's Journal: "sent unto me by friend."

CHAPTER III

The Achievement of Benjamin Tompson

The biographical sketches which precede this chapter admittedly consist of fragmentary threads stitched into the repeating pattern of the Tompsons' small victories and nagging frustrations. The scraps of genealogical information and legal data, the deeds, the wills, the few letters, can never adequately explain what it meant to be a zealous missionary in the wilderness or an aspiring poet in colonial Boston, or what it meant to participate in the Cambridge Synod or to announce *New Englands Crisis* to the world and to the mother-country. Vital records and church records for any New England town or congregation can never reveal the intellectual and emotional impact of important communal affairs upon the mind and heart of the individual citizen. Taken even in their entirety, the antiquarian's tools are useless in the effort to determine, for example, how the abandoned son of a deeply troubled zealot, a Harvard-educated schoolmaster, mathematician, physician, and sometime preacher, a man who had probably never traveled more than 20 miles at any one time in his entire life, came to write thousands of lines of genuine poetry in which he saw himself, his family, and his colony entangled in the grand sweep of secular and sacred history.

The documentary evidence of the first two chapters should not obscure equally fascinating and sometimes disturbing perspectives. The Tompsons were educated and genteel descendants of English nobility: they were the friends, the colleagues, and even the teachers of the most eminent New Englanders. Yet, they were perpetually frustrated in their attempts to be included within or sufficiently recognized by that higher strata of American society. Blind circumstance, not conspiracy, seems always to have kept them jostling at the edges of power and fame, making their century-long dilemma all the more exasperating. Perry Miller pinpointed Benjamin Tompson's problem when he said that the sons would spend their lives searching for a publisher in London in their desperate attempt to tell a heedless world, "Look, I exist!" Three centuries later we may be ready to hear Tompson's declarative plea.

Sacvan Bercovitch explained our contemporary failure to give Edward Taylor and Anne Bradstreet their due tribute as "something fairly commonplace—a 'cultural lag,' a period of adjustment, a season of gestation."[1] Reflective time serves this purpose on a smaller scale for the textual editor who, well before he begins his systematic task, must be firmly convinced that others will profit from a reliable and usable edition of a certain body of imaginative work. After Taylor and Bradstreet, there is no seventeenth-century American poet more entitled to due tribute—or at least careful and deliberate analysis—than Benjamin Tompson.

Not just another of that century's 250 practicing poets, who collectively produced over 2250 poems, as Harold Jantz and Harrison T. Meserole tell us,[2] Benjamin Tompson was himself an analyst of the New England Way, from the Golden Age to the beginning of the Rational Age. His poetry was the natural continuation of what Larzer Ziff has described as a "characteristic combination of plainness, passion, and allegory which crystallized in the century 1560–1660 and has ever since been a strong feature if not a separate tradition in our literature."[3] Above all, there is passion in Tompson's work—not quite like Taylor's for union with Christ or Bradstreet's for intimacy and beauty—but a passion for the means to articulate the American struggle for holiness and identity. To be sure, every student of our colonial period knows the standard outlines of the progress toward glorification: the means and ordinances of conversion, conviction, confession, and profession—every rung on the ladder to heaven. What we may not realize, however, is that beneath all our formalizations (and their own legalities) lies the bedrock of Puritanism: the quest for the sanctified life. Benjamin Tompson knew, besides the promises of the Covenant, the doctrines of predestination and election, and the willed belief in the free gifts of grace, that life in the New World consisted chiefly in what Jonathan Edwards later called the twelfth sign of the *Religious Affections*, Christian practice.

Tompson believed the poet's purpose, much like Emerson's inspired poet or Edwards's enlightened saint, was to cooperate with his newly regenerated faculties in first scrutinizing the matter and then relishing the life, the event, or the achievement which would serve as the subject of his verse. So seriously did the typical Puritan poet take his assignment that the event seemed to have no practical reality until he had duly examined and reported its meaning and consequences. The poet's particular task was to search for the symmetry and order in his world, sometimes bending physical reality in order to "reveal" exceptional cases of sacrifice, determination, and self-discipline. The poet might turn his wit to illustrate the uses of imagination and intellect among his peers, to congratulate those of the greatest vision or to chastise those blinded by self-exaltation or despair. Tompson's poetry, by these standards, may be described as quintessentially Puritan.

"The achievement of Puritan poetry, such as it is," said Roy Harvey Pearce in *The Continuity of American Poetry*, "lies in its hard, painstaking, often clumsy and overstrained search for that which could not be doubted: a sense of man's nature and destiny and his mission in the new world. If that achievement is in itself not great, its implications for the development of later American poetry are so great as to be definitive."[4] Certainly, the passionate, sometimes nervous, search for permanence and stability marks Tompson's every effort, particularly *New Englands Crisis*, the best known of his works.

Even if one concludes that Tompson's poetry has little inherent artistic merit (a position I would reject), and even if the traditions of American verse could not be traced to works like his, there would still be substance and reason enough to make his work available to students and scholars— especially to intellectual historians—for the kind of scrutiny Norman Grabo called for almost two decades ago in *The William & Mary Quarterly*. Arguing from the premise that ideas representing major aspects of human experience are expressed in symbolic forms of art and not merely in discursive communication, Grabo challenged contemporary historians to consider "belles-lettres" as "symbolic expressions, often involuntary, of the artist's emotional framework of ideas." The pursuit of such information, Grabo believes, is "not only useful, but essential to understanding the Puritan mind."[5] Because Tompson so often used the public persona and because he so fully absorbed the intellectual habits of his world, his poetry is ideally suited for the serious study of Puritan symbols, conventions, experience, and practice.

Consider, for example, "Remarks on the Bright, and dark side of Mr. William Tompson," which survives as his first mature poem. At age twenty-six, only six years after he had graduated from Harvard, Benjamin Tompson found in the elegy the symbolic means for emotionally expressing his ideas. Appealing to the sense of wonder so magnificently present in his audience, Tompson directs the imaginative eye of the reader over celestial and terrestrial worlds, through pleasant gardens, over craggy rocks, to the Sicilian mountains, to ancient Palestine, and from dismal vaults to the constellations and phosphorous rays of heaven. "Remarks on the Bright, and dark side" represents exactly what the Puritan mythology, by the second generation, was all about: celestial and terrestrial warfare. To the sons, the Patriarchs were soldiers in a historical drama, periodically basking in orbs of glorious light or shrunk in "Ember weeks of grief" and darkness. William Tompson was a general in the army of Christendom; he constantly struggled to meet some obscure challenge, or fell victim to the bitter accusations hurled by one of the factions of that tumultuous time. For this saintly man the world was an arena in which to display one's physical endurance and intellectual strength amid alarms, cries, ravishments, pushing, flocking, trembling, and thrusting of various supporters and detractors. Like many of Tompson's other poems, "Remarks on the Bright, and dark side" reflects what Roy Harvey Pearce called the Puritan "tension of a desperate certitude."[6] Here is the light versus the dark, the static converted by the dynamic, in a poetic form equally energetic and moving: here is the American Puritans' version of Genesis.

The Puritans' decision to flee England in the seventeenth century meant that some would forfeit comfort and security to engage in perhaps the most courageous, yet foolhardy, adventure in modern history. The flood tide of emigration to Massachusetts Bay Colony in the 1630s stands as one of history's unique events: in ten years, over ten thousand English scholars, soldiers, and statesmen, their minds filled with fear of mythological and actual beasts said to inhabit the American wilderness, embarked on a hazardous ocean journey with imprudent haste and impractical preparation. Their leaders, John Winthrop and Richard Mather among others, kept their vision focused on the promise of reward in the other world. Richard Mather warned them "experience shews that it is an easy thing in the middest of worldly business to lose the life and power of Religion, that nothing thereof should be left but only the external form, as it were the carcass or shell, worldiness having eaten out the kernell, and having consumed the very soul & life of godliness."[7] It was precisely this attention to godliness, as the leaders had predicted, which kept the Puritans from being consumed by failure. Only the monumental will to believe in Providence enabled them to survive the constant physical and psychological pressures of frontier existence. Perry Miller argues in all of his essays that New England was not "new" to the Puritan; it was the old, familiar world of sin and struggle and death. The Puritan elegy proves Miller correct.

Despite the fact that the average lifespan of the colonial leader was incredibly long—consider the Mathers: Richard died at seventy-three, Increase at eighty-four, and Cotton at sixty-five—epidemics, war, natural disaster, and infant mortality wreaked havoc with the colonists. The typical Puritan responded to catastrophe as he did to other realities: he met it squarely, mourned, reconciled himself, and went on as best he could. But the poets, and others who were particularly sensitive to the larger communal concerns of the New Israel, somehow managed to look beyond their personal sorrow and expand and vivify the event, as does the alchemist his base metals. Not that the poet or minister was hardhearted or dispassionate; on the contrary, he was so moved he could not overcome his sorrow unless he scrutinized death from every possible angle. He had to know the circumstances—the meteorological or astronomical signs, the last words of the deceased, his psychological state at the time of death, the people present at his deathbed, and so forth. Then he had to sift through these factors, carefully noting the prevailing patterns, marking the biographical and biblical parallels, and examining the integrity of an apparent coincidence for Providential significance.

His search for the surrounding aspects of a tragic death may appear to the modern reader as a "stretched passion,"[8] as Alan Simpson and Norman Grabo have rightly described it, but it was a stretching for the symbolic means of articulating the mysterious correspondences between human and divine life. A typical Puritan audience would have seen nothing ludicrous in John Cotton's description of the gracious experience as a fishlike wading and gliding into the River of Life;[9] nor would he have been shocked by Thomas Hooker's comparison of meditation—once an ancient, holy, profound experience—to rummaging in a deserted house or ship or watering a weedy and thorny garden.[10] Joshua Moody's "Souldiery Spiritualized" illustrates just how far afield the Puritan could go in his quest for the symbolic means: Moody says about his comparison of life to the strategies of war that

> As for my manner of speaking in the using of many Metaphorical Expressions, and Allusions unto the Calling, Postures, and motion of Souldiers . . . though it may possibly grate upon some Critical and captious Ears, yet I hope it will be at least excusable or tolerable to your selves . . . . Had I been to handle the same Head of Divinity on another Auditor, I could and should have sought out other words, . . . I conceive a man should take Measure of his Theam to cut out his Language by, and make it up something according to the mode of his Auditory. . . .
> The Lord takes care to make us spiritual in all our Imployments, by spiritualizing all our Imployments. Yea, all our Relations and Conditions . . . . [11]

Critical and captious ears did not, as far as we know, object to Moody's metaphors. His theory of the adaptability of language to audience ("I could and should have sought out other words") is perfectly consistent with the Puritans' efforts to build upon their emotional framework of ideas. In the construction of the elegy, the main beams—images of light and dark, anagramatic and acrostic designs, Biblical types, "invented" puns, "opened" texts, and Ramistic logic—supported the remarkable edifice of truth and meaning that sustained New England. The poet or sermon writer "cuts out his Language" according to that which he can discern in the details of God's created world, and he delights in the "laying open" of God's wisdom. As Miller and Pearce have demonstrated, the seventeenth century engaged in "Ramist poetics—a poetics of discovery, of examining and stating, of coming upon, of laying open to view. . . ."[12] His "inventiveness," that is, his artistic choice or selection of language and symbol, was exciting and satisfying; he was in a sense recreating.

While the poet or pastor set to work measuring his themes for an elegy or eulogy, other members of the family and community performed their own tasks. Coffins and tombs had to be constructed and tombstones engraved, hearses had to be draped, the horses harnessed and their heads painted white, gloves and rings had to be distributed to the pallbearers, and if the deceased were a dignitary, school children and the militia must be gathered to march in the procession. A colonial funeral, like a Thanksgiving day, Fast day, Election day, or Artillery sermon day, was an important social event and an opportunity for the poet, the engraver, and the printer to demonstrate their skills. The spectators at one of these communal events came expecting to hear highly conventionalized, almost formulaic recitations; they came to be consoled by the wit, the play of language, the sentiment or substance of poetic and prosaic reassurance. The funeral elegy or sermon provided early New Englanders with an opportunity to hear their spokesmen take stock of the colony's situation. They came to learn the purpose or meaning of a death, but they also came to be delightfully instructed. The deliberately hyperbolic elegy, sometimes composed of innumerable references to the marvelous, the wonderful, the strange and exotic, sometimes shockingly frank about disease, infection, bodily corruption and decomposition, and almost always governed by the voice of the grief-stricken persona, provided the Puritan with a kind of public entertainment into which he could invest his imaginative, mental, and emotional powers. Apparently seventeenth century audiences had distinct preferences for particular poets: Benjamin Tompson's tombstone lauds him as "the renowned poet of New England." If there is any concrete justification for this title, it probably lies in his elegiac canon.

In all, Tompson wrote twenty-three poems which can be classified as tributes to the deceased; fourteen for public audiences and nine for the consolation of the family. The elegies and epitaphs which I would label public efforts make up the largest group of poems in the Tompson corpus. This group includes the *Magnalia* elegies on William Tompson, Samuel Whiting, and John Wilson; broadsides on Ezekiel Chevers, John Winthrop, II, and Rebekah Sewall; the poems which may have appeared in contemporaneous broadsides but now exist only in manuscript form on Peter Hubbard, John Leverett, and Fitz-John Winthrop; the engraved epitaphs on Edward Tompson and Moses Fiske; and finally, the elegies on Winthrop and Simon Willard from *New-Englands Tears* and on James Allen from *Death is Certain* by Benjamin Wadsworth. The elegies which appear only in private notebooks, journals, or commonplace books of the family or close friends were probably never intended for publication. This group includes the epitaph on William Tompson and the tribute to Samuel Tompson from the Edward Tompson manuscript (Jantz catalogues these as "elegies of the Tompson family"); memorials of Mary and Elizabeth Tompson from the Joseph Tompson journal; the "first draft" elegies of Rebekah Sewall from the Winthrop Papers; the consolatory verse epistles addressed to Humphrey Davie from Samuel Sewall's commonplace book; and the Sarah Tompson memorial copied into her own journal.

In a few exceptional cases, such as that of the three poems on Rebekah Sewall and the two on the Davies, this classification is somewhat arbitrary. For the most part, however, there are clear and sustained differences in the two types of poem. In fact, the differences in literary approach are usually as distinct here as they are between Edward Taylor's Meditations and his topical verses or the *Christographia* sermons. In his public works, Tompson proudly proclaims to the world that New England is led by men of heroic stature, and in his private poems Benjamin, the son of a leader, tries to help his family and friends overcome their grief.

Tompson manages to control both poetic ranges through careful manipulation of the various techniques available to him. Several decades ago Edwin Fussell observed that Tompson was

> working within a tight and rigorously cultivated New England tradition. Conventional as many of these poems are, it is well to remember nevertheless the age's interest in "character" and the new art of biography, as well as the heroic light in which the New Englanders, from Bradford on down, habitually regarded their undertaking and its leaders. Working within this native tradition, then, Tompson would be a poet whose major task was the commemoration of heroic men and events. Like the great Mather, he would celebrate "the wonders of the Christian Religion," concentrating on the men and women whose heroism was making history in America in the seventeenth century.[13]

In recent years intellectual historians and literary critics have paid greater attention to the Puritans' use of typology to explain their mission, to justify their behavior, and to glorify their leaders. Of course, Edward Taylor, Edward Johnson, and Cotton Mather have been the primary subjects for typological analysis. Tompson, unfortunately, has been almost universally ignored. Yet he displays, in many of his poems, both elegiac and occasional, a thorough knowledge of the diversity of New England's use of typology. The clergymen, historians, and poets of New England, including Tompson, were well-versed in this Medieval method of exegesis, but in their own unique fashion they ingeniously transformed Old World methods to New World concerns. Thus they envisioned an interconnected universe in which nature and history participated in the cyclical pattern of adumbration and completion—antetype and type—first outlined in sacred scripture. John Wilson's biography is not analogous to Aaron's: he is another Aaron, and the rod he used also quelled rebellion. William Tompson is characterized by his son as another Lazarus because he was raised from the "death" of insanity to once again embrace his Savior and his church. Sometimes, as in "Remarks on the Bright, and dark side of that American Pillar Mr. William Tompson," the typological connections are multiple; certain events in the American's life parallel widely scattered biblical events. So, William Tompson is a kind of Melchizedek, John, Adam, Daniel, Nehemiah, and Boanerges. In some poems, one or possibly two biblical parallels are explored: John Winthrop, II, is a Moses, William Hubbard a Nathan, Peter Hubbard both Aaron and Abraham, and John Leverett both Joshua and Abraham. Typology also extends to nationalistic levels when Tompson compares the Great Migration of the 1630s and the Indian Wars ("New-Englands Travels through the bloudy Sea") to the liberation of the tribes of Israel, or when he characterizes American nature as "An Eden So long hid. . . ."

In addition to this varied use of typological matter, Tompson relied on a controlled structural pattern for most of his elegies. He traced, step by step, an individual's civil and spiritual progress. As models for public behavior, these representative men advanced within the Medieval framework of the great chain of being and the Puritan notion of vocation. In other words, individual heroes received Tompson's "assurance" of salvation because they struggled to meet the demands of their calling, and because they fulfilled their roles in both the social covenant and the covenant of grace. Society depends for its survival upon regenerated men and women who can commit themselves to an ecclesiastic, civic, or domestic leadership.

Tompson achieved in his poetry what Sacvan Bercovitch credits Mather with in the *Magnalia Christi Americana*: the eclectic Mather transforms all the traditional biographical and historical forms into "a distinctive concept of the representative American Saint."[14] "Nehemias Americanus," the title of Mather's life of John Winthrop, indicates that his biographical techniques will be comprised of elements of hagiographical "exemplar" wedded to historical portraiture. Mather's distinctively American methods draw upon, but do not slavishly imitate, the classical epic figure, the Medieval Saint's Life, Reformation Martyrology, Renaissance biography, Restoration Character, and chronicle history. In all of his public elegies, Benjamin Tompson, like Cotton Mather, extends the usefulness of exemplum to portray New England's leaders according to the Puritans'

two-fold concept of calling, the inward call to redemption and the summons to a social vocation, imposed on man by God for the common good. In keeping with their militant this-worldliness [Christian practice], the Puritans laid special emphasis upon vocation. Predictably, they drew their standards for the magistrate from the familiar Renaissance treatises; but they made one further, quintessentially Calvinist demand. Invoking various scriptural models, they distinguished the merely good ruler from the saintly ruler, and insisted that the saintly ruler reflect his inward calling in his social role. Faith, indeed, was crucial to the proper execution of his duties. As his vocation was a summons from God, so his belief led him to do well in public office.[15]

Once the poet has established the grounds upon which the elegiac tribute will be based, his next task is to find the poetic means of portraying the redemptive nature of the errand into the wilderness by the individual and the country. Tompson's favorite technique is to begin the poem dramatically and directly. He begins his elegy on the Very Reverend Samuel Whiting in this way: "MOunt *Fame*, the glorious Chariot of the *Sun*; / Through the *World's Cirque*, all you, her Herald's run" (11. 1–2). He similarly addresses the muses in his elegy on John Winthrop, II: "NIne Muses, get you all but one to sleep, / But spare *Melpomene*, with me to weep" (11. 193–194 *NET*). The direct address opening usually contains a phrase or an image which startles, even shocks, the reader; for example, in "Sudburies Fate" Tompson triggers the surprise with the word "Lacquey": "ONce more run Lacquey Muse the Councel tell, / What sad Defeat our hopeful Band befell" (11. 281–282 *NET*). The opening of Tompson's elegies gives the reader the impression that all the world participates in this tragedy, or that this is a moment of epic significance. In fact, what Bercovitch has described as a deliberate mixture of biographical models is here joined with "a baroque plethora of allusions . . . in an effort to blur the specific into a composite ideal of civic authority,"[16] or ministerial accomplishment, or military genius.

Tompson is also able to fix an image with precision and compactness. The well-turned, concise phrase, considered one of the Baroque poet's primary virtues, can rapidly and neatly summarize a series of ideas and images. For example, Tompson rounds off Samuel Whiting's scholarly attributes with this phrase: "By his closed Lips, / *Rhetoricks* Bright Body suffers an *Eclipse*" (11. 55–56). Playing on the figure of the elaborate necrological borders of the broadside elegy, Tompson calls Winthrop's death "ANother Black Parenthesis of woe" (1. 1). When Tompson pictures Winthrop, the alchemical scientist *par excellence* at work, he uses an exotic image to describe the signs of precious jewels: "Sometimes Earths veins creeping from endless holes / Would stop his plodding eyes" (11. 33–34). Shortly before the death of Governor John Leverett, Boston was pounded by an unseasonable and portentous thunderstorm, and Tompson turned this event to his own poetic advantage. He addresses the mourners of "Poor broken Boston" (1. 109), whose bleary eyes and doleful cries are "Griefs Hurricanes" (1. 111) forcing their way into New

England's door. In one or two lines Tompson can encapsulate a complex idea by drawing upon and combining biblical and pastoral images for their paradoxical effects, as he does in the last lines of the epitaph of William Tompson: "While thus the thundring Textman hidden lies / Some Virgins slumber: Others wantonize" (11. 5–6).

Owing perhaps to his familiarity with the human anatomy through practicing medicine, or to his knowledge of European literature and visual arts in which the human body became the subject of intense scrutiny, Tompson dwells frankly on images of physical deterioration. Peter Hubbard, says Tompson, often cried, "When will deaths curious claws these knots untie? / A crazie cage of bones curtaind with Skin / A Ruind Castle where great strength had beene" (11. 56–58). Horrified by Indian savagery, Tompson also used physical imagery to shock his audience, as in *New Englands Crisis*, which in a sense might be read as an elegy for New England at large:

> The field which nature hid is common laid,
> And Mothers bodies ript for lack of aid.
> The secret Cabinets which nature meant
> To hide her master piece is open rent,
> The half formd Infant there receives a death
> Before it sees the light or draws its breath, . . .
> (11. 247–252)

To describe the Indians' "monstrous rage," Tompson pushes his diction and imagery to the limits: the Indians "strip, they bind, they ravish, flea and roast," they burn, "Rob, kill and Roast, lead captive, flay, blaspheme." In *"Marlburyes* Fate," probably America's first "advice to a painter" poem, Tompson directs the artist to draw the Indians "besmear'd with Christian Bloud and oild / With fat out of white humane bodyes boil'd" (11. 433–434 *NEC*). The Indians are to be pictured "Like *Vulcans* anvilling *New-Englands* brains" (1. 436). This graphic vividness demonstrates that a Puritan poet could employ a diction and imagery as uninhibited and unrestrained as any of his English models.

The poet chooses language which will most interestingly and instructively affirm the indissoluble connections between the personal and the national, the singular and the corporate, the pilgrim and the plantation. Thus Tompson depicts the commonwealth as a place of Godly vigor, energy, and vitality in which the experiment will succeed and the people prevail. For example, there are scenes in which thousands of admirers flock to the sermons of a pastor, where multitudes press to catch a glimpse of an aged patriarch. In many of Tompson's poems the reader senses the dramatic flow, the swelling movement, a crescendo of activity from the chaos of war to the pomp of a colonial funeral procession.

William Tompson, Edmund Davie, John Wilson, Cotton Mather, and Samuel Whiting, to mention only a few of Tompson's heroes, move in "Orbs of Heavenly Glory" while comets blaze and stars beam their light to mark the saint's translation into pure, spiritual form. These founders cross bloody seas, draw swords on trembling Quakers, "snib" the outrages of the infidel, cut Gordian knots of confusion, and concoct alchemical balsams to cure disease. Their words are streams of nectar, conduits of wisdom, Asiatic stores of love, melting gleams of grace, produced in studious solitude, Attick nights, temples of the Levites, desert and wilderness tents. Repeatedly, he sets down his admiration for those virtuous habits outlined in John Winthrop's lay sermon, "A Modell of Christian Charity." The most important virtues are summarized in a couplet from *New Englands Crisis*: "Freeness in Judgment, union in affection, / Dear love, sound truth they were our grand protection" (11. 61–62). Just as the Phoenix could recreate itself, Christian rulers, writers, and teachers working in conjunction with a just and merciful God could wondrously and magnificently revitalize original principles. In passages where imagination, imagery, and diction form the Matherian concept of American sainthood, where parallels are drawn to biblical, classical, and Reformation heroes, where Tompson taps his knowledge of alchemy, astronomy, meteorology, and anatomy, the language, the form, and the creative vision coalesce. Admiration, sometimes filiopietism, marks Tompson's public voice as he emphasizes the existence of order, the potential for reformation, and the pervasiveness of meaning.

Sacvan Bercovitch is eloquent in his description of the magnitude of the Puritans' mythologizing of the American experience. The New England funeral elegy functions as "federal hagiography," says Bercovitch:

> . . .it constitutes an imaginative achievement of a very high order. Less than thirty years after the *Arabella* landed, before all the leaders of the Great Migration had died, there evolved a legend of a golden age, one that effectually transported all the archetypes of biblical and classical antiquity to the Massachusetts Bay shores. Its sustained intensity, its coherence, and the rapidity with which it grew, amounts to an astonishing, possibly unrivaled cultural maturation. . . . The orthodoxy had invested too much of themselves in their image of America: not only their hopes in founding a city on a hill, but their "national" background, their communal future, and their personal calling. Their recourse during this period of crisis to the legend of the fathers marks a momentous victory for their secular hermeneutics and, by implication, for the concept of American identity.[17]

In his public elegies, and in many of his occasional poems, Benjamin Tompson epitomizes this driving need to establish an American sense of a distinct identity. Insofar as he succeeded in capturing that intensity and coherence, as Bercovitch outlined it, Benjamin Tompson could be considered one of the first American poets to lead us toward cultural maturation.

The complete title of Tompson's elegy on Mary, his sister-in-law, illustrates the primary difference between the public and private elegies: "A short memoriall and Revew of sum / Vertues in that examplary Christian, / Mary Tompson, / who Dyed in march 22: 1679. / penned for the imitation of the liveing." Tompson's family elegies record the private virtues for emulation: secret prayer, tenderness, confession, personal charity, humility, control of the appetites and passions, sacrifice, and purity. In these private elegies the poetic voice speaks a willingness to empathize, to comfort, and to console; on several occasions Tompson himself shares the position of the bereaved—for example, when he tells the surviving children of Sarah Tompson, "Experience sad hath taught mee to confess / It's dolefull to bee left so Motherless" (11. 47–48). Similarly, he tries to soften the Sewalls' grief at the loss of young Rebekah by pointing out the commonality of such tragedy: "Pleasant Rebecka, heres to thee a Tear / Hugg my sweet Mary if you chance to see her" (11. 25–26).

Aside from Benjamin's nephew, Edward Tompson, and perhaps his brother Samuel, a deacon, the other members of his family, particularly the women, were not well-educated. Despite several decades of marriage to one of Boston's most learned schoolteachers, Susanna Kirkland Tompson signed her will with a mark. Tompson believed that philosophical speculation and intellectual language were not suited for farmers, children, and housewives. He therefore adopted a diction and a tone, somewhat sentimental but nevertheless effective, for these private elegies. The imagery, too, was carefully selected to appeal to the childlike sensibilities of the readers. "A Clowde of Tears" for Rebekah Sewall and "AD Deum veni" for Edmund Davie resemble a medieval poem, *The Pearl*, especially when they draw upon the imagery of Revelation to portray the New Jerusalem. In the elegies on Edmund Davie and Elizabeth Tompson, the structural design gives Tompson the freedom and flexibility of the Medieval dream-vision. "AD Deum veni" is headnoted with the standard seventeenth-century anagram, then moves into dramatic monologue by the departed and commentary by Tompson, followed by an epitaph and a Latin emblem. A similar pattern is repeated in the elegy on Elizabeth Tompson, who describes to her survivors "a Cyty filld with all delight" (1. 4), her translation into heaven, and her continued love for her parents. Within this framework, Tompson interjects the didactic commentary, thus judiciously mixing the delightful with the instructive. Such rich techniques as the heavenly epistle and monologue free Tompson from the literal, provide emotional impact, and soften the didactic strains. Moreover, in his private elegies Tompson seems to have been more willing to experiment with a variety of forms, perhaps because of their restricted circulation among close friends and relatives. Ironically, a few of Tompson's most effective conceits occur in the domestic elegies written primarily for exemplum and consolation. Benjamin tells his brother Samuel to consider the "Carcas" of his wife, Sarah, and "View it o'er well, Its but an empty Cage / Where shee was chain'd under a feavors Rage[.]" Then, to complete the metaphor, Tompson adds this image of the soul's ascension to heaven: "The Larke at length hath broke its fretting snare / And sings above your head Surpassing fair" (11. 59–62). There is a beauty and simplicity about the family elegies that often seem possible precisely because they were written for private purposes.

In a sense all of Tompson's elegies are occasional poems, but for the purposes of literary classification only those poems which have as their chief end the chronicling or celebration of colonial events should be categorized as topical (occasional) verse. More specifically, the occasional poems are of various lengths, written to preface and commend another writer's work, to welcome and celebrate the arrival of a colonial dignitary, to report to the world New England's providential and problematic condition, and to reawaken Americans to their puritanic goals of reformation and regeneration. While no one of these poems is exactly like another, all demonstrate Tompson's comprehensive sense of America's uniqueness as a nation. They show Tompson to be a man of complex sensibilities, capable of understanding the value of something outside his own immediate experience, of subtly manipulating tone and balancing ideas, and of laughing at those who take themselves too seriously. Above all, in the occasional poems Tompson reveals his humanity.

By 1675 New England had drastically fallen away from its original intention: the experiment had gone awry. Modern historians, following the lead of Perry Miller, call this period of internal strife and apostasy between 1660 and the Great Awakening the age of "declension." Miller, and more recently Emory Elliott, examined hundreds of printed sermons delivered by the second- and third-generation Puritans.[18] Although they discovered different motives for the composition of the "jeremiad," named for the prophet Jeremiah who bewailed the idolatrous condition of the Israelites, both Miller and Elliott would agree that such sermons reflect strong dissatisfaction with the progress of American Protestantism, specifically the New England Congregational Way. In these poems Tompson admits that he could not guarantee the rising glory of New England or the progress of Congregational-Protestant causes in America. Nor could he rest in the certain knowledge that the Holy Commonwealth had been firmly established on American soil. Massachusetts was a paradise constantly in the process of being lost and regained. New

England was to Tompson, as it was to so many of his generation, a place of promise and threat, of once virgin simplicity now threatened by internal and external enemies.

What ultimately worried the Puritans of this period, the members of the "Rising Generation," were the frequent evidences of Divine dissatisfaction with New England. Natural disasters, tragic and sudden deaths of the founders, epidemics, and political failures seemed to occur with greater frequency and intensity. More frightening yet were accounts of Indian raids and captivities: it seemed to the average frontiersman that God had purposely selected the Indian as His chief instrument of retribution. Once before, in 1637, God had whipped up the Pequot frenzy to punish the Puritans for allowing the Antinomian challenge to go so long unchecked. Now, in 1675–1676, God had unleashed a fearful weapon against them—the large but loose confederation of Algonquin tribes, the Narragansets, Nipmucks, Wampanoages, Mohegans, and others. As wilderness towns were set ablaze, women and children were assaulted in their homes and taken captive, while entire regiments of soldiers were ambushed in the woods or swamps. Now an unemployed resident of Charlestown and the father of three children, Benjamin Tompson decided that this war was an event of epic and potentially tragic dimensions—and he would describe the war to the world in just those terms.

There is nothing quite like *New Englands Crisis* in early American literature. Certainly, other poetic and prose narratives in the seventeenth century purported to describe the Englishman's conflict with the native American Indian. Edward Johnson, William Bradford, Roger Williams, John Josselyn, Peter Folger, Peter Hubbard, and many others had previously attempted to define the nature of the American Indian, his language, his religion, his military strategy, and even his origins. Wait Winthrop, son of Governor John Winthrop, II, celebrated the Great Swamp fight of 1675 with a news ballad entitled *Some Meditations Concerning our Honourable Gentlemen and Fellow-Souldiers, in Pursuit of those Barbarous Natives in Narragansit Country*. And when Benjamin Tompson wrote in 1676 that he hoped his humble efforts would inspire "quainter pens," the response was almost immediate—Philip Walker, a self-educated weaver and sawyer from Rehoboth, dashed off "Captan Perse & his coragios Company," one of the first attempts at an American epic. Diane Bornstein, who edited Walker's poem for the American Antiquarian Society, has persuasively traced Tompson's influence on Walker. Bornstein says, "It seems likely that Walker came to know *New Englands Crisis* through Noah Newman, whose dead father Samuel is the focus of 'Seaconck or Rehoboths Fate': . . . The resemblances between Walker's poem and Tompson's are too close to be coincidental."[19] However, these are essentially distinct poems, and parallels are primarily incidental.

Although we know that Tompson pledged allegiance to Massachusetts Bay and that he treated the wounded (and anatomized one of the enemy), he probably had little personal exposure to the actual fighting of the war. Nevertheless, in *New Englands Crisis* he used an almost journalistic approach to add power, verisimilitude, and immediacy to his descriptive passages. He does everything within his power to give the reader the impression that his reports come from the thick of things. The reader always has the sense that Tompson is both eyewitness and omniscient narrator as he ranges freely from Indian camp to Puritan garrison, from Irish bogs to deep forests, from virgin bowers to brumal dens, all the while mapping the movements and stratagems of the opposing forces. At one point he ambiguously refers to his position in reference to actual events:

> Methinks I see the *Trojan-horse* burst ope,
> And such rush forth as might with giants cope:
> These first the natives treachery felt, too fierce
> For any but eye-witness to rehearse.
> (11. 201–204 *NEC*)

As a result of passages like this, Tompson achieves a curious effect—a unique combination of epical and mythological stature on one hand, and an American realism on the other. In other words, he is adept at juggling the classical and the colloquial or familiar. Perhaps the greatest example of such imaginative fusion occurs in King Philip's set-speech, the only passage by Tompson which might honestly be called famous. To all the pomp and formality which usually characterizes the epic, Tompson adds the lowly and common to prepare the satiric groundwork:

> And here methinks I see this greasy *Lout*
> With all his pagan slaves coil'd round about,
> Assuming all the majesty his throne
> Of rotten stump, or of the rugged stone
> Could yield; casting some bacon-rine-like looks,
> Enough to fright a Student from his books,
> Thus treat his peers, and next to them his Commons,
> Kennel'd together all without a summons.
> (11. 103–110 *NEC*)

The idea of American Indians behaving like the grand diplomats and military strategists of ancient history—here in a barbarous and ludicrous way—must have amused the colonial reader. But in the speech King Philip delivers to his warriors, Tompson ingeniously undermines both the Indian and the Puritan: King Philip is angry, arrogant, irreverent, and lusty, and the Puritans are greedy, unlawful, intemperate, and hypocritical.

Tompson's entire "mock-epic," as it has been called, manages to sustain this double-edged wit, although it must be admitted that his sympathies are clearly with the European/American cause. There is no denying that Tompson took the popular, misinformed, stereotypical view of the American Indian, but a historical view may explain why Tompson wrote about the American Indians as he did. He thought of himself as the colonial bard, and, like his personified Fame, he took on the role of the announcer, the revealer, the scop with a printing press at his disposal. When he declared that his aim was to be of service to his country, he might have been thinking of the classical definition of poet as prophet in that he acts as a kind of interpreter of supernatural intercession into human affairs. He also knew that the epic poet was expected to chronicle national events with imagination and vitality. Finally, I believe Tompson considered it his duty to use literature to admonish those who failed to live up to the spiritual objectives and values of his country. In this manner he succeeds in maintaining some distance, some objectivity, in assigning blame and merit to both sides.

The most remarkable feature of *New Englands Crisis* (and *New-Englands Tears*) is that Tompson disproves in hundreds of lines of poetry the popular image of the Puritan as a lugubrious and pious bore. Even in this time of colonial disaster, during a war that killed over twenty percent of the adult male European population of America—a higher percentage than in any other American conflict—there was room for humor. Naturally, Tompson considered war and its consequent death and destruction hateful and pathetic; he said, "War digs a common grave for friends and foes" (1. 355 *NEC*). But he also saw that in every human affair, even war, people are still capable of the ridiculous and the humorous. For example, the poems on King Philip's War, especially "THE PROLOGUE" to *New Englands Crisis*, leave no one unscathed. Tompson deftly controls the satirical tone, so that finally he has maligned everyone imaginable. He attacks the ancient planters who said grace so long their hasty pudding grew cold, the new merchants who sinned away the golden age for love of gold, the prating women who ruined their complexions with imported delicacies, the "Grandee" missionaries who were dumped in Boston harbor on this new Thanksgiving Day, and the pretentious Harvard dons who now, almost incredibly, found themselves speechless. Tompson even finds an opportunity to criticize himself: "And men had better stomachs to religion / Than I to capon, turkey-cock or pigeon" (11. 27–28). Or Tompson can display a kind of gentle wit, through a series of stunningly appropriate and comic metaphors, to poke fun at those Amazonian dames who overcome their false femininity to sandbag Boston Neck. Harold Jantz called this last poem, "On *A FORTIFICATION At* Boston *begun by Women*," "jolly good fun

and worthy to be included in an anthology of Puritan humor. . . ."[20]
Brom Weber seconded Jantz's remark by including Tompson's poem in
his *Anthology of American Humor*.[21]

The satirical strokes of which Tompson proved himself capable in *New
Englands Crisis* were surrounded chronologically by other satirical ef-
forts. If, in fact, the earliest poem in this edition—on the ordination of
Samuel Arnold—was actually written by Tompson at age sixteen, we
have a clear indication that he had always cultivated the caustic side of
his temperament and talent. If we can believe Tompson when he wrote
in 1708 that "The Grammarians Funeral," an elegy on Ezekiel Chevers,
was first written in 1667 for John (Robert) Woodmancy, we have fur-
ther evidence of his early interest in wit and humor. If we doubt Tomp-
son's veracity, we are left with the proposition that he deliberately
created an elegy, which could easily be taken as irreverent, to "honor"
the man who was somewhat secretively offered his position at the Boston
Latin School. Ezekiel Chevers was one of New England's most revered
scholars: when he died at age ninety-four, he was universally respected
for his limitless knowledge, authority, and dignity. Singlehandedly, he
had prepared hundreds of young men for such institutions as Harvard,
Cambridge, and Padua. To pay tribute to such a man, Benjamin Tomp-
son published an elegy, larded with outrageous puns, in which Latin
personifications behave like peasants at a country wake. Except for the
final six lines of the poem, a unit radically different in tone and impact,
Tompson's elegy borders on mockery. One would think that a funeral
ceremony for a man like Ezekiel Chevers would have been an occasion
for great solemnity and mourning, but Tompson's personifications re-
semble the "pit" audiences in a Renaissance theater or the characters in a
Restoration comedy. "The Grammarians Funeral" is an early American
poem which ought to make us question our assumptions about social
behavior in the seventeenth century. More important, this poem chal-
lenges us to reexamine our ideas about Puritan poetry in general. Al-
though "The Grammarians Funeral" has been reprinted time and again,
it has never been subjected to critical analysis because, I suspect, it does
not fit standard definitions. In other elegies of this period, the linguistic
ploys, puns, anagrams, acrostics, and metaphors are decidedly functional.
They can be explained as manifestations of the Puritan's earnest disposi-
tion to dissect Providence, to reveal the order inherent in the universe.
The plainly comic impact of "The Grammarians Funeral" signifies that
Tompson either pushed this habit to an outlandish extreme (for satirical
reasons, perhaps), or that he simply did not share the prevailing aesthetic
goals. One thing is certain: "The Grammarians Funeral" goes beyond
the norms.

It does not seem unreasonable to argue that Tompson was having good fun at Ezekiel Chevers's expense. On several other occasions, Tompson was quite willing to come dangerously close to insulting important people. Cotton Mather has been called many things throughout history, but I doubt that anyone has ever described him as jovial. Yet when Tompson, Mather's former teacher, celebrated the publication of the *Magnalia Christi Americana* in 1702, he did not hesitate to poke fun at the author of one of America's most impressive histories. Again, Tompson illustrates his facility for controlling tone. He does this with such brilliance that he can take several quick jabs at his victim, usually through the pun, within the framework of generally complimentary verse. He obviously admires Mather's compendious volume, even as he admired William Hubbard's *Narrative of the Troubles with the Indians of New-England* (Boston, 1677). But in the former poem, Tompson gently eases across the thin line between sincere praise and conscious ridicule of Mather's learning. Just ten years after the Salem witchcraft trials, Tompson dared to "accuse" the Reverend Mather of practicing the "familiar arts" and necromancy. Lesser poets than Tompson might have been thrashed for this.

Harold Jantz remarked in *The First Century of New England Verse* that Tompson's poetry, and perhaps his public behavior, may have caused "the first native bard" some problems: "Popular and charming he no doubt was, able too as a schoolmaster, and always eager to stand well with the men in power, but his volatility and cleverness probably rendered him somewhat suspect to the more solid and unimaginative citizens of the province."[22] One historical event, in particular, supports Jantz's theory—the arrival of Lord Bellamont in Boston, May 1699. Bellamont had come to Massachusetts Bay, after a long stay in New York, to assume the governorship of the colony. In an effort to cement good relations between the British crown and the province, Boston arranged to greet Bellamont with full pageantry. Whether Tompson was actually commissioned to address the new governor and his lady is unknown. In any case we know that Tompson wrote a pastoral skit which Jantz says "came as near to a dramatic representation as anything ever did in Puritan New England."[23] Dressed in the costume of Nathaniel Ward's Simple Cobbler of Aggawam, Tompson recited a "rural Bitt" while shepherdesses offered the travelers nectar, flowers, and songs of welcome. This affair must have charmed many present, but to others it may have smacked of Morton's Maypole romps, Bartholomew Fair, and Restoration theater. It may have been the only day in the seventeenth century in which Boston officially sanctioned something reminiscent of merry old England. One may guess that Tompson was selected to write the address and play the part because he had previously been called upon to welcome Urian Oakes back to these shores in 1671, or because he had distinguished himself in 1662 when he delivered an amusing Latin oration at Harvard commencement. Unfortunately, little weight can be attached to this hypothesis since both the Oakes poem and the oration cannot be positively identified as Tompson's. Yet, without doubt, Tompson is the author of the address to Lord Bellamont, and it stands as one of his greatest achievements.

The address ought to be viewed as the best of Tompson's poetic career in microcosm: it is public, witty, rather bold in conception, but also honest and sincere in expression. It is sprinkled with classical and biblical allusions; it pauses to ridicule Harvard and Captain Kidd; it traces the progress of American civilization and outlines its paradisical beauty; and it pays tribute to those who would rule the country. The poem paints a picture of America as Tompson always imagined it should be—the place of joyful and open charity, love, and respect. Tompson's America was not without its problems: the university was floundering, the governors had lost the colonies' charter, and people were growing tired of English intrusion into their affairs. But beyond the crude provincialism apparent to all, Tompson could see that America had already established traditions and would some day rise to greatness, even in the arts. In the nineteenth century Channing, Emerson, and Whitman called for a poet who would celebrate America's traditions and potential. Had they looked back to the seventeenth century, they might have seen in Benjamin Tompson, the colonial bard, a perfect prototype.

Notes

1. Sacvan Bercovitch, ed., *The American Puritan Imagination: Essays in Revaluation* (Cambridge: Cambridge University Press, 1974), Introduction, p. 4.

2. Harrison T. Meserole, "New Voices from Seventeenth-Century America," in *Discoveries and Reconsiderations*, ed. Calvin Israel (Albany: State University of New York Press, 1976), p. 26.

3. Larzer Ziff, "The Literary Consequences of Puritanism," in *The American Puritan Imagination*, ed. Bercovitch, p. 43.

4. Roy Harvey Pearce, *The Continuity of American Poetry* (Princeton, N.J.: Princeton University Press, 1961), p. 24.

5. Norman S. Grabo, "The Veiled Vision: The Role of Aesthetics in Early American Intellectual History," in *The American Puritan Imagination*, ed. Bercovitch, p. 29.

6. Pearce, p. 19.

7. Richard Mather, *A Farewel-Exhortation To the Church and People of Dorchester in New-England* (1657), quoted from Perry Miller, *From Colony to Province* (Cambridge: Harvard University Press, 1953), p. 4.

8. Grabo, in *The American Puritan Imagination*, p. 25, and Alan Simpson, *Puritanism in Old and New England* (Chicago: University of Chicago Press, 1955), p. 21.

9. John Cotton, *The Way of Life* (London, 1641), quoted in *The Puritans: A Sourcebook of Their Writings*, eds. Perry Miller and Thomas H. Johnson (1938; rpt. New York: Harper and Row, 1963), p. 318.

10. Thomas Hooker, *The Application of Redemption* (London, 1659), quoted in Miller and Johnson, pp. 301–306.

11. Joshua Moody, *Souldiery Spiritualized* (Cambridge, 1674), quoted in Miller and Johnson, pp. 367–368.

12. Pearce, p. 34.

13. Edwin S. Fussell, "Benjamin Tompson, Public Poet," *The New England Quarterly*, 26 (1953), 498–499.

14. Sacvan Bercovitch, *The Puritan Origins of the American Self* (New Haven: Yale University Press, 1975), p. 2.

15. Ibid., p. 6.

16. Ibid., p. 5.

17. Ibid., pp. 122–123.

18. See note 2, Chapter 2 above.

19. Diane Bornstein, "Captan Perse & his coragios Company," *The Proceedings of the American Antiquarian Society*, 83 (1973), 72, 67–102.

20. Harold Jantz, *The First Century of New England Verse* (Worcester: 1943–44; rpt. Russell and Russell, 1962), p. 73.

21. *An Anthology of American Humor*, ed. Brom Weber (New York: Crowell, 1962).

22. Jantz, *The First Century*, p. 71.

23. Ibid., p. 164.

CHAPTER IV

The Historic Tompson: Textual and Critical Commentary

Benjamin Tompson wrote in 1695 that his brother Samuel's Christian "Examples set before this Age / And me in special wel deserv'd a Page[.]"[1] The same might also be said for the poetry of Benjamin Tompson: it well deserves a text. The "Renouned Poet of N: Engl" called himself a scribbler, a naked Sylvan, "guiltless as to Art," one who wrote with a "Rural Pen" to shed some "countrey tears." Yet if we read his poetry with the attention it merits, we cannot but be impressed with this indigent schoolmaster's urbanity, learning, wit, and sincerity. Nor can we ignore the plain facts of his poetic career: he published the first volume of American poetry to be reprinted in England; he was the first writer to use Anglo-Indian language for satirical purposes; he published prefatory poems in two of the greatest history books of the seventeenth century; he was the leading actor in his pastoral "play" performed in Boston in 1699; and he seems to have made absolutely no effort to preserve any of the poems which appear in this edition.

In some respects Tompson's poetic career is marked by its regularity and consistency. If we stand back from his individual poems and survey Tompson's career, several patterns become apparent. First, because he lived to the age of seventy-two, Tompson had the opportunity to produce a good deal of poetry over a long period of time. In the fifty-five years of his productivity, from the 1658 poem on Samuel Arnold to his "last lines" of 1713, Tompson wrote at least twenty-nine poems. His career can be divided into two major periods of activity neatly separated by twelve years of apparent passivity. From 1666, the year of his father's death, until 1682–83 when he wrote to Increase Mather about his financial problems, Tompson averaged one and sometimes two poems per year, if we count the poems in his volumes on King Philip's War as individual efforts. Between 1683 and 1695 it appears that Tompson was either preoccupied with his duties as the Braintree schoolmaster or he was despondent over his financial plight to such an extent that he ceased writing. Of course the possibility always exists that Tompson's work from this time, written perhaps in his own journal, will someday be uncovered. In the final stage of his career, 1695 to 1713, Tompson wrote about one poem every other year, or, more exactly, eleven different poems in eighteen years. These verses, however, are shorter and obviously less ambitious than those of his younger years.

The fairly regular appearance of Tompson's poetry is matched by a discernible pattern in the major sources for his extant work. Over half of Tompson's verses were preserved by relatives or close friends of his family: Joseph Tompson, Benjamin's elder brother by two years, preserved three poems in his journal; Samuel Tompson (Harvard, A.B. 1710), Benjamin's grandnephew from Newbury, Massachusetts, copied four of his uncle's verses into a manuscript of twelve duodecimo pages which were given to the Massachusetts Historical Society by Edward Tompson, another of Benjamin's descendants; one elegy was discovered in Sarah Tompson's journal; Samuel Sewall and Cotton Mather, two of Benjamin's associates, preserved six more poems; and the Winthrops, who I believe were close to the Tompsons, treasured at least two of Benjamin's elegies.

It is difficult, however, to determine Tompson's interest in having his work published or circulated through the community. Some of the poems, like *New Englands Crisis* or the *Magnalia* contributions, were obviously intended for publication. The elegies on public figures, if not printed, may have been read at funeral ceremonies or distributed among the family of the deceased, as was customary in New England in the seventeenth century. Certainly, though, the elegies which Tompson produced for the consolation of his own family were intended to give private solace: in tone, direction, and diction they are significantly and consciously different from the public elegies.

Several elegies on such eminent colonial figures as Fitz-John Winthrop or John Leverett may never have been published during Tompson's lifetime, or they may have appeared in broadsides which are now irretrievable. These possibilities, in turn, lead one to believe that Tompson may have written many more verses of a similar nature which are no longer extant. For example, it seems highly unlikely that he could have silently accepted the death of Richard Mather, an old friend of the Tompsons. Mather died in 1669, and that date falls into a nine-year gap, 1667 to 1676, in the Tompson corpus. Is it possible that Tompson had nothing to say about Governors Bellingham (d. 1672), Phips (d. 1695), Bradstreet (d. 1697), Stoughton (d.1701), or Sir Edmund Andros (ruled 1686–1689); could Tompson have ignored the deaths of Harvard College Presidents Chauncy (d. 1671), Hoar (d. 1675, buried at Braintree), Oakes (d. 1681), Rogers (d. 1684), or Samuel Willard (d. 1707) ? Also disturbing is the fact that Tompson made little or no mention of other colonial poets. We know that Samuel Danforth (d. 1674) was a good friend of the Tompson family and wrote several anagrams in their honor, and that Tompson was a close friend of Samuel Sewall, who enjoyed the company and work of Edward Johnson (d. 1677), Nicholas Noyes (d. 1717), and the Mathers. John Fiske of Chelmsford was, like Tompson, a poet, physician, and schoolmaster, but Tompson was silent about his death in 1677. Michael Wigglesworth (d. 1705), perhaps New England's most popular poet, was also a physician and a renowned minister, yet Tompson never mentioned him. It is difficult to estimate Tompson's interest in important ecclesiastical events and controversies, but the Half-Way Covenant, the Reforming Synod, and the witchcraft trials could have provoked Tompson's satiric pen. In brief, then, it seems probable that Tompson wrote many more poems than are extant; certainly, material appropriate to Tompson's poetic temperament and ambition was readily available to him. Speculation about the kinds of topics which may have appealed to Tompson is possible and reasonable given his consistent interest in three major areas: an event of colonial significance, the death of a family member or patriarch, and the follies of the pretentious. The overwhelming majority of Tompson's poems can be classified as either occasional, elegiac, or satirical.

Fortunately, a number of dedicated scholars took pains to keep Tompson's name alive in our literary history. In 1829 Samuel Kettell excerpted passages from *New Englands Crisis* and concluded that Tompson "must be allowed considerable praise; he is exceeded by none of his contemporaries for correct and smooth versification."[2] Rufus Griswold also recognized the literary virtues of the "first native bard"[3] but dismissed him with a critical flourish: "He wrote besides his 'great epic,' three shorter poems, neither of which have much merit."[4] Evert A. and George L. Duyckinck published in 1855 the *Cyclopaedia of American Literature; Embracing Personal and Critical Notices of Authors.* The Duyckincks had the good sense to go beyond Kettell and Griswold by reprinting and focusing critical attention upon two of Tompson's lesser known poems: "On *A FORTIFICATION At* Boston *begun by Women*" (from *New Englands Crisis*) and the witty "Celeberrimi Cottoni Matheri."[5]

All students of American literature are indebted to Moses Coit Tyler, whose *A History of American Literature: 1607–1765* appeared in 1878. Unable to locate Kettell's copy of *New Englands Crisis*, Tyler had to confine his comments to the extracts given by Kettell; nevertheless, his critical opinions are worth quoting at length:

This poet's best vein is satiric,—his favorite organ being the rhymed pentameter couplet, with a flow, a vigor, and an edge obviously caught from the contemporaneous verse of John Dryden. He has the partisanship, the exaggeration, the choleric injustice, that are common in satire; and like other satirists, failing to note the moral perspectives of history, he utters over again the stale and easy lie, wherein the past is held up as wiser and holier than the present. Though New England has had a life but little more than fifty years long, the poet sees within it the tokens of a hurrying degeneracy, in customs, in morals, in valor, in piety. He turns back, with reverent and eyeless homage, to the good old times of the Founders. . . .[6]

In 1894, through the bibliographic and critical scholarship of John Langdon Sibley and Samuel A. Green, the only known copy of *New Englands Crisis* was located in the Boston Athenaeum and published by the Club of Odd Volumes. *New-Englands Tears* was also located in the library of John Nicholas Brown.

More than any other scholar of the nineteenth century, Samuel A. Green deserves recognition for his careful scrutiny of the literary matter of New England. It was Dr. Green, in conjunction with the Massachusetts Historical Society, who first began serious inquiry into Tompson's literary career. In the 1895–96 *Proceedings of the Massachusetts Historical Society*, Green traced the relationship between *New Englands Crisis* and *New-Englands Tears*, identified Tompson as the author of both, provided bibliographical descriptions and excerpts, brought to light "The Grammarians Funeral" and the three elegies on Rebekah Sewall, and supplied biographical and historical commentary.[7] Perhaps the most important consequence of Green's scholarship was that it inspired others, notably Edward W. E. Tompson, to contribute to the rediscovery of Benjamin Tompson. Edward Tompson, a member of the Suffolk County bar and a collateral descendant of Benjamin Tompson, sent to the Massachusetts Historical Society a manuscript of twelve duodecimo pages containing four more of Tompson's poems, as well as poems by Edward Tompson (Benjamin's nephew) and Samuel Danforth.[8]

While the quantity of Tompson's poetry increased, the frequency of critical response abated until 1924 when Howard Judson Hall produced one of the first editions of the verse of a seventeenth-century American.[9] Before Thomas H. Johnson's discovery of Edward Taylor, prior even to the pioneering work of Miller, Morison, and Murdock, Hall assembled all of Tompson's extant poetry into one critical edition. Seventeen of Tompson's poems were included—several from private collections, two from the *Magnalia*, four from the Edward Tompson manuscript, and all the poems previously catalogued by Green. Although Hall was a careful and diligent scholar, his work was marred in several respects: he included Samuel Danforth's anagram among Tompson's poems; he could not locate Tompson's elegy on Governor John Leverett, which had previously been catalogued by Sibley; his textual transcriptions were occasionally inaccurate; and his annotations, cast in the form of brief introductory comments, were inadequate. But perhaps ultimately more damaging to Tompson's reputation were Hall's introductory remarks on Tompson's poetic ability. Partially as a result of the temper and taste of the times, Hall concluded that Tompson's "work is not art; it is the handicraft of a people in the second and third generations of those who have suppressed in themselves all art for conscience's sake. Even in its crudeness and yearning for form it proves the human impossibility of denying art altogether. . . . If it be questioned why Tompson, knowing, as a schoolmaster, the best of classic authors, wrote such bad verses in English, the same query may be put concerning many an English poet of that day."[10] Of course, Hall thought he was defending Tompson against the majority who still believed that puritanism and poetry were completely antithetical, particularly in America.

Despite its shortcomings, Hall's edition accomplished one of the primary objectives of textual criticism: the discovery of more manuscript material. Immediately following the 1924 publication of *Benjamin Tompson . . . His Poems*, C. E. Goodspeed of Boston notified Kenneth Murdock of Harvard University of the existence of Joseph Tompson's manuscript journal which included two previously unpublished poems by Benjamin Tompson, one by Anna Hayden, and four by John Wilson. In all, the journal contained eleven poems, seven of which had never before been published. Moreover, the journal identified Samuel Danforth, not Benjamin Tompson, as the author of the anagram "lo now i am past ill." Murdock, eventually to become one of America's most respected scholars, pronounced Tompson able "to write better verse than his contemporaries. If one reads New England colonial poetry, one finds no one save the English-born Anne Bradstreet, and, perhaps, Samuel Danforth, who comes nearer than he to mastery in verse."[11] Few today would deny that Edward Taylor is the most interesting and capable of the colonial poets, but Taylor's poems were not discovered until 1937. When Murdock published *Literature and Theology in Colonial New England* in 1949, he stated unequivocally, "The best poet of Puritan New England, and one whose finest passages are memorable, is Edward Taylor."[12]

Curiously, though, Murdock made no mention of Benjamin Tompson in 1949, perhaps because Harold Jantz had already given Tompson a good deal of attention in his *The First Century of New England Verse*, published in 1943–44 in the *Proceedings of the American Antiquarian Society*. Jantz's bibliography of seventeenth-century American verse is one of those indispensable, scholarly tools, which must be consulted throughout any textual project. Eight more poems were added to the Tompson corpus by Jantz, including the Davie poems, the lost Leverett elegy, and the Lord Bellamont celebration, all of which he transcribed for *The First Century.* In the evaluative section of his study, Jantz praised Tompson's learning, his secular temperament and wit, his Baroque sensibility, his American vigor, and his domestic simplicity; in other words, Jantz admired Tompson's poetic and intellectual range. One of his most intriguing remarks, however, was that "unpublished poems of his [Tompson's] have been turning up regularly in the most widely dispersed localities."[13] While I am convinced that Tompson wrote many more poems than we now have, unless we can locate his commonplace book, journal, or diary, only accidental discoveries are likely.

Trusting in their own critical instincts, a host of twentieth-century literary scholars recognized Tompson's talents and importance and included a wide variety of his poems in their anthologies of American literature. Perry Miller and Thomas H. Johnson, Russel B. Nye and Norman S. Grabo, Kenneth Silverman, Roy Harvey Pearce, and Brom Weber have selected, transcribed, and annotated, besides *New Englands Crisis*, such historically underrated work as "The Grammarians Funeral," "On *A FORTIFICATION At* Boston," and "*Upon the setting of that Occidental Star* John Winthrop *Esq.*"[14] In his anthology, *Seventeenth-Century American Poetry* (1968), Harrison T. Meserole included *New Englands Crisis*, the Davie poems, and a facsimile of "The Grammarians Funeral." Throughout the Introduction to his anthology, Meserole spoke of Tompson as representative of certain characteristics of seventeenth-century American poetry: Tompson's art was consciously and patiently practiced; his work was popular and acceptable to English audiences; he was not a sober, pious minister who harangued his readers with narrow dogmatics but a poor schoolmaster who wrote with "a lively, hard-driving pace and a perceptive eye for situations. . . . It is his ability to take a whole view of situations and events, and to fix them with graphic completeness, that makes Tompson an important poet of early America."[15]

Extended critical response to Tompson's poetry in the years following Jantz's work has been stimulating but too infrequent. In fact, only three articles have been written on Tompson in the last thirty years, and longer studies of American poetry most often mention Tompson only in passing. In 1953 Edwin S. Fussell published "Benjamin Tompson, Public Poet" in *The New England Quarterly.* Fussell's overview of Tompson's career is an extremely comprehensive and sympathetic estimation of his art, concluding in this manner: "Underrating his own talent, he [Tompson] has been nearly forgotten by literary historians and all but ignored by antiquarians. He deserves better. Poem by poem, he is representative of certain aspects of Puritan culture that need attention; in a few passages, he measures up to the best that Puritan literature can show."[16]

Roy Harvey Pearce, in *The Continuity of American Poetry*, and Larzer

Ziff, in *Puritanism in America: New Culture in a New World*, appear to have followed Fussell's suggestion that Tompson be considered a representative poet and thinker. Pearce, who wrote that some of Wigglesworth's and Tompson's poems are "crude, overinsistent, even vulgar,"[17] would nevertheless credit Tompson with originality in turning wit to use in the normally morose elegy (for example, in "The Grammarians Funeral") and with achieving a "certain directness and realism in his portrayal of Indians as creatures of Satan."[18] Pearce further argued that Tompson was a representative Puritan poet in that he captured in his poetry "the tension of desperate certitude," the meaning of the history the Puritans were in the process of making, and employed all the artistic and technical skill of which he was capable to something higher than merely aesthetic ends: Tompson had that "characteristic Puritan insistence on fixing once and for all the meaning of the event as that event is somehow bound up in a communal experience."[19] Working from a similar understanding of Tompson's literary aims, Larzer Ziff analyzed the significance of Tompson's appeal to the Golden Age in *New Englands Crisis*, a poem which Ziff says "fixed his countrymen's image of themselves."[20]

The most recent work on Tompson is that of Professor Neil T. Eckstein, who edited Tompson's elegy on Sarah Tompson and who analyzed the pastoral and primitive elements in Tompson's poetry, particularly in the address "To Lord Bellamont."[21] Eckstein believes that Tompson's use of pastoral conventions in this address suggests a deliberate effort on the part of the poet to adapt his poetry to the latest European literary vogue—the neoclassical imitation and adaption of the Virgilian pastoral."[22]

Although the critical and scholarly works of Jantz, Meserole, Pearce, and others have provided us with a solid introduction to Tompson's literary methods and talents, interesting and profitable approaches still remain. One could, for example, subject "The Grammarians Funeral" to further linguistic analysis and place that work within the larger context of the Puritan elegy; or examine Tompson's alchemical, medical, theological, and historical allusions and references to discover more about his Baroque qualities; or place him squarely within a classical framework with its reliance upon standard rhetorical techniques. We still know little about the exact nature and extent of Tompson's commerce with the Sewalls, the Mathers, the Winthrops, the Davies, or other colonial poets such as Saffin, Noyes, and Wigglesworth. Closer scrutiny of Tompson's sometimes exotic diction and imagery—particularly of his realistic and metaphoric portrayal of the American Indian—might further clarify both our understanding of Puritan poetic practices and their emotionally heightened fear and hatred of the American "savage," especially as he was seen by the common man. A detailed study of the relationship among the three *New Englands Crisis* texts could reveal more about the ways in which an American poet's work might appear under English imprint. The primary purpose in making Benjamin Tompson's poetry readily available is to raise these and other important questions.

Notes

1. Benjamin Tompson, "A Character of . . . Mr. Samuel Tompson," ll. 5–6. All further references to Tompson's poetry are based on my edition and are cited, within the text of this chapter, by line numbers.

2. Samuel Kettell, *Specimens of American Poetry with Critical and Biographical Notices* 3 vols., (Boston: S. G. Goodrich and Co., 1829), I, xlii.

3. Harold Jantz, *The First Century of New England Verse* (Worcester, 1943–44; rpt. Russell and Russell, 1962), p. 57, says, "We can add here that he [Josiah Winslow (1629–1680)] was also, to our present knowledge, the first native-born writer of verse, being thirteen years older than Benjamin Tompson, who has long enjoyed that frankly meaningless rank but is actually about in eighth place."

4. Rufus Wilmont Griswold, *The Poets and Poetry of America, To the Middle of the Nineteenth Century* (Philadelphia: A. Hart, Late Carey & Hart, 1852), p. xxi.

5. Evert A. and George L. Duyckinck, *Cyclopaedia of American Literature; Embracing Personal and Critical Notices of Authors, and Selections from Their Writings*, 2 vols. (New York: Charles Scribner, 1866), I, 66–68.

6. Moses Coit Tyler, *A History of American Literature: 1607–1765*, 2 vols. (1878; rpt. Ithaca: Cornell University Press, 1949), I, 274–275.

7. Samuel A. Green, untitled paper on Benjamin Tompson, *The Proceedings of the Massachusetts Historical Society*, 2nd ser., 10 (1895), 263–285.

8. Ibid.

9. *Benjamin Tompson . . . His Poems*, ed. Howard Judson Hall (Boston: Houghton Mifflin, 1924).

10. Ibid., p. 27.

11. *Handkerchiefs from Paul*, ed. Kenneth B. Murdock (Cambridge: Harvard University Press, 1927), p. xxxi.

12. Kenneth B. Murdock, *Literature and Theology in Colonial New England* (Cambridge: Harvard University Press, 1949), p. 152.

13. Jantz, p. 71.

14. Tompson's poems have appeared in *The Puritans: A Sourcebook of their Writings*, ed. Perry Miller and Thomas H. Johnson (New York: Harper and Row, 1938); *American Thought and Writing*, ed. Russel B. Nye and Norman S. Grabo (Boston: Houghton Mifflin, 1965); *Colonial American Poetry*, ed. Kenneth Silverman (New York: Hafner Publishing Co., 1968); *Colonial American Writing*, 2nd. Ed., ed. Roy Harvey Pearce (New York: Holt, Rinehart, and Winston, 1969); *An Anthology of American Humor*, ed. Brom Weber (New York: Crowell, 1962).

15. *Seventeenth-Century American Poetry*, ed. Harrison T. Meserole (Garden City, N.Y.: Doubleday, 1968), p. 222.

16. Edwin S. Fussell, "Benjamin Tompson, Public Poet," *New England Quarterly*, 26 (1953), 494–511.

17. Roy Harvey Pearce, *The Continuity of American Poetry* (Princeton, N.J.: Princeton University Press, 1961), p. 24.

18. Ibid., p. 21.

19. Ibid., pp. 19, 24.

20. Larzer Ziff, *Puritanism in America: New Culture in a New World* (New York: Viking Press, 1973), p. 161.

21. Neil T. Eckstein, "Benjamin Tompson's Elegy, 'A Short But Sorrowfull Memoriall of My Dear Sister Sarah Tompson,'" *Connecticut Historical Society Bulletin*, 36 (July 1971), 72–76; and "The Pastoral and the Primitive in Benjamin Tompson's 'Address to Lord Bellamont,'" *Early American Literature*, 8 (Feb. 1973), 111–116.

22. Eckstein, "The Pastoral and the Primitive," p. 113.

CHAPTER V

Editorial Principles

The poems in this edition have been arranged chronologically, according to the certain or probable date of composition or publication. In many cases I have assumed that Tompson composed the elegies within a few days of the subject's death, and I have trusted Tompson's statement that "The Grammarians Funeral" was originally written for John (Robert) Woodmancy. The poems on Rebekah Sewall are ordered as they were in the Winthrop Papers, with the published broadside appearing last since it may have been a conflation of the two manuscript versions. I have placed the poems on Samuel Arnold, Moses Fiske, Edward Tompson, Urian Oakes, and John Wilson in an appendix, labeling them "Poems Probably by Tompson." Although all internal evidence, and some external evidence, leads to the conclusion that Tompson was in fact the author, some editorial caution still seems necessary. Further research may soon solve the problem of attribution.

I may perhaps add a parenthetical word here about the identification and short-title designations of the major family sources of Tompson's poetry. Because a number of scholars, over a period of two centuries, have considered the family journals and commonplace books which contain Tompson's poems, they have been assigned different and admittedly confusing names. In every case, I have tried to be clear and complete in my identification of these main manuscript sources: (1) The Massachusetts Historical Society, twelve-page, duodecimo manuscript, is a fragile fragment which appears to have been the work of Samuel Tompson (Harvard College, 1710), the grandnephew of Benjamin Tompson and the grandson of Samuel Tompson of Braintree. Jantz calls this manuscript "elegies of the Tompson family," but I have given it the designation "Edward Tompson manuscript" because it was given to the Massachusetts Historical Society by Edward Tompson in June 1895. (2) The second major source is the Joseph Tompson journal now located at the Houghton Library, Harvard University. Kenneth Murdock has described this book and its author in *Handkerchiefs from Paul* (Cambridge, Mass., 1927). (3) The Sarah Tompson manuscript, located in the collections of the Connecticut Historical Society, may have been compiled by John Pierce or Benjamin Allen, sons-in-law of Sarah Tompson. Sarah was the wife of Samuel Tompson, Benjamin's brother. Neil T. Eckstein describes this journal in the *Connecticut Historical Society Bulletin*, 36 (July 1971), 72–76.

In many cases, the selection of a copy-text was a simple matter because we possess only one source for an astonishingly large number of Tompson's poems. But in a few cases, selection of the copy-text involved editorial judgment: one poem, "Gulielmi Tompsoni Braintreensis," exists in two manuscript versions; two poems, "Remarks on the Bright, and dark side of that American Pillar Mr. William Tompson" and "A Neighbour's TEARS," exist in both manuscript and printed form; and three other poems, *New Englands Crisis*, "UPON the *NATIVES*," and "JOHN WILSON," went through more than one printing, the second in London.

I chose to use the Edward Tompson manuscript, rather than the Joseph Tompson journal, for "Gulielmi Tompsoni Braintreensis" because Samuel Tompson was more aware of contemporary practices of capitalization, spelling, and punctuation in the Bay Colony in the late seventeenth century. Furthermore, we know that Joseph Tompson, Benjamin's brother and a resident of relatively distant Billerica, did not begin his journal until fairly late in life, and it is apparent that he had little formal or advanced education.

I chose the Edward Tompson manuscript for "Remarks on the Bright, and dark side of that American Pillar Mr. William Tompson" over the *Magnalia* version for a number of reasons which are fully explained in the note to the poem. I may summarize my argument here by simply saying that Tompson, like his student Cotton Mather, had no authorial control over the printing of his poems in the *Magnalia Christi Americana*. For the same reason, I chose the Boston, 1695, *Johannes in Eremo* for the elegy on John Wilson which appears in Appendix A of this book.

The bibliographical problems surrounding Tompson's "UPON the *NATIVES*" are more complex. As my note to the text will reveal, I chose the Boston (1677) edition as the copy-text because I believe, here too, that Benjamin Tompson and William Hubbard had no control over the editions printed in London (1677). As is so often the case in early American literature, the three thousand miles which separated Massachusetts Bay from England, and the eight weeks required to travel that distance, kept colonial authors from exercising their prerogatives as writers—witness the case of Anne Bradstreet's *The Tenth Muse*. Although I have supplied references to textual and bibliographical studies of Hubbard's *Narrative* of 1677, which contains Tompson's "UPON the *NATIVES*," I decided in this complex case to modify my editorial principles and list accidental variants as well as substantive ones in the London edition. Fortunately, the variants in Tompson's poem are few in comparison to the entire text of the *Narrative*.

This edition presents three elegies on Rebekah Sewall, two in the handwriting of John Winthrop, Fellow of the Royal Society, and one from the 1710 broadside, which is almost certainly a conflation of the two with some completely new additions. I provided all three versions so that scholars might further examine the evolutionary sequence of the poem or argue, as has Howard Judson Hall, that Samuel Sewall or perhaps one of the Winthrops combined the manuscript versions into the printed broadside. There are two extant copies of the broadside on Rebekah Sewall, but comparison on the Lindstrand comparator at Harvard University indicates that they are identical imprints.

The Lindstrand comparator at Harvard was also used for the two extant texts of *New Englands Crisis*, the Boston Athenaeum and the Huntington copies. The Boston Athenaeum copy is imperfect, missing a title page and address to the reader, and the ink has begun to bleed through the fragile pages. The Huntington copy, however, was photoduplicated quite successfully and was therefore selected as the copy-text. Comparator examination of the two copies showed no substantive or accidental variations. I have noted substantive variations in the possibly pirated, London (1676) *Sad and Deplorable NEWES from NEW ENGLAND*. This abbreviated version of Tompson's famous work is a mysterious and hastily printed document that seems to serve as a link between *New Englands Crisis* and *New-Englands Tears* (London, 1676). *Sad and Deplorable NEWES*, as the title page announces, was "Newly sent over to a Merchant in London," a reference that defies explanation at this time. I have only listed the variants in the intermediate edition, but I have reproduced and edited the entire text of *New-Englands Tears* because that London edition (1676) contains seven new poems and altered versions of poems previously published in *New Englands Crisis*.

Several of Benjamin Tompson's poems appeared in late seventeenth-century or early eighteenth-century histories, broadsides, or printed sermons, such as Hubbard's *Narrative*, Mather's *Magnalia*, or Mather's *Johannes in Eremo*. Many copies of these works exist in public and private libraries, personal collections, and historical institutions. Under these circumstances, collation of all extant imprints was impractical, if not impossible. In order to insure textual reliability, I performed firsthand and photoduplication collation against a representative sample of copies, most of which were obtained from libraries with the largest holdings in Tompson's other poetic material, such as The Massachusetts Historical Society(MHi), American Antiquarian Society (MWA), Essex Institute (MSaE), Boston Athenaeum (MBAt), Harvard University (MH), Yale University (CtY), The Pennsylvania State University (PSt),

The John Carter Brown Library (RPJCB), Boston Public Library (MB), Henry E. Huntington Library (CSmH), and the New England Historical and Genealogical Society (MBNEH). The reader will find a list of collated texts in the individual notes following the poems.

I felt such an arrangement to be more convenient for both scholar and student. Following the identification of copy-text and collated texts, I have included other bibliographical information and references to clarify such textual complexities as those which exist in the William Hubbard history, or to provide the reader with interesting and relevant material on the loss or recovery of a manuscript or printed edition. I have also listed many of the well-known texts, periodicals, anthologies, and critical editions from both the nineteenth and twentieth centuries which contain transcriptions or editions of Tompson's poems. These works are identified by asterisk in the List of Works Consulted at the end of this edition. I have not attempted to be comprehensive in the section of textual notes to the poems, merely directing the reader to available and helpful textual and critical commentary. I have also supplied references to the Evans or Sabin bibliographies, commentary by those who have preserved the poems or by scholars who have identified them, some historical information about seventeeth-century printing and engraving practices, and explanations of any irregularities in the texts or editorial procedures. My textual notes also record any substantive variations between the copy-texts and any other contemporary texts, that is, any copies written or published within the poet's lifetime.

In preparing this edition my primary ambition was to give the reader all the information necessary to reconstruct the copy-text. For this reason I have adopted the following editorial procedures: this edition preserves the running titles of the original sources, original stanzaic structure (stanza breaks at the bottom of the page are indicated in brackets), original indentation, underscoring, italic type, capitalization, and standard seventeenth-century spelling and usage. I have retained Tompson's occasional use of "then" for "than," "least" for "lest," and "there" for "their."

Because we have Tompson's work from many different hands, however, I have avoided rigid reproduction in my text of scribal slips, printing errors, and peculiarities of seventeenth-century shorthand and typography. In a list of emendations following the textual notes to each poem, I have recorded any accidental or substantive correction of the copy-text. These emendations include line-by-line identification of the following changes: correction of spelling to restore the proper or intended sense to a word or line, expansion of manuscript shorthand or abbreviations in printed or handwritten texts, insertion or deletion of punctuation, correction of scribal errors as in the accidental repetition of a word, and end-of-line emendation to correct the printer's hyphenation and compounding. I have silently substituted modern "s" for the earlier long form, "and" for ampersand, capital "W" for capital double "V," and I have regularized "u" and "v" and "i" and "j" and employed them as in modern usage. No attempt has been made to reproduce black-letter or bold-face type, ornamental initials, or varied sizes of majuscules. To facilitate reading and discussion of the poems, I have numbered every fifth line of poems of ten lines or longer, except in the case of the earliest poem ("Samuel Arnold") where line numbers would have interfered with the unusual format.

Following the list of emendations, I have attempted to annotate the poems so that student and scholar might better understand the context or peculiarities of any given poem. I have designed these annotations so that they will be of service to a variety of readers. Allusions to persons, places, or events have been explained in the notes by reference to many of the standard intellectual histories, local histories, the *Dictionary of American Biography* and the *Dictionary of National Biography*, the excellent recent biographies, and literary studies. I have also made reference to older and less easily obtained documents, such as those in the *Proceedings, Collections*, and *Publications of the Massachusetts Historical Society* or contemporary biographical sketches and diaries. If a particular biblical allusion has bearing upon a poetic passage, it has been cited or explained in the notes. Latin words, lines, and phrases have been translated in the notes. In presenting a translation of Benjamin Tompson's Latin Salutatory Oration of 1662, my primary objective was to supply the student with a usable translation. George Lyman Kitteridge has fully annotated the Latin address in the *Transactions of the Colonial Society of Massachusetts*.

While I have relied heavily upon the bibliographical work of Green, Hall, Murdock, and Jantz to establish the canon of Tompson's poetry, I have also searched extensively to find more of Tompson's work. Besides making a number of visits to the Boston area and to New England generally, I wrote well over two hundred and fifty letters to public and private libraries, museums, genealogical societies, and historical institutions, with specific queries concerning poems or letters I thought likely to be extant in a particular geographical area. I was fortunate to have made the acquaintance of Ralph Newel Thompson, a direct descendant of the Tompson family, who has been assembling material relating to the family for several years. Although Mr. Thompson was unable to direct me to any new poems by his ancestor, I am grateful for his cheerful encouragement and his willingness to share biographical gleanings. This edition does, however, make several significant additions to our knowledge of Tompson's corpus, for example the discovery of the Peter Hubbard manuscript at the Essex Institute in Salem, Massachusetts.

AN EDITION OF THE POETRY
OF BENJAMIN TOMPSON

Remarks on the Bright, and
dark side of that American Pillar
Mr. William Tompson.
Pastor of the Church in Braintree.
Who Triumphed December 10th. 1666 Aetat 68.

But may a Rural Pen try to set forth
Such a Great Fathers Ancient Grace and worth
I undertake a no less Arduous Theme
Then the Old Sages found the Chaldae Dream[1]
'Tis more then Tythes of a profound respect   5
That must be paid such a Melchizedeck[2]
Oxford this light with tongues and Arts doth trim
And then his Northern Town[3] doth Challeng him
His Time and Strength he Center'd there in this
To do good works, and be what now he is.   10
His fulgent Virtues there and learned Strains
Tall comely Presence, Life unsoil'd with Stains
Things most on WORTHIES[4] in their Stories writ
Did him to move in Orbs of Service fitt
Things more peculiar yet, my muse intend   15
Say stranger things then these, so weep and End
When he forsook first his Oxonian Cell
Some Scores at once from Popish darkness fell
So this Reformer studied! rare first fruits![5]
Shakeing a <u>Crab-tree</u>[6] thus by hot disputes   20
The acid juice by miracle turn'd wine
And rais'd the Spirits of our young Divine
Hearers like Doves flock'd with contentios wing
Who should be first, feed most: most homeward bring
Laden with honey like Hyblaean Bees[7]   25
They knead it into combs upon their knees.
Why he from Europes pleasant Garden fled
In the Next Age will be with horrour said
Braintree was of this Jewel then possest
Untill himself he labour'd into Rest   30
His Inventory then with Johns was took
His rough Coat, Girdle with the Sacred Book
When Reverend <u>Knowles</u> and he sail'd hand in hand
To Christ, Espousing the Virginian Land
Upon a ledge of Craggy Rocks near stav'd   35

His Bible in his bosome thrusting sav'd[8]
The Bible, the best cordial of his Heart
Come floods, come flames (cry'd he) we'l never part
A constellation of great converts there
Shone round him and his Heav'nly Glory where   40
With a Rare Skill in hearts, this Doctor cou'd
Steal into them words that should do them good
His Balsom's from the Tree of Life distill'd[9]
Hearts cleans'd and heal'd, and with rich comforts fill'd
But here's the wo! Balsoms which others cur'd   45
Would in his Own Turn hardly be endur'd
Apollyon[10] Owing him a cursed Spleen
Who an Apollos[11] in the Church had been
Dreading his Traffick here would be undone
By Numerous proselites he daily won   50
Accus'd him of Imaginary faults
And push'd him down so into dismal Vaults
Vaults where he kept long Ember weeks of grief
'Till Heav'n alarm'd sent him in relief
Then was a Daniel in the lyons Den   55
A man, oh how belov'd of God and men
By his beds-side an Hebrew sword there lay
With which at last he drove the Devil away.
Quaker's too durst not bear his keen replies
But fearing it half drawn the trembler flyes   60
Like Lazarus new rais'd from Death appears
The Saint that had been dead for many years
Our Nehemiah[12] said, shall such as I
Desert my flock, and like a Coward fly
Long had the Churches begg'd the Saints release   65
Releas'd at last, he dies in Glorious peace
The Night is not so long, but phosphors ray
Approaching Glories doth on high display
Faith's Eye in him discern'd the Morning Star
His heart leap'd; Sure the Sun cannot be far   70
In Extasies of Joy, he Ravish'd Cryes
Love, Love the Lamb, the Lamb, in whome he dies.

December. 10. 1666.

TEXT
MS contemporaneous copy from the Massachusetts Historical Society, Edward
Tompson manuscript (for further identification of this manuscript, see Chapter

Four of the Introduction to this edition and the Editorial Principles). This poem is printed in Cotton Mather, *Magnalia Christi Americana* (London, 1702), Bk. III, Ch. XVII, pp. 119–120. I have chosen the Edward Tompson manuscript as the copy-text for several reasons. First, as Kenneth B. Murdock's Introduction to the Harvard Edition of the *Magnalia* (Cambridge: Harvard University Press, 1977) makes clear, Mather exercised very little control over his own manuscript, which, in fact, has never been recovered. Although Mather dashed off a list of errata, his own proofreading was halfhearted and hasty. Second, the spelling, punctuation, and use of italics more closely resemble Mather's than Tompson's. But perhaps even more persuasive evidence that the Edward Tompson text is truer to the original may be found in the substantive variants in the 1702 *Magnalia:* Mather's title reads "Remarks on the *Bright* and the *Dark* Side, of that *American* Pillar, The Reverend Mr. *William Thompson;* Pastor of the Church at *Braintree.* Who *Triumphed* on Dec. 10. 1666." In an effort to make the title more informative and polite, Mather may have added "The Reverend" to Mr. Tompson's name. After line 40, I believe that Mather added this couplet: "GOOKINS was one of these: By Thompson's Pains, / CHRIST and NEW-ENGLAND, a dear GOOKIN'S gains." Mather here refers to William Tompson's conversion of Daniel Gookin, who became a missionary to the Indians on Deer Island in Boston Harbor during King Philip's War. We know that Benjamin Tompson held no great love for Gookin, "the Indian sympathizer." See Tompson's *New-Englands Tears*, "M. J. Antonomies *the Grand Sachems* Death[,]" wherein Tompson declares a new Thanksgiving Day to celebrate the capsizing of Gookin's boat. In addition, it seems that the couplet on Gookin was inserted into the original poem with little regard for the continuity of the passage. Line 40 Mather leaves as "were," but I think Tompson intended lines 40 and 41 to read, "Shone round him and his Heav'nly Glory w[h]ere/ With a Rare Skill in hearts, this Doctor cou'd. . . ." Reading "were" instead of "w[h]ere" completely distorts the rhyme. This poem is also printed in *Proceedings of the Massachusetts Historical Society*, 2nd ser., 10 (1895–96), 281–283, and Howard Judson Hall, *Benjamin Tompson . . . His Poems* (Boston: Houghton Mifflin, 1924), pp. 105–107.

Collation of the *Magnalia* copies at PSt, MHi, CtY, MH, MBAt, and CSmH against the Essex Institute copy showed no substantive variants.

EMENDATIONS
title: M^r/ Mr.
title: Decemb^r/ December
  40: were/ where
  73: Decemb.^{r}/ December.

COMMENTARY
  1. Chaldae Dream: see Daniel 2: 1–49.
  2. Melchizedeck was probably a Canaanite king of pre-Israelite Jerusalem. In Genesis 14:18–20 he prepares a meal for Abraham, receives him in the name of the God Most High, and receives his tithe.
  3. William Tompson matriculated at Brasenose College, Oxford, 28 January 1620, at the age of twenty-two, and was granted a B.A. in 1621/22. The Northern Town referred to in line 8 is probably Winwick, a parish in his native Lancashire. Tompson preached there before coming to America in 1636. See James Savage, *A Genealogical Dictionary of the First Settlers of New England*, 4 vols. (Boston: Little, Brown and Co., 1862), IV, 289, and Samuel Eliot Mori-

son, *The Founding of Harvard College* (Cambridge: Harvard University Press, 1935), p. 402.

4. WORTHIES: nine heroes—three from the Bible, three from the classics, and three from romance.

5. Perhaps a general reference to Exodus 22:29, but it may be an anachronistic reference to *New Englands First Fruits* (London, 1643). On page 9 of that work William Tompson is praised for his missionary work in Agamenticus, Maine:"1. First at *Agamenticus* (a Plantation out of our jurisdiction) to which one of our Preachers comming and labouring amongst them, was a means under God, not only to sparkle heavenly knowledge, and worke conviction and reformation in divers of them, but conversion also to Christ in some of them, that blesse God to this day, that ever he came thither."

6. <u>Crab-Tree</u>: It seems that Benjamin Tompson had a particular person in mind, but I have not been able to identify this satirical reference. We do know, however, that William Tompson faced serious opposition in Agamenticus as can be seen from his letter to John Winthrop in 1638. See Chapter 1 of this book for more on William Tompson's troubles in the northern outpost.

7. Hyblaean Bees: Hybla, a mountain and city of Sicily, abounds in flowers and bees. See Virgil's Eclogue 7.

8. In 1642 William Tompson, John Knowles, and Thomas James were sent to Virginia as missionaries, but in 1643 the Virginia assembly forbade nonconformists to preach in that colony. The assembly required Governor Sir William Berkeley to order all nonconformists to depart. See John Winthrop, *The History of New England from 1603 to 1648*, ed. J. K. Hosmer, 2 vols. (1908; rpt. New York: Barnes and Noble, 1959), II, 94, for an account of the politics and physical perils of Tompson's journey to Virginia. See also Mather, *Magnalia*, Bk. III, Ch. XVII, p. 118, and see Chapter 1 above.

9. The Tree of Life: Philosopher's Tree, elixer, parallel to the fountain of youth, an alchemical term. In Eirenaeus Philoponos Philalethes, *The Marrow of Alchemy* (London, 1654–55), ed. Cheryl Z. Oreovicz, Diss., The Pennsylvania State University, 1972, p. 45, the Tree of Life is poetically described:

This is the Tree of Life which doth preserve
From sickenesse humane body, and renews
The youth, it suffereth Nature not to swerve,
But it doth keep intire; this good accrues
By this rare Art, riches, with length of daies,
Freedom from sickness, which men most dismaies.

(ll. 19–24)

10. Apollyon: The Greek name of the angel of the underworld, the king of the locusts in Joel 1:4ff.

11. See I Corinthians 1:12. Apollos appears to be the focus of partisan loyalty in the Corinthian Church.

12. Nehemiah was the son of Hecaliah. When his kinsman Hanani told him of the plight of the Jews in Jerusalem, Nehemiah became ill with grief and was allowed to go to Jerusalem as governor. See Nehemiah 1:1–2; see also Tompson's letter to Winthrop, Chapter 1 above, and Sacvan Bercovitch, *The Puritan Origins of the American Self* (New Haven: Yale University Press, 1975).

Gulielmi Tompsoni Braintreensis.
Ecclesiae Pastoris in Angliâ utraque
Celeberimi vice. Epitaphium.[1]

Judicious Zeale: New-Englands Boanerges[2]
Lies Tombless: not to Spare the Churches Charges
But that the world may know he lacks no Tomb
Who in Ten thousand hearts commanded room.
While thus the thundring Textman hidden lies
Some Virgins slumber: Others wantonize.[3]

B. T.

TEXT

MS contemporaneous copy from The Massachusetts Historical Society, Edward Tompson manuscript. The Joseph Tompson manuscript, Houghton Library, Harvard University, does not include the title, and reads "wants" for "lacks" in line 3. In that same MS the word "tomb," appearing after "know" in line 3, has two lines drawn through it. This poem is printed in *Proc. M.H.S.*, 2nd ser., 10 (1895–96), 238; Hall, p. 107; and Kenneth B. Murdock, *Handkerchiefs from Paul* (Cambridge: Harvard University Press, 1927), p. 20; Roy Harvey Pearce, ed., *Colonial American Writing*, 2nd ed. (New York: Holt, Rinehart and Winston, 1969), p. 436; and Kenneth Silverman, ed., *Colonial American Poetry* (New York: Hafner 1968), p. 144.

EMENDATIONS
2: Tombles/ Tombless
4: room/ room.

COMMENTARY

1. Epitaph of William Tompson of Braintree, Very Illustrious Pastor of a Church in both Englands in turn. This is a Latin version of the English epitaph carved on William Tompson's gravestone in Quincy, Mass. While the early records of his parish are no longer extant, we do know that William Tompson's financial condition in his last years was not sound, and that the family could not afford, even with the congregation's help, to purchase a more expensive and elaborately carved vaulted tomb or tablestone, such as the one in which the Reverend Moses Fiske is interred in Quincy. See Tompson's epitaph on Moses Fiske in Appendix A of this edition.

2. See Mark 3:17: "And James the son of Zebedee, and John the brother of James; and he surnamed them Boanerges, which is, the sons of thunder."

3. Probably a reference to the parable of the virgins, Matthew 25:1–14.

The Grammarians Funeral,
OR,
An ELEGY composed upon the Death of Mr. *John Woodmancy*,[1]
formerly a School-Master in *Boston*: But now Published upon
the DEATH of the Venerable
Mr. Ezekiel Chevers,[2]
The late and famous School-Master of *Boston* in *New-England*; Who
Departed this Life the [end line] *Twenty-first* of *August* 1708. Early in
the Morning. In the Ninety-fourth Year of his Age.

Eight Parts of *Speech* this Day wear *Mourning Gowns*
Declin'd *Verbs, Pronouns, Participles, Nouns.*
And not declined, *Adverbs* and *Conjunctions*,
In *Lillies*[3] Porch they stand to do their functions.
With *Preposition*; but the most affection   5
Was still observed in the *Interjection.*
The *Substantive*[4] seeming the limbed best,
Would set an hand to bear him to his Rest.
The *Adjective* with very grief did say,
Hold me by strength, or I shall faint away.[5]   10
The Clouds of Tears did over-cast their faces,
Yea all were in most lamentable *Cases.*
The five *Declensions* did the Work decline,
And *Told* the *Pronoun Tu*, The work is thine:
But in this case those have no call to go   15
That want the *Vocative*, and can't say O!
The *Pronouns* said that if the *Nouns* were there,
There was no need of them, they might them spare:
But for the sake of *Emphasis* they would,
In their Discretion do what ere they could.   20
Great honour was confer'd on *Conjugations*,[6]
They were to follow next to the *Relations.*
Amo did love him best, and *Doceo* might
Alledge he was his Glory and Delight.
But *Lego* said by me he got his skill,   25
And therefore next the *Herse* I follow will.
Audio said little, hearing them so hot,
Yet knew by him much Learning he had got.
O Verbs the *Active* were, Or *Passive* sure,
Sum to be *Neuter*[7] could not well endure.   30
But this was common to them all to Moan

Their load of grief they could not soon *Depone*.[8]
A doleful Day for *Verbs*, they look so *moody*,
They drove Spectators to a Mournful Study.
The *Verbs* irregular, 'twas thought by some,   35
Would break no rule, if they were pleas'd to come.
Gaudeo could not be found; fearing disgrace
He had with-drawn, sent *Maereo* in his Place.
Possum did to the utmost he was able,
And bore as Stout as if he'd been A *Table*.   40
Volo was willing, *Nolo* some-what stout,
But *Malo* rather chose, not to stand out.
Possum and *Volo* wish'd all might afford
Their help, but had not an *Imperative Word*.
Edo from Service would by no means Swerve,   45
Rather than fail, he thought the *Cakes* to Serve.
Fio was taken in a fit,[9] and said,
By him a Mournful *POEM* should be made.
Fero was willing for to bear a part,
Altho' he did it with an aking heart.   50
Feror excus'd, with grief he was so Torn,
He could not bear, he needed to be born.

Such *Nouns* and *Verbs* as we defective[10] find,
No *Grammar* Rule did their attendance bind.
They were excepted, and exempted hence,   55
But *Supines*,[11] all did blame for negligence.
Verbs Offspring, *Participles* hand-in-hand,
Follow, and by the same direction stand:
The rest Promiscuously did croud and cumber,
Such Multitudes of each, they wanted Number.   60
Next to the Corpse to make th' attendance even,
Jove, *Mercury*, *Apollo* came from heaven.
And *Virgil*, *Cato*, gods, men, Rivers, Winds,
With *Elegies*, Tears, Sighs, came in their kinds.
Ovid from *Pontus* hast's Apparrell'd thus,   65
In Exile-weeds bringing *De Tristibus*:[12]
And *Homer* sure had been among the Rout,
But that the Stories say his Eyes were out.
Queens, *Cities*, *Countries*, *Islands*, Come
All Trees, Birds, Fishes, and each Word in *Um*.[13]   70

What *Syntax* here can you expect to find?
Where each one bears such discomposed mind.

Figures of Diction and Construction,
Do little: Yet stand sadly looking on.
That such a Train may in their motion *chord*, 75
Prosodia gives the measure Word for Word.

Sic Maestus Cecinit,[14]
Benj. Tompson.

TEXT

Broadside, Massachusetts Historical Society. This poem is printed (with a facsimile) in Hall, pp. 115–117; *Old South Leaflets* (Boston: D.C. Heath Co., n.d.), 8, Gen. Ser., No. 177, pp. 31–34; and facsimiles appear in Evans (E 1376); Samuel A. Green, *Ten Fac-simile Reproductions* . . . (Boston, 1902); Ola Winslow, *American Broadside Verse* (London: Oxford University Press, 1930), p. 25; Harrison T. Meserole, ed., *Seventeenth-Century American Poetry*, Anchor Seventeenth-Century Series (Garden City, N.Y.: Doubleday, 1968), p. 257; *Proc. M.H.S.*, 2nd ser., 5 (1889–1890), 2–4, and Brom Weber, ed., *An Anthology of American Humor* (New York: Crowell, 1962), pp. 33–34.

EMENDATION

61: Corps/Corpse

COMMENTARY

1. Probably the printer of this broadside (either John Foster or Samuel Green) confused John Woodmansey, a successful merchant and official of Boston who died in 1684, with Robert Woodmansey, headmaster of the Boston Latin School, who died in 1667. See Hall, pp. 111–113, and Dr. Samuel Green, *Proc. M.H.S.*, 2nd ser., 5 (1889–1890), 2–4.

2. Ezekiel Chevers (Cheever) (25 Jan. 1614/15–21 Aug. 1708) emigrated to Boston in June 1637, was appointed master of the New Haven school in 1638, the Ipswich Free School in 1650, and the Charlestown School in 1661. He replaced Tompson as the master of the Boston Latin School in 1670. Chevers's *Accidence, a short Introduction to the Latin Tongue* had gone through twenty editions by 1785.

3. William Lily (1468?–1522) was the first headmaster of St. Paul's School, London, a Latin and Greek scholar, and author of *Grammatica Rudimenta*, a Latin syntax with the rules in English. With the aid of Erasmus, Lily produced the *Absolutissimus*, a syntax with rules in Latin. These two works were revised and combined into a national grammar for the use of Edward IV.

4. Substantive: a word functioning syntactically as a noun.

5. Adjective: In Latin, as in English, adjectives are generally placed next to the noun they modify.

6. *Amo-amare, Doceo-docere, Lego-legere*, and *Audio-audire* represent each of the four Latin conjugations.

7. *Sum*, I am, is neither active nor passive.

8. *Depone*, to put down or lay aside, may also echo deponent verbs, verbs occurring with passive or middle voice forms but with active voice meaning.

9. *Fit* is third person singular form of *Fio*, I become; also, a division of a poem.

10. Defective verbs: verbs lacking in one or more of the usual forms of grammatical inflection.

11. Supines: Latin verbal nouns having an accusative of purpose in *-um* and an ablative of specification in *-u*. Thus, *video* (to see) becomes *visu* (in the seeing) and *visum* (to be seen). Having only two cases, supines are lazy, "negligent"; they lie on their backs (L. *supinus*).

12. Augustus sentenced Ovid to banishment at Tomis where he composed the *Tristia* (Poems of Sorrow) and *Epistulae Ex Ponto*.

13. *Um:* perhaps the printer shortened *unum* (in one place) to *Um*. In Latin neuter words of the second declension end in *-um*, and often these words are referred to as "words in *-um*," a phrase that Tompson, as master of the Boston Latin School, may have used often.

14. *Sic Maestus Cecinit:* thus sings the afflicted one.

New Englands Crisis

Or a Brief
Narrative,
of *NEW-ENGLANDS* Lamentable
Estate at present, compar'd with the for-
mer (but few) years of
Prosperity.

Occasioned by many unheard of *Cruel-*
tyes practiced upon the *Persons* and *Estates*
of its united *Colonyes*, without respect of
Sex, *Age* or *Quality* of Persons, by the
Barbarous *Heathen* thereof.

Poetically Described.

By a Well wisher to his
Countrey.
BOSTON.
Printed and sold by *John Foster*, over against
the Sign of the *Dove*. 1676

TO THE
READER

Courteous Reader,

   I *never thought this* Babe
of my weak Phantasie
worthy of an Imprima-
tur; *but being an* Abortive,
it was beg'd in these perplexing
Times to be cherished by the
Charity *of others. If its* Li-
neaments *please not the* Rea-
der *better than the* Writer,
I shall be glad to see it prest
to death: but if it displease not
many and satisfie any, its to me
a glorious Reward, who am
more willing than able to any
Service to my Countrey and
Friend,

                    Farewell

New Englands Crisis
THE
PROLOGUE.

THe times wherein old *Pompion* was a Saint,
When men far'd hardly yet without complaint
On vilest *Cates*;[1] the dainty *Indian Maize*
Was eat with *Clamp-shells* out of wooden Trayes
Under thatcht *Hutts* without the cry of *Rent*,   5
And the best *Sawce* to every Dish, *Content*.
When Flesh was food, and hairy skins made coats,
And men as wel as birds had chirping Notes.
When Cimnels[2] were accounted noble bloud
Among the tribes of common herbage food.   10
Of *Ceres* bounty form'd was many a knack
Enough to fill *poor Robins Almanack*.
These golden times (too fortunate to hold)
Were quickly sin'd away for love of gold.
Twas then among the bushes, not the street   15
If one in place did an inferiour meet,
Good morrow Brother, is there ought you want?
Take freely of me, what I have you ha'nt.
Plain *Tom* and *Dick* would pass as currant now,
As ever since *Your Servant Sir* and bow.   20
Deep-skirted doublets, *puritanick* capes
Which now would render men like upright Apes,
Was comlier wear our wiser Fathers thought
Than the cast fashions from all *Europe* brought.
Twas in those dayes an honest *Grace* would hold   25
Till an hot puddin grew at heart a cold.
And men had better stomachs to religion
Than I to capon, turkey-cock or pigeon.
When honest Sisters met to pray not prate
About their own and not their neighbours state.   30
During *Plain Dealings*[3] Reign, that worthy Stud
Of th' ancient planters race before the flood
These times were good, Merchants car'd not a rush
For other fare than *Jonakin*[4] *and Mush*.
Although men far'd and lodged very hard   35
Yet Innocence was better than a Guard.
Twas long before spiders and wormes had drawn
Their dungy webs or hid with cheating Lawne

New-Englands beautyes, which stil seem'd to me
Illustrious in their own simplicity.   40
Twas ere the neighbouring *Virgin-land* had broke
The Hogsheads of her worse than hellish smoak.
Twas ere the Islands sent their Presents in,
Which but to use was counted next to sin.
Twas ere a *Barge* had made so rich a fraight   45
As *Chocholatte*, dust-gold and bitts of eight.
Ere wines from *France* and *Moscovadoe* too
Without the which the drink will scarsly doe,
From western Isles, ere fruits and dilicacies,
Did rot maids teeth and spoil their hansome faces.   50
Or ere these times did chance the noise of war
Was from our towns and hearts removed far.
No Bugbear Comets in the chrystal air
To drive our christian Planters to despair.
No sooner pagan malice peeped forth   55
But Valour snib'd⁵ it; then were men of worth
Who by their prayers slew thousands Angel like,
Their weapons are unseen with which they strike.
Then had the Churches rest, as yet the coales
Were covered up in most contentious souls.   60
Freeness in Judgment, union in affection,
Dear love, sound truth they were our grand protection.
These were the twins which in our Councells sate,
These gave prognosticks of our future fate,
If these be longer liv'd our hopes increase,   65
These warrs will usher in a longer peace:
But if *New-Englands* love die in its youth
The grave will open next for blessed Truth.
This *Theame* is out of date, the peacefull hours
When Castles needed not but pleasant bowers.   70
Not ink, but bloud and tears now serve the turn
To draw the figure of *New-Englands* Urne.
New Englands hour of passion is at hand,
No power except Divine can it withstand;
Scarce hath her glass of fifty years run out,   75
But her old prosperous Steeds turn heads about,
Tracking themselves back to their poor beginnings,
To fear and fare upon their fruits of sinnings:
So that the mirrour of the Christian world
Lyes burnt to heaps in part, her Streamers furl'd   80
Grief reigns, joyes flee and dismal fears surprize,

Not dastard spirits only but the wise.
Thus have the fairest hopes deceiv'd the eye
Of the big swoln Expectant standing by.
Thus the proud Ship after a little turn   85
Sinks into *Neptunes* arms to find its Urn.
Thus hath the heir to many thousands born
Been in an instant from the mother torn.
Ev'n thus thine infant cheeks begin to pale,
And thy supporters through great losses fail.   90
This is the *Prologue* to thy future woe,
The *Epilogue* no mortal yet can know.

New-Englands Crisis.

IN seventy five the *Critick* of our years
Commenc'd our war with *Phillip* and his peers.[6]
Whither the sun in *Leo*[7] had inspir'd   95
A feav'rish heat, and *Pagan* spirits fir'd?
Whither some Romish Agent hatcht the plot?
Or whither they themselves? appeareth not.
Whither our infant thrivings did invite?
Or whither to our lands pretended right?   100
Is hard to say; but *Indian spirits* need
No grounds but lust to make a Christian bleed.

    And here methinks I see this greazy *Lout*
With all his pagan slaves coil'd round about,
Assuming all the majesty his throne   105
Of rotten stump, or of the rugged stone
Could yield; casting some bacon-rine-like looks,
Enough to fright a Student from his books,
Thus treat his peers, and next to them his Commons,
Kennel'd together all without a summons.   110
"My friends,[8] our Fathers were not half so wise
As we our selves who see with younger eyes.
They sel our land to english man who teach
Our nation all so fast to pray and preach:
Of all our countrey they enjoy the best,   115
And quickly they intend to have the rest.
This no wunnegin, so big matchit law,
Which our old fathers fathers never saw.
These english make and we must keep them too,
Which is too hard for them or us to doe,   120

We drink we so big whipt, but english they
Go sneep, no more, or else a little pay.
Me meddle Squaw me hang'd, our fathers kept
What Squaws they would whither they wakt or slept.
Now if you'le fight Ile get you english coats,   125
And wine to drink out of their Captains throats.
The richest merchants houses shall be ours,
Wee'l ly no more on matts or dwell in bowers
Wee'l have their silken wives take they our Squaws,
They shall be whipt by virtue of our laws.   130
If ere we strike tis now before they swell
To greater swarmes then we know how to quell.
This my resolve, let neighbouring *Sachems*[9] know,
And every one that hath club, gun or bow."
This was assented to, and for a close   135
He strokt his smutty beard and curst his foes.
This counsel lightning like their tribes invade,
And something like a muster's quickly made,
A ragged regiment, a naked swarm,
Whome hopes of booty doth with courage arm,   140
Set forthwith bloody hearts, the first they meet
Of men or beasts they butcher at their feet.
They round our skirts, they pare, they fleece they kil,
And to our bordering towns do what they will.
Poor Hovills (better far then *Caesars* court   145
In the experience of the meaner sort)
Receive from them their doom next execution,
By flames reduc'd to horror and confusion:
Here might be seen the smoking funeral piles
Of wildred towns pitcht distant many miles.   150
Here might be seen the infant from the breast
Snatcht by a pagan hand to lasting rest:
The mother *Rachel*-like[10] shrieks out my child
She wrings her hands and raves as she were wild.
The bruitish wolves suppress her anxious moan   155
By crueltyes more deadly of her own.
Will she or nill the chastest turtle must
Tast of the pangs of their unbridled lust.
From farmes to farmes, from towns to towns they post,
They strip, they bind, they ravish, flea[11] and roast.   160
The beasts which wont their masters crib to know,
Over the ashes of their shelters low.
What the inexorable flames doe spare

More cruel *Heathen* lug away for fare.
These tidings ebbing from the outward parts   165
Makes trades-men cast aside their wonted Arts
And study armes: the craving merchants plot
Not to augment but keep what they have got.
And every soul which hath but common sence
Thinks it the time to make a just defence.   170
Alarums every where resound in streets,
From *West* sad tidings with the *Eastern* meets.
Our common fathers in their Councels close
A martial treaty with the pagan foes,
All answers center here that fire and sword   175
Must make their *Sachem* universal Lord.
This armes the english with a resolution
To give the vaporing *Scab* a retribution.
Heav'ns they consult by prayer, the best design
A furious foe to quel or undermine.   180
RESOLV'D that from the *Massachusets* bands
Be prest on service some *Herculean* hands
And certainly he wel deserv'd a jerke
That slipt the Collar from so good a work.
Some Volunteers, some by compulsion goe   185
To range the hideous forrest for a foe.
The tender Mother now's all bowels grown,
Clings to her son as if they'd melt in one.
Wives claspe about their husbands as the vine
Huggs the fair elm, while tears burst out like wine.   190
The new-sprung love in many a virgin heart
Swels to a mountain when the lovers part.
Nephews and kindred turn all springs of tears,
Their hearts are so surpriz'd with panick fears.
But dolefull shrieks of captives summon forth   195
Our walking castles, men of noted worth,
Made all of life, each Captain was a *Mars*,
His name too strong to stand on waterish verse:
Due praise I leave to some poetick hand
Whose pen and witts are better at command.   200
Methinks I see the *Trojan-horse* burst ope,
And such rush forth as might with giants cope:
These first the natives treachery felt, too fierce
For any but eye-witness to rehearse.
Yet sundry times in places where they came   205
Upon the Indian skins they carv'd their name.

The trees stood Centinels and bullets flew
From every bush (a shelter for their crew)
Hence came our wounds and deaths from every side
While skulking enemies squat undiscri'd,   210
That every stump shot like a musketeer,
And bowes with arrows every tree did bear
The swamps were Courts of Guard, thither retir'd
The stragling blew-coats when their guns were fir'd,
In dark Meanders, and these winding groves,   215
Where Beares and panthers with their Monarch moves
These far more cruel slily hidden lay,
Expecting english men to move that way.
One party lets them slip, the other greets
Them with the next thing to their winding-sheets;   220
Most fall, the rest thus startled back return,
And from their by past foes receive an urn.
Here fel a Captain, to be nam'd with tears,
Who for his Courage left not many peers,
With many more who scarce a number left   225
To tell how treacherously they were bereft.
This flusht the pagan courage, now they think
The victory theirs, not lacking meat or drink.
The ranging wolves find here and there a prey,
And having fil'd their paunch they run away   230
By their Hosts light, the thanks which they return
Is to lead Captives and their taverns burn.
Many whose thrift had stor'd for after use
Sustain their wicked plunder and abuse.
Poor people spying an unwonted light,   235
Fearing a Martyrdom, in sudden fright
Leap to the door to fly, but all in vain,
They are surrounded with a pagan train;
Their first salute is death, which if they shun
Some are condemn'd the Gauntelet to run;   240
Death would a mercy prove to such as those
Who feel the rigour of such hellish foes.
Posts daily on their *Pegasean* Steeds
Bring sad reports of worse then *Nero's* deeds,
Such bruitish Murthers as would paper stain   245
Not to be heard in a Domitians Reign.[12]
The field which nature hid is common laid,
And Mothers bodies ript for lack of aid.
The secret Cabinets which nature meant

To hide her master piece is open rent,   250
The half formd Infant there receives a death
Before it sees the light or draws its breath,
Many hot welcomes from the natives arms
Hid in their sculking holes many alarms
Our brethren had, and weary weary trants,[13]   255
Sometimes in melting heats and pinching wants:
Sometimes the clouds with sympathizing tears
Ready to burst discharg'd about their ears:
Sometimes on craggy hills, anon in bogs
And miery swamps better befitting hogs,   260
And after tedious Marches little boast
Is to be heard of stewd or bakt or roast,
Their beds are hurdles, open house they keep
Through shady boughs the stars upon them peep,
Their chrystal drink drawn from the mothers breast   265
Disposes not to mirth but sleep and rest.
Thus many dayes and weeks, some months run out
To find and quell the vagabonding rout,
Who like inchanted Castles fair appear,
But all is vanisht if you come but near,   270
Just so we might the *Pagan* Archers track
With towns and merchandize upon their back;
And thousands in the *South* who settled down
To all the points and winds are quickly blown.
At many meetings of their fleeting crew,   275
From whom like haile arrows and bullets flew:
The *English* courage with whole swarms dispute,
Hundreds they hack in pieces in pursuit.
Sed haud impunè,[14] English sides do feel
As well as tawny skins the lead and steel   280
And some such gallant Sparks by bullets fell,
As might have curst the powder back to Hell:
Had only Swords these skirmishes decided
All *Pagan Sculls* had been long since divided.
The lingring war out-lives the Summer sun,   285
Who hence departs hoping it might be done,
Ere his return at *Spring* but ah hee'l find
The Sword still drawn, men of unchanged mind.
Cold winter now nibbles at hands and toes
And shrewdly pinches both our friends and foes.   290
Fierce *Boreas* whips the *Pagan* tribe together
Advising them to fit for foes and weather:

The axe which late had tasted Christian bloud
Now sets its steely teeth to feast on wood.
The forests suffer now, by waight constrein'd   295
To kiss the earth with souldiers lately brain'd.
The lofty oakes and ash doe wagge the head
To see so many of their neighbours dead;
Their fallen carcasses are caried thence
To stand our enemies in their defence.   300
Their Myrmidons inclos'd with clefts of trees
Are busie like the ants or nimble bees:
And first they limber poles fix in the ground,
In figure of the heavens convex: all round
They draw their arras-matts and skins of beasts,   305
And under these the Elves do make their nests.
Rome took more time to grow then twice six hours,
But half that time will serve for indian bowers.
A Citty shall be rear'd in one dayes space
As shall an hundred english men out-face.   310
Canonicus[15] precincts there swarmes unite,
Rather to keep a winter guard then fight.
A dern[16] and dismal swamp some Scout had found
Whose bosome was a spot of rising ground
Hedg'd up with mighty oakes, maples and ashes,   315
Nurst up with springs, quick boggs and miery plashes,
A place which nature coyn'd on very nonce[17]
For tygers not for men to be a sconce.
Twas here these Monsters shapt and fac'd like men
Took up there Rendezvouz and brumal[18] den,   320
Deeming the depth of snow, hail, frost and ice
Would make our Infantry more tame and wise
Then by forsaking beds and loving wives,
Meerly for indian skins to hazzard lives:
These hopes had something calm'd the boiling passion   325
Of this incorrigible warlike nation.
During this short *Parenthesis* of peace
Our forces found, but left him not at ease.
Here english valour most illustrious shone,
Finding their numbers ten times ten to one.   330
A shower of leaden hail our captains feel
Which made the bravest blades among us reel.
Like to some ant-hill newly spurn'd abroad,
Where each takes heels and bears away his load:
Instead of plate and jewels, indian trayes   335

With baskets up they snatch and run their wayes.
Sundry the flames arrest and some the blade,
By bullets heaps on heaps of Indians laid.
The Flames like lightening in their narrow streets
Dart in the face of every one it meets.   340
Here might be heard an hideous indian cry,
Of wounded ones who in the Wigwams fry.
Had we been *Canibals* here might we feast
On brave *Westphalia* gammons ready drest.
The tauny hue is Ethiopick made   345
Of such on whome *Vulcan* his clutches laid.
There fate was sudden, our advantage great
To give them once for all a grand defeat;
But tedious travell had so crampt our toes
It was too hard a task to chase the foes.   350
Distinctness in the numbers of the slain,
Or the account of Pagans which remain
Are both uncertain, losses of our own
Are too too sadly felt, too sadly known.
War digs a common grave for friends and foes,   355
Captains in with the common souldier throws.
Six of our Leaders in the first assault
Crave readmission to their Mothers Vault
Who had they fell in antient *Homers* dayes
Had been enrol'd with *Hecatombs* of praise.   360
As clouds disperst, the natives troops divide,
And like the streames along the thickets glide.
Some breathing time we had, and short God knowes
But new alarums from recruited foes
Bounce at our eares, the mounting clouds of smoak   365
From martyr'd townes the heav'ns for aid invoke:
Churches, barns, houses with most ponderous things
Made volatile fly ore the land with wings.
Hundreds of cattle now they sacrifice
For aiery spirits up to gormandize;   370
And to the *Molech* of their hellish guts,
Which craves the flesh in gross, their ale in butts.
Lancaster, *Medfield*, *Mendon* wildred *Groton*,
With many Villages by me not thought on
Dy in their youth by fire that usefull foe,   375
Which this grand cheat the world will overflow.
The wandring Priest to every one he meets
Preaches his Churches funeral in the streets.

Sheep from their fold are frighted, Keepers too
Put to their trumps not knowing what to doe.   380
This monster Warre hath hatcht a beauteous dove
In dogged hearts, of most unfeigned love,
Fraternal love the livery of a Saint
Being come in fashion though by sad constraint,
Which if it thrive and prosper with us long   385
Will make *New-England* forty thousand strong.

But off the Table hand, let this suffice
As the abridgment of our miseryes.
If Mildew, Famine, Sword, and fired Townes,
If Slaughter, Captivating, Deaths and wounds,   390
If daily whippings once reform our wayes,
These all will issue in our Fathers Praise;
If otherwise, the sword must never rest
Till all New-Englands *Glory it divest.*

A Supplement.

WHat meanes this silence of *Harvardine* quils   395
While *Mars* triumphant thunders on our hills.
Have pagan priests their Eloquence confin'd
To no mans use but the mysterious mind?
Have Pawaws[19] charm'd that art which was so rife
To crouch to every Don that lost his life?   400
But now whole towns and Churches fire and dy
Without the pitty of an *Elegy.*
Nay rather should my quils were they all swords
Wear to the hilts in some lamenting words.
I dare not stile them poetry but truth,   405
The dwindling products of my crazy youth.
If these essayes shall raise some quainter pens
Twil to the Writer make a rich amends.

Marlburyes Fate

When *Londons* fatal bills were blown abroad
And few but Specters travel'd on the road,   410
Not towns but men in the black bill enrol'd
Were in *Gazetts* by *Typographers* sold:
But our *Gazetts* without *Errataes* must
Report the plague[20] of towns reduct to dust:
And feavers formerly to tenants sent   415
Arrest the timbers of the tenement.

Ere the late ruines of old *Groton's* cold,
Of *Marlbury's* peracute disease we're told.
The feet of such who neighbouring dwellings urnd
Unto her ashes, not her doors return'd   420
And what remaind of tears as yet unspent
Are to its final gasps a tribute lent.
If painter overtrack my pen let him
An olive colour mix these elves to trim:
Of such an hue let many thousand thieves   425
Be drawn like Scare-crows clad with oaken leaves,
Exhausted of their verdant life and blown
From place to place without an home to own.
Draw Devils like themselves, upon their cheeks
The banks for grease and mud, a place for leeks.   430
Whose locks *Medusaes* snakes, do ropes resemble,
And ghostly looks would make *Achilles* tremble.
Limm[21] them besmear'd with Christian Bloud and oild
With fat out of white humane bodyes boil'd.
Draw them with clubs like maules and full of stains,   435
Like *Vulcans* anvilling *New-Englands* brains.
Let round be gloomy forrests with crag'd rocks
Where like to castles they may hide their flocks,
Till oppertunity their cautious friend
Shall jogge them fiery worship to attend.   440
Shew them like serpents in an avious[22] path
Seeking to sow the fire-brands of their wrath.
Most like AEneas in his cloak of mist,
Who undiscover'd move where ere they list
Cupid they tell us hath too sorts of darts.   445
One sharp and one obtuse, one causing wounds,
One piercing deep the other dull rebounds,
But we feel none but such as drill our hearts.
From Indian sheaves which to their shoulders cling,
Upon the word they quickly feel the string.   450
Let earth be made a screen to hide our woe
From Heavens Monarch and his Ladyes too;
And least our Jealousie think they partake,
For the red stage with clouds a curtain make.
Let dogs be gag'd and every quickning sound   455
Be charm'd to silence, here and there all round
The town to suffer, from a thousand holes
Let crawle these fiends with brands and fired poles,
Paint here the house and there the barn on fire,

With holocausts ascending in a spire.   460
Here granaries, yonder the Churches smoak
Which vengeance on the actors doth invoke.
Let *Morpheus* with his leaden keyes have bound
In feather-beds some, some upon the ground,
That none may burst his drowsie shackles till   465
The bruitish pagans have obtain'd their will,
And *Vulcan* files them off then *Zeuxis* paint
The phrenzy glances of the sinking saint.
Draw there the Pastor for his bible crying,
The souldier for his sword, The Glutton frying   470
With streams of glory-fat,[23] the thin-jaw'd Miser
Oh had I given this I had been wiser.
Let here the Mother seem a statue turn'd
At the sad object of her bowels burn'd.
Let the unstable weakling in belief   475
Be mounting *Ashurs* horses for relief.
Let the half Convert seem suspended twixt
The dens of darkness, and the Planets fixt,
Ready to quit his hold, and yet hold fast
By the great *Atlas* of the Heavens vast.   480
Paint Papists mutterring ore their apish beads
Whome the blind follow while the blind man leads.
Let *Ataxy*[24] be mounted on a throne
Imposing her Commands on every one,
A many-headed monster without eyes   485
To see the wayes which wont to make men wise.
Give her a thousand tongues with wings and hands
To be ubiquitary in Commands,
But let the concave of her skull appear
Clean washt and empty quite of all but fear,   490
One she bids flee, another stay, a third
She bids betake him to his rusty sword,
This to his treasure, th'other to his knees,
Some counsels she to fry and some to freeze,
These to the garison, those to the road,   495
Some to run empty, some to take their load:
Thus while confusion most mens hearts divide
Fire doth their small exchecquer soon decide.
Thus all things seeming ope or secret foes,
An Infant may grow old before a close,   500
But yet my hopes abide in perfect strength.
New England will be prosperous once at length.[25]

The Town called *Providence*
Its fate.

Why muse wee thus to see the wheeles run cross
Since *Providence* it self sustaines a loss:
And yet should *Providence* forget to watch 505
I fear the enemy would all dispatch;
Celestial lights would soon forget their line,
The wandering planets would forget to shine,
The stars run all out of their common spheres,
And quickly fall together by the eares: 510
Kingdoms would jostle out their Kings and set
The poor Mechanick up whome next they met,
Or rather would whole kingdoms with the world
Into a *Chaos* their first egge be hurl'd.
Ther's none this Providence of the Most High 515
Who can survive and write its Elegie:
But of a solitary town I write,
A place of darkness yet receiving light
From pagan hands, a miscellanious nest
Of errors Hectors, where they sought a rest 520
Out of the reach of Lawes but not of God,[26]
Since they have felt the smart of common rod.
Twas much I thought they did escape so long,
Who Gospel truth so manifestly wronge:
For one *Lots* sake perhaps, or else I think 525
Justice did at greatest offenders wink
But now the shott is paid, I hope the dross
Will be cashiered in this common loss.
Houses with substance feel uplifting wings,
The earth remains, the last of humane things: 530
But know the dismal day draws neer wherein
The fire shall earth it self dissolve and sin.

Seaconk Plain Engagement.

On our *Pharsalian Plaines*, comprizing space
For *Caesars* host brave *Pompey* to outface,
An handfull of our men are walled round 535
With Indian swarmes; anon their pieces sound
A *Madrigal* like heav'ns artilery
Lightning and thunderbolts their bullets fly.
Her's hosts to handfulls, of a few they leave
Fewer to tell how many they bereave. 540

Fool-hardy fortitude it had been sure
Fierce storms of shot and arrows to endure
Without all hopes of some requital to
So numerous and pestilent a foe.
Some musing a retreat and thence to run,   545
Have in an instant all their business done,
They sink and all their sorrows ponderous weight
Down at their feet they cast and tumble straight.
Such who outliv'd the fate of others fly
Into the Irish bogs of misery.   550
Such who might dye like men like beasts do range
Uncertain whither for a better change,
These Natives hunt and chase with currish mind,
And plague with crueltyes such as they find.

When shall this shower of Bloud be over? When?   555
Quickly we pray oh Lord! say thou Amen.

Seaconk or Rehoboths Fate.

I once conjectur'd that those tygers hard
To reverend *Newmans*[27] bones would have regard,
But were all *SAINTS* they met twere all one case,
They have no rev'rence to an Angels face: 560
But where they fix their griping lions paws
They rend without remorse or heed to laws.
Rehoboth here in common english, Rest
They ransack, *Newmans* Relicts to molest.
Here all the town is made a publick stage   565
Whereon these *Nimrods* act their monstrous rage.
All crueltyes which paper stain'd before
Are acted to the life here ore and ore.

Chelmsfords Fate.

Ere famous *Winthrops*[28] bones are laid to rest
The pagans *Chelmsford* with sad flames arrest,   570
Making an artificial day of night
By that plantations formidable light.
Here's midnight shrieks and Soul-amazing moanes,
Enough to melt the very marble stones:
Fire-brands and bullets, darts and deaths and wounds   575
Confusive outcryes every where resounds:

97

The natives shooting with the mixed cryes,
With all the crueltyes the foes devise
Might fill a volume, but I leave a space
For mercyes still successive in there place   580
Not doubting but the foes have done their worst,
And shall by heaven suddenly be curst.

Let this dear Lord the sad Conclusion be
Of poor New-Englands *dismal tragedy.*
Let not the glory of thy former work   585
Blasphemed be by pagan Jew or Turk:
But in its funeral ashes write thy Name
So fair all Nations may expound the same:
Out of her ashes let a Phoenix rise
That may outshine the first and be more wise.   590

B. Tompson.

On
A FORTIFICATION
At Boston *begun by Women.*
Dux Foemina Facti.[29]

A Grand attempt some Amazonian Dames
Contrive whereby to glorify their names,
A Ruff for *Boston* Neck of mud and turfe,
Reaching from side to side from surfe to surfe,
Their nimble hands spin up like Christmas pyes,   595
Their pastry by degrees on high doth rise.
The wheel at home counts it an holiday,
Since while the Mistris worketh it may play.
A tribe of female hands, but manly hearts
Forsake at home their pasty-crust and tarts   600
To knead the dirt, the samplers down they hurle,
Their undulating silks they closely furle.
The pick-axe one as a Commandress holds,
While t'other at her awkness gently scolds.
One puffs and sweats, the other mutters why   605
Cant you promove[30] your work so fast as I?
Some dig, some delve, and others hands do feel
The little waggons weight with single wheel.
And least some fainting fits the weak surprize,
They want no sack nor cakes, they are more wise.   610

98

THE POETRY OF BENJAMIN TOMPSON

These brave essayes draw forth Male stronger hands
More like to Dawbers then to Martial bands:
These do the work, and sturdy bulwarks raise,
But the beginners well deserve the praise.

TEXT

From the Boston, 1676 edition, Henry E. Huntington Library. Comparison of photostats of the Boston Athenaeum copy (imperfect) with the H. E. Huntington copy on the Lindstrand comparator at Harvard University showed no variation in the texts. This transcription is based upon the Huntington copy, which contains the title page and address to the reader, both missing in the Athenaeum copy. This poem is also printed in Evans Microcards (E 225); *The Club of Odd Volumes*, I (Boston: University Press, John Wilson and Son, Cambridge, 1894); Hall, pp. 41–71; Meserole, pp. 225–241; and Silverman, pp. 96–112. The first two parts of *New Englands Crisis* appeared in London (1676) under the title: Sad and Deplorable/NEWES/FROM/NEW ENGLAND./ Poetically Related by an Inhabitant there,/and Newly sent over to a Merchant/in London,/BEING A/TRUE NARRATIVE/OF/NEW-ENGLANDS Lamentable Estate at present, Occa-/sioned by many un-heard of Cruelties, Practiced upon the/Persons and Estates of its United Colonies, with-/out Respect of Sex, Age or Quality of Persons/by the barbarous Heathen thereof./ *With Allowance/LONDON,/* Printed for H. J. Anno Dom. 1676./ *Sad and Deplorable NEWES* does not contain the address "TO THE READER," but it does reprint, with the exception of two lines, "THE PROLOGUE" and "New-Englands Crisis" from the Boston, 1676 edition. Thus, *Sad and Deplorable NEWES* supplied English readers with the introductory sections missing in *New-Englands Tears*, published later that same year. The London edition, *Sad and Deplorable NEWES*, remained unidentified until the appearance of Harold S. Jantz's *The First Century of New England Verse* (Worcester: American Antiquarian Society, 1943–44). Jantz discovered the work in the collections of the Henry E. Huntington Library, San Marino, California. *Sad and Deplorable NEWES* contains the following variants: l. 11 NEC—many a knack/ *SDN*—many knack; ll. 37–38 missing; l. 113 english man, who/ English Men, who; l. 114 nation all so fast/ nation also fast; l. 132 know how to quell/ know to quell; l. 219 lets them ip/ lets them slip; l. 297 wagge the head/ wag their head; l. 311 Canonicus precincts/ In several precincts; l. 323 Then by by forsaking/ Then by forsaking; l. 356 the common souldier/ the private souldier; l. 365 the mounting clouds/ the mountain clouds; l. 373 *Lancaster, Medfield, Mendon/ Lancaster, Mendon, Medfield*. Considering the nature of these variants, many of them corrections, it is possible that the English printer was working from a corrected copy and that *Sad and Deplorable NEWES* was printed *With Allowance*, as the title page says. On the other hand, certain changes reflect some possible confusion on the part of the printer, as in the substitution of the word "several" for the name "Canonicus." This substitution resembles the one made in *New-Englands Tears*, where the printer changed Miontonimo to M.J. Antonomies. In my opinion the English printer of *Sad and Deplorable NEWES* corrected some obvious mistakes in the Boston edition and may have substituted more familiar words for the English audience, whether purposefully or inadvertently I do not know.

EMENDATIONS in Boston, 1676 NEC

2: com-plaint; hyphenated "plaint" raised from l. 3.
23: "i" in wiser changed to Roman
32: of th' ancient; apostrophe reversed; printer probably used inverted comma
33: car'd; apostrophe reversed
62: protecti-on; hyphenated "on" lowered from l. 61.
104: with / With
111 to 134: quotation marks added
123: hang'd; apostrophe reversed
124: Sqaws / Squaws
125: you'le; apostrophe reversed
129: Wee'l; apostrophe reversed
130: Wee'l; apostrophe reversed
159: post,; lowered from l. 158.
198: "n" in "stand" inverted
201: "u" in "burst" inverted
219: ip/ slip
235: peeple/ people
258: discharg'd; apostrophe reversed
262: he/ be
288: Swotd/ Sword
323: by by/ by
325: passi-on; hyphenated "on" raised from l. 326.
395: hills.; raised from l. 396.
406: dwingling/ dwindling
459: there there/ there
461: Churhes/ Churches
466: obtain'd; apostrophe reversed
468: of of/ of
471: thin-jaw'd; apostrophe reversed
473: turn'd; apostrophe reversed
474: burn'd; apostrophe reversed
487: thousands/ thousand
502: line 110 added from NET
511: jostles/ jostle
514: hurl'd; apostrophe reversed

COMMENTARY

1. Cates: provisions, foods.
2. Cimnels: biscuits.
3. *Plain Dealings:* perhaps a reference to Thomas Lechford's *Plain Dealing: or News from New England* (1642). Lechford (fl. 1629–1642) came to America in 1629, one year before the start of the Great Migration, which lasted for approximately ten years. While he was no great supporter of the Puritan experiment in New England, Lechford did recognize the benefits of plantations there.
4. Jonakin: Johnnycake.
5. snib'd: rebuffed
6. Philip, whose Indian name was Metacomet, was chief of the Wampanoags in 1675 when war broke out in New England.
7. The Indian attack on Swansea on 24 June 1675 signaled the beginning of the war. Perhaps Tompson's reference to Leo is only meant to suggest the

approximate time of the start of hostilities. On the other hand, astronomical-astrological evidence indicates that Tompson might have intended a somewhat more precise dating of the war. Today, the sun enters Leo on 23 July, but if one takes into consideration the eleven-day change in the calendar (the Julian then in use was eleven days earlier than the Georgian) and the precession of the equinoxes, the correlation between month and zodiacal series was quite different in 1675. The first point of Aries begins at the moment the sun crosses the equator going north, and the other zodiacal phases follow Aries in 30-degree intervals. The effect of precession is slight—1 degree in 72 years—but in 305 years, and with the change to the Georgian calendar, Tompson could have intended to place the date in early July.

8. At this point in the poem, King Philip addresses his warriors. Tompson was obviously familiar with the linguistic traits of the Algonquin natives, and he assumed that his audience would have no difficulty in following Philip's formal or set speech. The words "wunnegin" (good) and "matchit" (bad) are Narraganset words, but "sneep" represents Tompson's attempt to reproduce, as well as ridicule, the Indians' difficulty pronouncing the letter "L"; thus "sneep" means "sleep." In lines 121–122 Philip refers to the colonists' liquor laws: if the Indians drink they are whipped, but if the colonists drink they either go to sleep with impunity, or they pay a small fine. See Ives Goddard, "Some Early Examples of American Indian Pidgin English from New England," *International Journal of American Linguistics*, 43 (1977), 37–41.

9. Sachems: from the Narraganset and Pequot word "sachima," a sachem is a tribal chief, especially the chief of a confederation of the Algonquin tribes of the North Atlantic coast.

10. *Rachel*-like: Rachel, the wife of Jacob, died soon after giving birth to Benjamin. Perhaps, though, Tompson is also referring to the death of Rachel Mann and her infant daughter, which occurred at Swansea on 24 June 1675.

11. flea: flay.

12. Domitians Reign: Roman emperor, A.D. 81 to 96. Domitian was notorious for ordering persecution of the Christians.

13. trants: cunning action, trickery; a stratagem.

14. *Sed haud impunè:* but not safely.

15. *Canonicus:* Narraganset Indian chief (c. 1565–1647), friend of the early colonists. Possibly Tompson confused Canonicus with Canonchet, leader of the Narragansets in King Philip's War. In 1676 Canonchet was captured by a group of colonists and Indians, and was eventually killed by the Indians. In *New-Englands Tears* Tompson confused Canonchet with Miontonomo (M. J. Antonomies), Canonchet's father.

16. dern: drear.

17. on very nonce: possibly Tompson means at the very nonce, or at the very moment, but more likely on very nonce should be read "for the express purpose." "Nonce" (once) had become a conventional filler-word in poetry, and its meaning is inconsequential here.

18. brumal: wintry.

19. Pawaws: Powah, Powaw, Powwow, an Indian medicine man, priest, wizard, or magician who officiates at tribal ceremonies. See Edward Winslow, *Good News from New England: or a true Relation* (London, 1624), p. 22: "The actor of this fact was a Powah, one of special note amongst them."

20. In 1603, 1625, 1647, and 1665–66 London was the center of the Great Plague. The bills of mortality reveal that almost 70,000 people died of the

bubonic plague. London typographers (printers) sold the first official English journal—*The Oxford Gazette*—in November 1665, when the court was at Oxford because of the plague.

21. Limm: limn, to draw or paint lightly.

22. avious: twisting.

23. glory-fat: glor-fat, soft fat; the most greasy and transparent fat in cooked animal food. Glore-fat: glowing fat, usually applied to "dripping," partially set, bacon fat.

24. *Ataxy:* disorder, confusion, want of discipline.

25. Tompson obviously meant to finish this couplet, and in all probability the printer made the omission. I have inserted the appropriate line from *New-Englands Tears*. For more on this omission, see the textual note to *New-Englands Tears*.

26. Tompson here refers to the dissenting followers of Roger Williams, who was dismissed from Salem, Massachusetts, October 1635, and founded Providence, Rhode Island, in 1636.

27. Reverend Samuel Newman (1602–1663), ordained in Rehoboth (1644) as its first minister, changed that town's name from Seekonk to Rehoboth.

28. John Winthrop (1606–1676) was governor of Connecticut and the subject of two of Tompson's elegies.

29. *Dux Foemina Facti:* the leader is a woman. See Virgil, *Aeneid* I. 364, also quoted by Winthrop in *A Short Story . . . of the Antinomians* (London, 1644), p. 157.

30. promove: to promote, to move forward.

New-Englands Tears
FOR HER
Present Miseries:
OR,
A Late and True RELATION of
the CALAMITIES of
NEW-ENGLAND
Since *APRIL* last past.
With an Account of the Battel between the
English and *Indians* upon *Seaconk Plain:*

And of the *Indians* Burning and Destroying of
Marlbury, Rehoboth, Chelmsford, Sudbury,
and *Providence.*

With the Death of *Antonomies* the Grand *Indian* Sachem;
And a RELATION of a Fortification begun by
Women upon *Boston Neck.* Together with an Elegy on
the Death of *John Winthrop* Esq; late Governour of *Con-*
necticott, and Fellow of the *Royal Society.*

Written by an Inhabitant of Boston *in* New England
to his Friend in London. With Allowance.

LONDON Printed for *N.S.* 1676.

A
NARRATIVE
OF
New Englands
PRESENT
CALAMITIES.
15 *April* 1676.

WHAT means this silence of *Harvardine* Quills [*NEC* 395–408]
Whilst *Mars* Triumphant thunders on our Hills?
Have *Pagan* Priests their Eloquence confin'd
To no mans use but the mysterious Mind?
Have *PAWAWS* charm'd that Art which was so rife 5
To crouch to every *DON* that lost his life?
But now whole Towns and Churches fire and die,
Without the pity of an Elegy.
Nay, rather should my Quills, were they all Swords,
Wear to the Hilts in some lamenting words: 10
I dare not stile them Poetry, but Truth,
The dwindling products of my crazie youth;
If these Essays shall rouze some quainter Pens
'Twill to the Author make a rich amends.

    Marlburies Fate. [*NEC* 409–502]

WHen *London's* fatal Bills were blown abroad, 15
And few but Specters travel'd on the Road,
Not Towns, but Men in the black page inroll'd
Were in Gazets by *Typographers* sold;
But our Gazets without Errata's Must
Report the Plague of Towns reduc'd to Dust: 20
And Feavors, but ere while to Tenants sent
Arrest the Timbers of the Tenement.

Ere the late ruines of poor *Groton's* cold,
Of *Marlburies* peracute Disease we're told;
The feet of such, who neighb'ring dwellings urn'd 25
Unto its ashes, not its doors return'd.
So what remain'd of Tears as yet unspent
Are to its final gasps a Tribute lent.

If Painter ever track my Pen, let him
An Olive colour mix, these Elves to trim; 30

Of such an hue, let many hundred Thieves
Be drawn like Scarecrows clad with Oaken leaves,
Exhausted of their Verdant Life, and blown
From place to place without a home to own:
Draw Devils like themselves, upon their cheeks   35
Those Banks of Grease and Mud a plat for Leeks;
Whose dangling Locks *Medusa's* Snakes resemble,
With grizly looks would make *Achilles* tremble.
Limn them besmear'd with Christian blood, and oyl'd
With fat out of white humane Bodies boyld.   40
Draw them with Clubs like Mauls, all full of stains;
Like *Vulcan's* anvelling *New Englands* brains:
Let round be gloomy Forrests, and thick Rocks;
Where like to Castles they may hide their Flocks:
Till opportunity their constant friend,   45
Shall jogge them *Vulcan's* Worship to attend.
Shew them like Serpents in an avious path,
Waiting to sow the Fire-balls of their wrath.
Much like *AEneas*, in his cloak of mist,
Who undiscover'd, move where ere they list.   50
Cupid some tell us, had two sorts of Darts,
But we feel none, but such as drill our hearts;
From *Indian* sheaves which to their shoulders cling,
Upon the Word they quickly feel the string.
Hide first the *Sun* beneath the Earth, and quench   55
In *Thetis* boul[1] the Stars; the *Lunar* Wench
So mutable in fashions, make her happe
To lie a slumbering in *Apollo's* lappe.
Let Earth be made a Screen to hide our woe,
From Heaven's Monarch, and his Ladies too: 60
And least our jealousie think they partake,
For the Red Stage with Clouds a Curtain make.
Let Doggs be gagg'd, and every quickning sound,
Be charm'd to silence: here and there all round,
The Town, to suffer. From a thousand holes   65
Let crawl those Fiends with brands and firing Poles.
Paint here an House and there a Barn on fire,
With Holocausts ascending in a spire.
Here Granaries, yonder the Churches smoke,
Which Vengeance on the Actors did invoke.   70
Let *Morpheus* with his Leaden Keys have bound
In Feather beds some, some upon the Ground,
That none may burst his drousie Shackles till

The Bruitish Pagans have obtain'd their will,
And *Vulcan* files them off. Then *Zeuxis* paint   75
The phrensie glances of the Sinking Saint.
Draw there the Pastor for his Bible crying,
The Souldier for his Sword, the Glutton frying
With Streams of glory fat. The thin-jaw'd Miser,
Ah had I given this, I had been wiser.   80
Let here the Mother seem a Statue turn'd,
At the sad object of her Bowels burn'd.
Let the unstable Weakling in belief,
Be mounting *Ashur's* Horses for relief.
Let the half Convert seem suspended 'twixt   85
The Dens of Darkness and the Planets fixt.
Ready to quit his hold and yet hold fast
By the great *Atlas* of the Heavens vast.
Paint Papists mutt'ring over apish Beads,
Whom the Blind follow while the Blindman leads.   90
Let *ATTAXIE* be mounted on a Throne,
Imposing her Commands on every one:
A many-headed Monster without Eyes,
To see the Wayes which wont to make men wise.
Give her a Thousand Tongues with Wings and Hands   95
To be Ubiquitary in commands:
But let the Concave of her Soul appear,
Washt Clean and Empty, quite of all but fear.
One she bids run, another stay, a third
She bids betake him to his rusty Sword;   100
This to his treasure, t'other to his Knees,
Some Counsels she to fry, and some to freeze:
These to the Garrisons, those to the Load;
Some to run empty, some to take the Load.
Thus while Confusion, most mens hearts divide,   105
Fire doth the small Exchequer soon decide.
Thus all things seeming ope or secret foes,
An Infant may grow gray before a close.
But yet my hopes remain in perfect strength,
New England will be prosperous once at length.   110

Providences Fate.   [NEC 503–532]

WHy muse we thus, to see the Wheels run cross,
Since Providence it self, sustains a loss:
Should Providence, but one day miss its watch,

106

I fear the Enemy would all dispatch.
Resplendent *Phoebus* would forget to shine,   115
The wandring Planets, to forget their Line.
The Stars run all out of their proper spheres,
And quickly fall together by the eares;
The Ocean would forget to ebbe and flow,
The Mother cease the tender babe to know.   120
Kingdoms would jostle out their Kings and set,
The Vile Mechanick up who next they met:
Or rather Kings, and Kingdoms, with the World,
Would into Chaos its first rise be turn'd:
This sacred Providence of the Most High,   125
None can outlive and write its Elegy.
But of a solitary Town I write,
A place of darkness, yet receiving light
From Pagans hands; a miscellaneous nest
Of Errours, Hectors, where they sought a rest   130
Out of the reach of Laws, but not of God;
Since they have smarted by the common Rod.
'Twas much I thought it did escape so long,
Which sacred truth did manifestly wrong;
For one *Lots* sake perhaps, or else I think,   135
Justice did long at great offenders wink.
'Tis happy for them, if their filth and dross,
Be cleansed off, though by a common loss.

                   Seaconk Plain Engagement.   [NEC 533–556]

ON our *Pharsalian* Plain, containing space
For *Caesar's* Armies, *Pompey's* to outface,   140
An handful of our men are walled round,
With Tawny Bands, anon their pieces sound
A Madrigal; like Hail the Bullets fly,
An Emblem of Heavens Artillery.
Heres Hosts to Handfuls, of a few they leave   145
Fewer to tell how many they bereave.
Fool hardy Fortitude, it had been sure,
Thousands of Shot, and Arrows to endure:
Without all hopes of some requital too,
So numerous and pestilent a foe.   150
Most Fought like *Dragons;* through this *Indian* mist,
The Beams of Valour break where e'r they list.
Who died ('tis thought) sold lives at such a rate,

                            107

As doth the fury of the foes abate.
Some musing a Retreat, and thence to run,   155
Have in an instant, all their business done.
They Sink, and Die, their wonted sorrows weight,
They Tumble at their Feet, and follow strait.
Here Captious ones, without their Queries lie,
The Quaker here, the Presbiterian by.   160
The Scruple dormant lies of thee and thou,
And most as one to Deaths dominion bow.
Such who out-live the fate of others fly,
Into the Neighbouring Swamps of misery.
Those who might die like men, like beasts must range,   165
Uncertain whither for a better change.
Such Natives hunt and chase with Tygers mind,
And plague with Cruelties such as they find.
When shall this showre of Blood be over? when?
Quickly we pray (good Lord) say thou *Amen*.   170

           Rehoboth's Fate.   [*NEC* 557–568]

I Once conjectur'd that these Figures hard,
To reverend *Newman's* Bones would have regard.
But were all Saints they met, it were all one case,
They owe no Reverence to an Angels Face.
But where they fix their Monstrous Lion Paw's,   175
They Rend without remorse or heed to Laws
Rehoboth here in our plain English Rest,
They ransack, *NEWMAN*'s Reliques they molest.
Here all the Town is made a publick stage,
Whereon these *Nimrods* act their Monstrous rage;   180
And Cruelties which Paper stain'd before,
Are acted to the life here ore and ore.
Let this, dear Lord, the sad Conclusion be   [*NEC* 583–590]
Of poor *New-Englands* fatal Tragedie.
Let not the Glory of thy former work,   185
Blasphemed lie by *Pagan*, *Jew*, or *Turk*.
But in *New-Englands* Ashes write thy Name,
So fair all Nations may expound the same.
Out of these Ruins, let a Phoenix rise,
That may outshine the first, and be more wise.   190

Another black Parenthesis of woe,
The Printer wills that all the world should know.

Upon the setting of that Occidental Star John Win-
throp *Esq; Governour of* Connecticott *Colony,*
Member of the Royal Society; who deceased in his
Countreys Service 6 April 1676.[2]

NIne Muses, get you all but one to sleep,
But spare *Melpomene*, with me to weep.
From you whose bleared Eyes have Lectures read, 195
Of many of our *English* Heroe's dead.
I beg a glance from Spectacles of Woe,
(Quotidian Gazets) Brave *Winthrop* to.
Whose death Terrestrial Comets did portend,
To every one who was his Countreys friend. 200
The Blaze of Towns was up like Torches light,
To guide him to his Grave, who was so fit
To rule, or to obey, to live or die:
(A special Favorite of the Most High)
Monarch of Natures Secrets, who did hold, 205
Its grand Elixir named the *Star* of GOLD.[3]
Or else the World mistakes, and by his deeds,
Of Daily Charities Expence he needs.
But had he it, he wiser was than so,
That every Ape of Artists should it know. 210
He had the System of the Universe,
Too Glorious for any to Rehearse.
As *Moses* took the Law in Clouds and Fire;
Which Vulgars barr'd at distance much admire.
Thus was he taught the precious Art of healing, 215
(Judge we but by success) at Gods revealing.
He mounted up the Stairs of Sciences,
Unto the place of Visions which did please.
Where on the Pinacle of worldly skill,
On Kingdoms of all Arts, he gaz'd his fill. 220
Into his Thoughts Alembick[4] we may think,
He crouded Stars to make a Diet Drink.
(I mean) Terrestrial Stars which in the Earth,
Receive their vitals and a Mineral Birth:[5]
That *Proteus, Mercury*, he could compel, 225
Most soberly well fixt at home to dwell.[6]
Of Salt[7] (which Cooks do use for Eggs and Fishes)
He made a Balsom better than all Riches;
And Sulphur[8] too provided for mens woe,
He made an Antidote Diseases to. 230

This Terrene three, were made by Fire his friends,
To bring about his *ARCHIATRICK* ends.[9]
He saw the World, which first had only shade,
And after rich Embroideries on it laid,
Of Glorious Light; how the Homogeneal spark,[10]   235
Did first Rebell against the Central dark.
He saw the Jemms how first they budded, and
The Birth of Minerals, which put to stand
Natures grand Courtiers.[11] He knew the Womb
From whom the Various Tribes of Herbs did come.[12]   240
He had been round the Philosophick sea,
And knew the Tincture[13] if there any be:
But all his Art must lie, there's no Disease
Predominant, where he doth take his Ease:
Outliving *Theophrast*,[14] he shew'd thereby   245
Himself Hermetick, more surpassing high
TRISMEGESTOS[15] I'll stile him; first in Grace,
Thrice great in *ART*, the next deserving place;
Thrice High in humble Carriage, and who,
Would not to Highest Meekness ready bow?   250
England and *Holland* did great *Winthrop* woe;
Both had experienc'd Wonders he could doe.
But poor *New-England* stole his humble Heart,
From whose deep Wounds he never would depart:
His Councel Balsome like, he poured in,   255
And plaistred up its Breaches made by sin.
Natives themselves, in parlies would confess,
Brave *Winthrops* Charity and Holiness.
The Time he rul'd, War never toucht his bound,
When Fire, and Sword, and Death, raged all round.   260
Above whose reach he reigns in Glories Rays,
Singing with all the Saints his Makers praise.

EPITAPHIUM

GReater Renown than Boston *could contain,*
Doth underneath this Marble-stone remain:
Which could it feel but half so well as we,   265
'Twould melt to Tears and let its Prisoner free.

Chelmsfords Fate.   [NEC 569–582]

ERe Famous *Winthrops* Bones are laid to rest,
The Pagans *Chelmsford* with sad Flames arrest;

Making an artificial day of night,
By that Plantations formidable light.   270
Here's midnight shreekes, and soul amazing groanes,
Enough to melt the very Marble-stones:
Fire-brands, and Bullets, Darts, and Deaths, and Wounds,
Confusive Noyses every where resounds:
The Natives shouting, with the English cries: 275
With all the Cruelties the Foes devise,
Might fill a Volume: but I leave a space,
For mercies yet successive in their place:
Not doubting but the foes have done their worst,
And shall by Heaven, suddainly be curst.   280

Sudburies Fate.

ONce more run Lacquey[16] Muse the Councel tell,
What sad Defeat our hopeful Band befell:
Since Fifty odd of Valours choicest Sons,
Sinke into Deaths retiring Room at once.
The Natives Scouts, like living baits were trail'd,   285
With Umbrages of mighty Rocks and Holes;
(Fit Pallaces for such perfideous souls.
Some to our Linx-ey'd Centinels appear,
And quickly run as if possest with fear:
Ours chase, they halt; We gain, they lightly fly,   290
As if some *Gad*[17] be stung upon the Thigh.
One while they linger, falsly to give hope,
While to trapan, is their disguized scope;
Into a Labyrinth) or a natural maze,
Of hideous thickets and unbeaten wayes;   295
Ours close pursue them, and as close their fate,
Smelling their Treachery when 'twas too late,
A Race of Natives, as if newly hatcht,
Starts from their Dens, and soon our friends dispatch,
Here was of *Indians* too a plenteous Fair,   300
The Chapmen Devils, hovering in the Air:
But ah with Tears I may the Reader tell,
A little Host of English down there fell:
Two hardy Captains, many manly hearts,
Then felt the Bullets with the venom'd darts,   305
The Parents Vesture with the purple stain'd
Of his *Ascanius*[18] by him newly braind.
Euryalus[19] his Soul reaks through the wound,

Of *Nisus*[20] gasping by upon the ground;
While the *Rutilian*[21] like enraged bears,   310
The Garments; with Mens Skins, asunder tears:
One seeks his Head, scrambling for breathing room,
By *Lethal*[22] pangs; a second reads his doom
In Vellome Rolls, flead off his right hand man:
Which they send home for Sagamores to tan;   315
With Scalpes, according to whose number they,
Receive brave Titles and some rich Array:
Our numerous Scars, like stars in bodies shone,
Who have for each a glorious Trophie wone:
From this *Aceldama* they post away,   320
To the Grand General for their ready pay:
While fellow Soudiers who escape the dint,
Bounce our Exchecquers, but find little in't.

CELEUSMA MILITARE.[23]

BUt know stout hearts that Diadems and Crowns,
Will powre down from Heaven after your wounds;   325
And you shall find in Honours Lists a place,
Where Dastard Spirits dare not shew their Face.

About this time Died Major *Willard* Esq; who had continued one
of our Senators many years, and Head of the *Massachuset* Bands.
In 23 *April* 1676.[24]

EPITAPHIUM.

GReat, Good, and Just, Valiant, and Wise,
New-Englands *common Sacrifice:*
The Prince of War, the Bond of Love,   330
A True Heroic *Martial Dove:*
Pardon I croud his Parts so close,
Which all the World in measure knows.
We envy Death, and well we may,
Who keeps him under Lock and Key.   335

His Praises will, or are more largely celebrated; but let this be ac-
cepted according to the Nature of my Writings, which are but
Brief and General.

The Indians *threaten to Dine at* Boston *on our Election.*

THe hungry Dogs, scenting the bay good Cheer,
Give out Bravadoes that they will be here.

But hopes we have of an Election day,
Although their Votes and Proxies keep away.
We think they will our Ammunition smell,   340
Which from our friends beyond Sea us befell.

M. J. Antonomies[25] *the Grand Sachems Death.*

A Breathing time of silence had my Pen,
But finds a scribling matter once agen.
In *Narraganset* Land near *Paquetuck,*
The English with the Natives try a pluck: 345
Here in an Isthmus pitcht the foes their tents,
Here quartered their naked Regiments:
Some grope for Lobsters, some to clamp banks run,
And some lie beautifying in the Sun:
Some sit in Council, others treating squaws;   350
Some grinding parcht Corn with the Querns their Jawes.
Some sing their Captains dooms, others are lousing,
Some pawawing, some wenching, and some drousing.
And herein *ANTONOMIE* among the rest,
All up in Wampam Belts, most richly drest: 355
Sate as the Dagon of their motley crew,
Not thinking that his downfal would insue:
Whose Pedegree should I presume to write,
To *Hesiods Theognis*[26] run I might.
Our Checquer'd Bands of Whites and Tawnies joyn'd,   360
These in their close Retirements quickly find;
Down to the Earth our Martial gallants fall,
And like to insects on the Natives crawl.
Old *UNCUS*[27] tribe who ever had been true,
Upon the moving Forrest nimbly flew.   365
The English them as they are flying meet,
And multitudes they tumble at their feet.
Some captiv'd, others wounded, many slain,
Like *Hydra's* Heads, yet ne'r the less remain.
And here that *Lucifer* receives defeat,   370
Who scorns with any less then Princes treat.
What Necklace could *New-England* better please,
Then Heads strung thick upon a thred of these,
Him they dispatch, and hundreds more are hurl'd,
Him to attend upon in th'other world: 375
Whose hunting bouts will heavily go on,
His Legs must stay until the Head come on.

That phansie which so stifly they maintain,
That such on hunting go who hence are slain:
I hope ere long will quite convinced be,   380
By many Heads chopt off as fine as he:
His (a brave present) kist the grateful Hand,
Of Dons who in our Southern Tract command.

Least such *Moecaenas's* beyond Sea should,
Restrain their yearly showrs of Goods and Gold,   385
Be pleas'd to know there is an hopeful race,
Who as you oft have been inform'd have grace.[28]
These are confin'd under Christian Wings,
And hopes we have never to feel their stings.
A natural Prison wall'd with Sea and Isles,   390
From our Metropolis not many miles,
Contains their swarms:[29] hither upon advice,
Some Grandees venturing powerful and wise;
In a small Vessel on a time did tend,
Three Dons with their great Apostolick friend: 395
Ere they arrive a Barge runs down their Boat,
Mean-while these Worthies three must sink or float.[30]

Their Loaves for comfort round about them swam,
And from their Bottles Neptune drinks a dram,
He gap'd for men and all, but as God pleas'd   400
By sturdy tackles of that care he's eas'd,
With like observance to *November's* day,
Keep the remembrance of this passage pray.

On the Fortifications began by Women upon
Boston *Neck.*

[NEC 591–614]

A Grand attempt the *Amazonian* dames,
Contrive, whereby to glorify their names.   405
A Ruffe for *Bostons* Neck of mud and turfe,
Reaching from side to side, from surfe to surfe.
Their nimble Hands spin up like Christmass Pies.
Their pastry by degrees on high doth rise.
Their Wheeles at home count it an Holyday   410
While Mistresses are working they may play.
A tribe of Peticoates with manly hearts,
Forsake at home their Pasticrust and Tarts:

To knead the dirt, their Samplers down they hurle,
Their undulating Silks they closely furle.   415
The Pickaxe one as a Commandress holds,
Another at her awkness gently scolds.
One holds her side, while *Hypocondrick* fumes,
Do tympanize her Pericardian roomes[31]
This puffs and sweats, the other grumbles why   420
Can't you promote your work so fast as I.
Some dig and delve, while others hands do feel,
The little Waggons weight with single wheel;
And least some fainting fit, the weak surprize,
They want not Sack and Cakes; they are more wise.   425
These brave Essays drew forth mens nervous hands,
More like to Daubers than to Martial Bands.
These do the work and sturdy Bulwarks raise,
But those who first began deserve the praise.

FINIS.

TEXT

From the London, 1676 edition, in the John Carter Brown Library, Brown University, Providence, Rhode Island; printed in Hall, pp. 76–93. *New-Englands Tears* is composed of fourteen separate poems, seven of which appeared in *New Englands Crisis* (Boston, 1676). Only "A Supplement" remains unchanged from the Boston edition; thus, this present edition includes all fourteen poems in the London, 1676, *New-Englands Tears*.

As Howard Judson Hall remarked in his edition of Tompson's poetry, *New-Englands Tears* cannot be considered a reprint of *New Englands Crisis*. In his note to *New Englands Crisis*, Hall provides the reader with an accurate summary of the chronological relationship between events of the war and the publication of *New Englands Crisis* and *New-Englands Tears*, essentially concluding that the former poem covers the period from 10 February to 6 April, 1676, and the latter from late March to late April, perhaps the 23rd. Hall specifically reasoned that "A careful examination of the poems in common to both the little booklets shows the 'Tears' to be more accurately printed, more uniform in punctuation and capitalization, less old-fashioned, and somewhat less rugged where differences exist between the two texts. Some interpolations in the London edition do not seem like Tompson's. Perhaps the changes were made by Tompson's London friend or by the printer" (Hall, pp. 43–44). My comparison of the texts confirms Hall's opinions: *New-Englands Tears* seems not to have been printed from a corrected copy of *New Englands Crisis*. The common poems have been substantially revised, sometimes by the addition of a pair of couplets, the deletion of a couplet, rearrangement of lines, reordering of larger sections (for example, the end of *Chelmsfords* Fate was moved to the end of *Rehoboth's Fate* in *New-Englands Tears*), revision of individual words, and regularization of accidentals. Such revision goes beyond the mere correction of the Boston edition, although the London edition does correct certain obvious mistakes in the Boston; for example, *Tears* finishes the incomplete couplet at line 502 in *Crisis*. Based upon our enlarged collection of Tompson's poetry, I take issue with Hall's remark that some of the interpolations do not seem like Tompson's. While it is certainly possible that Tompson's London friend "improved" the text, it seems more likely that Tompson sent over to London a holograph incorporating his own extensive revisions and new poems. Many of the changes reflect a desire to make the poem more classical by allusion and reference to mythological characters or events, and some changes appear to have been made for the benefit of a British audience; for example, line 550 of *Crisis* reads "Into the Irish bogs of misery," and line 164 of *Tears* reads "Into the Neighbouring Swamps of misery." Further, Tompson is critical of those ministers who befriended the Indians on Deer Island, and *New-Englands Tears* includes other allusions and references that American readers might not have sanctioned or understood; for example, Tompson changed "A tribe of female hands" (line 599, *Crisis*) to "A tribe of Peticoates" (line 412, *Tears*). The effect of the changes is to make *New-Englands Tears* more appropriate to an English audience and to make it appear a more learned poem.

I have cross-referenced the poems that are common to both texts with bracketed line numbers from my edition of *New Englands Crisis*.

EMENDATIONS

title: *Antononies/ Antonomies*
  1: Quills; raised from l. 2.
  2: Hills?; raised from l. 3.
  5: was so rife; raised from l. 6.
 57: mutab'e/ mutable
189: Phaenix/ Phoenix
253: hamble/ humble
331: Herorick/ Heroic
414: Samplets/ Samplers

COMMENTARY

   1. In Greek and Roman myth Thetis was one of the Nereids or sea nymphs.
   2. John Winthrop, Jr. (12 Feb. 1605/6–5 April 1676) was the eldest son of John Winthrop (12 Jan. 1587/88–26 March 1649), the first governor of Massachusetts Bay, and the father of John Winthrop, III (14 March 1638–27 Nov. 1707), who is usually known as Fitz-John Winthrop. John Winthrop, Jr., the subject of two of Tompson's elegies, was one of the most enlightened and versatile figures in early New England. In England Winthrop had been admitted as a barrister at the Inner Temple and had accepted an appointment in the Royal Navy, but in New England he turned his attention to political, industrial, and scientific matters. He governed Connecticut for nineteen years (1657, 1659–1676), incorporated the New Haven Colony, and secured an extremely liberal charter. He set up smelting furnaces in Lynn and Braintree, Massachusetts, and in 1644 the General Court granted him 3000 acres for his iron works. In 1663 he was elected a member of the Royal Society, as the first resident member in America. See also Samuel Eliot Morison, *Builders of the Bay Colony*, 2nd ed. (Boston: Houghton Mifflin, 1958); Robert C. Black, III, *The Younger John Winthrop* (New York: Columbia University Press, 1966); Pearce, *Colonial American Writing*, 2nd ed., pp. 437–438; and Silverman, pp. 145–147.
   3. See Arthur Edward Waite, ed., *The Hermetic And Alchemical Writings of*

Aureolus Philippus Theophrastus Bombast, Of Hohenheim, Called Paracelsus The Great, vol. II (New York: University Books, 1967), who provides the reader with "A Short Lexicon of Alchemy." Star of GOLD was perhaps Tompson'sterm for Sphere of the Sun, the dual matter of the stone, the heaven, that is, the quintessence (p. 381). Gold was considered by the alchemists the most nearly perfect of all metals and was called Sun, Apollo, Phoebus when it was considered "philosophically." (See Waite, II, 368–369; 382–383; and see note 5 below.)

4. Alembic: the upper part of an alchemist's still; also called limbeck, or helm, because of its resemblance to a helmet. (See also Waite, II, 351.)

5. In lines 221–224 Tompson is referring to the process of preparing the Philosophic Tincture (see note 13 below). See also Paracelsus, in "Concerning the Nature of Things" (Waite, I, 181, 186).

6. In lines 225–226 Tompson credits Winthrop with the ability to capture and stabilize elemental Mercury, out of which "all the virtue of the art is extracted. . . . The whole secret of Hermetic philosophy and the Great Work consists in the wonderful sympathy between those Mercuries [there are many] and this [fluidic] earth." (See Waite, II, 374.)

7. Salt was one of the most common elements used by the alchemists; it was believed to consist of a small quantity of sulfurous earth and a large proportion of mercurial water. (See Waite, II, 379.) See Black, p. 100, for evidence that Winthrop spent at least three years absorbed in the development and supervision of a saltworks beside the estuaries of Salem, Massachusetts.

8. Sulfur was as common to alchemists as salt, and according to Waite, II, 382, there are at least twenty different names and functions for philosophic sulfur, many of which were medicinal.

9. Minerals, salt, and sulfur are the terrene (earthy) three which Winthrop fired in his laboratory. The Fire of the Philosophers is "said to be the greatest crux of the art. It is a close, aërial, circular, bright fire, which the philosophers call their sun." (See Waite, II, 366.) ARCHIATRICK (from the Greek ἀρχιατρός, compounded of ἄρχων, a chief, and ἰατρός, a physician) refers to a medical title given under the Roman emperors. Winthrop was a highly respected physician.

10. Homogeneal spark probably refers to one of the essential processes of alchemy; perhaps Tompson had in mind fulmination, "so called because the metals become brilliant and diffuse radiance from time to time during the process. A red pellicle forms above, and when it disappears little sparkles are manifested at intervals." (See Waite, II, 368.)

11. Tompson's references to "Mineral Birth," "budding," "Womb," and perhaps a pun on "egg" probably revolve around the term "Philosophical Egg." According to Waite, II, 377, most chemists have misunderstood the egg to be simply a vessel; "The egg of the philosophers is not that which contains; it is that which is contained; that is, the true vessel of Nature." Winthrop, as the successful alchemist, achieved the desired creations and regenerations through his mastery of the virtues of Nature, something of which other "Courtiers" were incapable.

12. See Paracelsus' "Concerning Degrees and Compositions in Alchemy," in Waite, II, 190–195, for a discussion of the seven species, locations, and functions of herbs.

13. When in the form of the Elixir Vitae or Red Tincture, the Philosophic Stone was depicted as an agent for curing human ills and conferring longevity.

14. Theophrastus (c. 370–288 B.C.) of Eresos in Lesbos was a pupil, col-

laborator, and successor of Aristotle and was primarily known for his botanical observations. But Tompson is probably referring to Paracelsus The Great, Aureolus Philippus Theophrastus Bombast.

15. *TRISMEGESTOS:* Hermes Trismegistus, "Hermes thrice greatest," was the reputed author of the philosophical treatises known collectively as *Hermetica,* also several works on astrology, magic, and alchemy. See Black, p. 102, for Winthrop's reading of Paracelsus and pp. 156–157 for intriguing speculation that Winthrop may have been the noted alchemist "Eirenaeus Philalethes."

16. Lacquey: lackey.

17. *Gad*: gadabout; gadfly.

18. Ascanius was the son of Aeneas.

19. Euryalus, the son of Mecisteus, marched with Epigoni, sailed with the Argonauts, and went to Troy with Diomedes.

20. Nisus was the king of Megara; Nisus' daughter, Scylla, knowing that Nisus' life depended on keeping his lock of red hair, betrayed him and cut it off.

21. The Rutulians led Latin tribes against Aeneas and the Trojans.

22. *Lethal*: Lethe, an underworld river.

23. Military Command.

24. Major Simon Willard (1605–24 April 1676), fur trader, founder of Concord, local magistrate, Indian agent, and officer in the colonial militia, took charge of the defense of the Merrimac frontier during King Philip's War. He heroically relieved Brookfield on 4 August 1675, and defended Groton, Chelmsford, and Lancaster.

25. M. J. Antonomies: Tompson confused Miontonomo, leader of the Narragansets during the Pequot War in 1643, with Canonchet, leader of the Narragansets during King Philip's War. In 1676 Canonchet was captured by a group of colonists and Indians and was killed by the Indians. The colonists sent his head to Hartford, Connecticut, as evidence of their victory.

26. Hesiod's *Theogony* deals with the origins and genealogies of the gods. From Chaos and Earth, in two separate lines, some 300 gods descend, including personified abstracts.

27. Uncus (c. 1588–c. 1683) was sachem of the Mohegan Indians.

28. The so-called Praying Indians were converted and ministered to by John Eliot, Daniel Gookin, Samuel Danforth, Jr., or William Stoughton.

29. Deer Island in Boston Harbor.

30. In the *Sixth Report of the* [Boston] *Records Commissioners*, Roxbury Church Records, p. 193 (quoted by Hall, p. 93), the Apostle to the Indians, John Eliot, explains the accident which took place in Boston Harbor: a fourteen-ton barge, "weth^r wilfully or by negligence, God he knoweth," rammed a boat carrying Eliot, Gookin, Stoughton, and Danforth to the Praying Indians on Deer Island. All were saved, "some thanked God and some wished we had been drowned," and they continued on their mission. According to Eliot, "one y^t wished we had bene drowned, was himself drowned about the same place w^r we w^r so wonderfully delivered. . . . "

A
FUNERAL TRIBUTE
To the Honourable Dust of that most Charitable Christian,
Unbiassed Politician, [end line]
And unimitable Pyrotechnist
John Winthrope esq:

A Member of the Royal Society, and Governour *of* Conecticut
Colony *in* [end line]
NEW-ENGLAND.
Who expired in his Countreys Service, *April.* 6th. 1676.[1]

ANother Black Parenthesis of woe
The *Printer* wills that all the World should know
Sage *Winthrop* prest with publick sorrow Dies
As the Sum total of our Miseries:
A Man of worth who well may ranked be   5
Not with the thirty but the peerless three
Of *Western Worthies*,[2] Heir to all the Stock
Of praise his Sire received from his Flock:
GREAT *WINTHROPS* Name shall never be forgotten
Till all *NEW-ENGLANDS* Race be dead and rotten;   10
That Common Stock of all his Countries weal
Whom Grave and Tomb-stone never can conceal.
Three Colonies[3] his *PATIENTS* bleeding lie
Deserted by their great *PHYSICIANS* eye;
Whose common sluice is poized for their tears,   15
And Gates fly open to a Sea of fears.
His Christian Modesty would never let
His Name be near unto his *SAVIOURS* set:
Yet Miracles set by, hee'd act his part
Better to LIFE then Doctors of his Art.   20
Projections various by fire he made[4]
Where Nature had her common Treasure laid.
Some thought the tincture *Philosophick*[5] lay
Hatcht by the Mineral Sun in *WINTHROPS* way;
And clear it shines to me he had a Stone[6]   25
Grav'd with his Name which he could read alone.
To say how like a *SCEVOLA*[7] in Court
Or ancient *CONSULS* Histories report
I here forbear, hoping some learned Tongue

119

Will quaintly write, and not his Honour wrong.   30
His common Acts with brightest lustre shone,
But in *Apollo's* Art[8] he was alone.
Sometimes Earths veins creeping from endless holes
Would stop his plodding eyes:[9] anon the Coals
Must search his Treasure, conversant in use   35
Not of the Mettals only but the juice.[10]
Sometimes his wary steps, but wandring too
Would carry him the Christal Mountains to
Where Nature locks her Gems, each costly spark
Mocking the Stars, spher'd in their Cloisters dark.   40
Sometimes the Hough, anon the Gardners Spade
He deign'd to use, and tools of th'Chymick trade.
His fruit of Toyl Hermetically done[11]
Stream to the poor as light doth from the Sun.
The lavish Garb of silks, Rich Plush and Rings   45
Physitians Livery, at his feet he flings.
One hand the Bellows hold, by t'other Coals
Disposes he to hatch the health of Souls;
Which Mysteries this *Chiron* was more wise
Then unto ideots to Anatomize.[12]   50
But in a second person hopes I have
His Art will live though he possess the Grave.
To treat the *MORALS* of this Healer *Luke*
Were to essay to write a *PENTATUKE*,
Since all the Law as to the *MORAL* part   55
Had its impression in his spotless heart:
The vertues shining brightest in his Crown
Were self depression, scorning all renown;
Meekness and Justice were together laid
When any Subject from good order straid.   60
Neither did ever Artificial fire
Boyle up the Choler of his temper higher
Then modest bounds. In Church and Common-wealth
Who was the Balsome of his Countries Health.
Europe sure knew his worth who fixt his Name   65
Among its glorious Stars of present fame.
Here Royal *CHARLES* leads up, stands *WINTHROPE* there
Amongst the *Virtuosi* in the Rear:
But for his Art with hundreds of the rest
He might be plac'd in Front and come a Breast.   70
What Soul in fouldings t'other side the Scene
With Souls turn'd Angels guess we to have been

When first his Chariot wheels the threshold felt
Where *WINTHROPS, DUDLYS, COTTONS*[13] Spirits dwelt?
What melting joys are there? Sorrows below,   75
Should adequately from *New-England* flow:
If Saints be intercessors, heres our hope
We need not be beholding to the Pope.
We have as good our selves, an honest Brother
Outvies their Saintship, there or any other.   80
Now *Helmonts*[14] lines so learned and abstruse
Are laid aside and quite cast out of use:
And Authors which such vast expenses spent
Lye like his Corpse; his Ear is only lent
To Heavenly Harmonies, all things his Eye   85
Views in the platforme whence all forms did fly;
His labours cease for ever, but the fruit
He reaps at Fountain head without dispute.

B. Thompson.

TEXT
Broadside, Massachusetts Historical Society; printed in Hall, pp. 99–102; and in Evans (E 224).

EMENDATIONS
Italicized "W" changed to full upper-case throughout the text.
15: sluce/sluice
40: spher'd; apostrophe reversed
42: deign'd; apostrophe reversed
47: t'other; apostrophe reversed
67: there; lowered from l. 66.
70: be be/ be; plac'd; apostrophe reversed
71: 'tother/ t'other
72: turn'd; apostrophe reversed
84: Corps/ Corpse
signature: *B. Th ompson/ B. Thompson*

COMMENTARY
1. For biographical information, see Tompson's elegy on John Winthrop, Jr., in *New-Englands Tears*. The opening couplet in this elegy is identical with the couplet which precedes the Winthrop elegy in *New-Englands Tears*, 11. 191–192.
2. The peerless three of the Nine Worthies are Hector, Alexander, and Julius Caesar.
3. Massachusetts, Connecticut, and probably Plymouth.
4. In alchemy, projection is the casting of the powder of the philosopher's stone upon a metal in fusion to transmute it into gold or silver.
5. See note 13 for *New Englands Crisis*.
6. Philosopher's stone: a reputed solid substance or preparation used in the transmutation processes of alchemy. (See also Waite, II, 377; cf. Rev. 2:17.)

121

7. Quintus Mucius Scaevola, called "Pontifex," an eminent Roman lawyer, orator, and a model proconsul and governor of Asia.

8. Alchemy.

9. See Paracelsus, in "Concerning the Nature of Things" (Waite, I, 183–186).

10. The Elixir Vitae, Balsam, or Tincture.

11. See note 15 for *New-Englands Tears*.

12. Winthrop, as a wise alchemist, carefully guarded the secrets of The Great Work. However, Tompson may have been alluding to Cardinal Nicolaus Cusanus's *The Idiot in Four Books* (1543: rpt. London, 1650), a scientific treatise cast in the Socratic form. The Idiot, a "practical man," argues with and insults a philosopher in the Roman forum.

13. John Winthrop (12 Jan. 1587/88–26 March 1649), the first governor of Massachusetts Bay; Thomas Dudley (1576–31 July 1653), the second governor of Massachusetts Bay; John Cotton (4 Dec. 1584–23 Dec. 1652), Teacher of the First Church in Boston and one of New England's most influential clergymen.

14. Either Franciscus Mercurius van Helmont (1618–1699) or Jean Baptiste van Helmont (1577–1644). While both were eminent physicians, chemists, and philosophers, Jean Baptiste's works were probably better known and more accessible in New England in 1676. This passage (11. 81–84) seems to refer to a deceased author whose works had been older and more established than Franciscus Mercurius van Helmont's.

UPON

The elaborate *Survey* of *New-Englands* Passions from the
NATIVES
By the impartial *Pen* of that worthy *Divine*
Mr. WILLIAM HUBBARD.[1]

A *Countreys Thanks with Garlands ready lye*
To wreathe the Brows of your Divinity
Renowned Sir: to write the Churches Warre
In ancient times fell to the Prophets *share*
New-Englands Chronicles *are to be had*   5
From Nathans *Pen, or Manuscript of* Gad.[2]
Purchase[3] *wrote much,* Hacluyt *traversed farr,*
Smith *and* Dutch John de Laet *famous are,*
Martyr, *with learn'd* Acosta *thousands too,*
Here's noveltyes and stile which all out-doe,   10
Wrote by exacter hand then ever took
Historians Pen *since* Europe *wee forsooke.*
I took your Muse *for old* Columbus Ghost,
Who scrapt acquaintance with this western Coast,
But in converse some pages I might find   15
Then all Columbus Gemms *a brighter mind.*
Former Adventures did at best beguile
About these Natives Rise (*obscure as* Nile)
Their grand Apostle[4] *writes of their return;*
Williams *their Language;*[5] Hubbard *how they burn,*   20
Rob, kill and Roast, lead Captive, *flay, blaspheme;*
Of English valour *too he makes his* Theme,
Whose tragical account may Christned be
New-Englands Travels through the bloudy Sea.
Drake *gat renown by creeping round the old;*   25
To treat of this New World *our Author's bold.*
Names uncouth which ne'r Minshew[6] *could reduce*
By's Polyglotton *to the vulgar use.*
Unheard of places like some New-Atlantis,
Before in fancy only, now Newlandis: 30
New found and subtle Stratagems of Warre,
We can quaint Elton[7] *and brave* Barriffe[8] *spare:*
New Discipline and Charges of Command
Are cloath'd in Indian *by this* English hand.
Moxon[9] *who drew two Globes, or whosoere*   35

Must make a third, or else the old ones tear,
To find a Roome for thy new Map by which
Thy friends and Country all thou dost enrich.

Gratitudinis ergò apposuit[10]
B.T.

TEXT

Prefixed to William Hubbard's *A Narrative of the Troubles with the Indians in New-England* (Boston, 1677); printed in Hall, pp. 121–122. The bibliographical problems surrounding the Boston and London, 1677, editions of Hubbard's history are enormous. Randolph C. Adams, in "William Hubbard's 'Narrative,' 1677," *The Papers of the Bibliographic Society of America*, 33 (1939), 25–39, has comprehensively described and analysed the problem of variant printings in both the Boston and the London (*The Present state of New England*) editions. Adams listed the typographical and textual variants for all the Boston and London "issues," but he did not find any accidental or substantive variants for Tompson's poem in any of the "issues." I have based my transcription of Tompson's prefatory poem upon the Boston, 1677, Essex Institute copy of Hubbard's narrative. My own collation of the Essex Institute copy against copies at MHi, MBAt, CSmH, RPJCB, CtY, and MH showed no substantive variants.

The London, 1677, Boston Public Library copy of *The Present state of New England* contains the following variants: title: Hubbard (no period); l. 1 Countries; l. 2 wreath . . . Divinity,; l. 3 Write . . . War; l. 4 times, . . . share.; l. 7 far,; l. 8 are:; l. 9 Acosta,; l. 10 Novelties . . . Stile . . . out-do,; l. 12 we . . . forsook.; l. 14 scrap'd . . . Western . . . Coast:; l. 15 Pages . . . find,; l. 16 Gemms,; l. 17 beguile,; l. 20 William's; l. 21 Flay, Blaspheme;; l. 22 Valour; l. 23 Tragical . . . be,; l. 24 Bloody; l. 26 Treat; l. 29 places,; l. 31 New-found . . . War,; l. 35 whosoere,; l. 37 Room . . . Map,; l. 38 Friends.

COMMENTARY

1. William Hubbard (c. 1621-14 Sept. 1704), a Congregational clergyman and historian, served as a substitute for John Rogers as president of Harvard College in 1684. For more biographical information see John Langdon Sibley, *Biographical Sketches of Graduates of Harvard University* (Cambridge: Harvard University Press, 1873); and Viola F. Barnes on William Hubbard in *The Dictionary of American Biography*, IX, ed. Dumas Malone (New York: Scribners, 1932).

2. See I Chronicles 29:29, "Now the acts of David the King, first and last, behold, they are written in the book of Samuel the seer, and in the book of Nathan the prophet, and in the book of Gad the seer."

3. One could assemble a respectable library of geographical, historical, and travel literature from the references scattered throughout this short poem. Samuel Purchase (1577–1626), an English compiler of travel books, published *Purchas His Pilgrimage* (1613) and *Purchas His Pilgrim* (1619); Richard Hakluyt (1552?–1616), an English geographer, promoted colonization and exploration in North America and published *The Principall Navigations, Voyages and Discoveries of the English Nation;* John Smith (c. 1579–1631), an English adventurer and explorer, and an organizer of the Virginia Company of London, wrote histories and accounts of explorations in Virginia, New England, Europe, Asia, and

Africa; John de Laet (d. 1649), a native of Antwerp, was director of the Dutch East India Company and author of numerous travel books on North and South America; Pietro d'Anghiera Martire (d. 1526), an Italian historian, wrote *De Rebus Oceanicis et Novo Orbe* (1516), the first known written account of the discovery of America; José de Acosta (c. 1539–1600), a Spanish historian, cosmographer, and poet, was sent to Peru as a missionary and there produced his most important work, *Historia natural y moral de las Indias*, translated into English in 1604; Sir Francis Drake (c. 1540–1596), the founder of the English naval tradition, was knighted in 1580 as the first captain to have circumnavigated the globe. The narrative of Drake's voyage was written by the ship's chaplain, Francis Fletcher, and printed by Hakluyt.

4. John Eliot (1604–1690), called "Apostle to the Indians," translated the Bible, religious treatises, and catechisms into the language of the Massachusetts Indians.

5. Roger Williams (c. 1600–1683) wrote *A Key Into the Language of America* (London, 1643).

6. John Minsheu (fl. 1617), an English lexicographer and teacher, published *A Dictionarie in Spanish and English* (London, 1599); *A Spanish Grammar* (London, 1599); *Vocabularium Hispanico-Latinum et Englicum copiosissimum* (London, 1617?); and *The Guide to Tongues* (London, 1617?), containing equivalents in eleven languages.

7. Richard Elton (fl. 1650) wrote *The Compleat Body of the Art Military* (London, 1650). (See note 8 below.)

8. William Barriffe (1601?–1643), author of *Mars, His Triumph* (London, 1639); and *Military Discipline, or the Young Artillery Man* (London, 1635). In Boston, 1701, Nicholas Boone (1679–1738) published *Military Discipline. The Compleat Souldier, or expert artillery-man. . . . Being a collection from Col. Elton, Bariff, and others.*

9. Joseph Moxon (1627–1700), an English hydrographer and mathematician, published numerous scientific and geographical works, including *A Tutor to Astronomie and Geographie; or an easy and speedy way to know the use of both the Globes, celestial and terrestrial* (London, 1659). His younger brother, James Moxon, pursued the same career.

10. He sets this down in gratitude.

The Reverend man of God Mr. Peter Hubbard[1]
Pastor of Hingam church his transla-
tion or 'Αηοθέωσις
23: 11: 1678.[2]

Deepe Hubbard, next Religious awe to thine
Is due, what men allow Virtues Divine.
I in remembrance of thy name essayd
A first and second time but was afraid:
Too big for my poore shell to Comprehend   5
Where to begin or where to make an end.
Nor Could an Ephod[3] cut by humane witt
This Aaron's gravity compleatly fitt.
I could not trace so deepe and spacious stream
Up to Its head, the name's sufficient Theame   10
Of such antiquity beyond sea knowne
By persecutions from an Eden blowne
Into a milder clime, yet even there
From Truth-Professing friends hee had his share.[4]
Yet like a Marble pelted by the waves   15
Hee kept his soundness where some found their graves.[5]
[   ] alone with truth on's side
Than by whole Synods to bee dignified.
The common places of Divines desert
Perfection in the tongues: brave skill in Art   20
May here adapted bee, for at his Grave
Their excellencies they divested have.
His trade was Jewells: which hee fetcht above:
All his Returnes, Faith, Currant[6] prayers and love.
Mans full allowance, threescore years and Ten   25
Spent most in pulpit toyles this man of men
[   ] honour to supply the needs
Of his great Charge, without the Reverend weeds
Of purest Lawne, which else might well become
This sufferer in his petty Martyrdome.   30
His words were Oracles his fervent prayers
Like mighty Angels climbd the Heavnly stairs
Bat'red heavns Frontiers, entred and Came back
With all the blessings which the Church did lack.
His life was Gospel copied out by line,

The Reverend man of God Mr. Peter Hubbard

In 1860 S. P. Fowler of Danvers-port, Massachusetts, sent this autograph manuscript to the *New England Historical and Genealogical Society*. It was transcribed and printed in the *Register* that year and then given as part of the Fowler papers to the Essex Institute in Salem. All previous transcriptions and descriptions of this poem have been based upon the *Register* "edition" of 1860. See "William and Benjamin Tompson: the Light and the Dark" in *SCN*, Winter 1978, 96–99 for a further account of the discovery and condition of the manuscript. (*Courtesty of the Essex Institute, Salem, Mass.*)

Exactness best becomes the best Divine.
His Doctrine plaine, yet pungent: free but pure,
Whose efficacy could both kill and Cure.
This Abram kept his bosom Opend Wide
As Jesus armes for babes which some deny'd.   40
What many pray for only, not indeav'or,
Christs Kingdom's growth hee durst not would not sever.
Infants unborne may well lament his Death
Who saincted all when first they drew their breath
Barring those Temples, least the World or sin   45
Or Hells great Champion should enter in.
Zeale to the Levits work, the vineyards call
Moved him pay more than tithes of sons nigh all[7]
Greate Benefactor to the Learned sort
This Western World hath cause to bless him for't.   50
Before this heavnly Hydra[8] Feels his fate
Four heads of the old stock doe Germinate,
True Issue of his braines and Learned loynes
By grace and practise both, Lively Divines.
The Vesper of his life's a constant Cry: 55
When will deaths curious claws these knots untie?
A crazie cage of bones curtaind with Skin
A Ruind Castle where great strength had beene.[9]
A Blaze of Heavn A beame Divine, A mind
Of the first Magnitude some time Confin'd.   60
When Aarons Tabernacle work is done
Hee strips his Vestures to adorne his Son
Thus hee uncased himselfe: Resignes the Keys
With (Nunc dimittis)[10] finishing his days.
The travells of almost a double age   65
Hoary with toyle, and time thus quitts the stage.
Heavns Charioteers, hence with an unseene traine
Up in great Honour Convoy him to Reigne.
And what remains imbalmd in Teares is dust
Not lost but sowne: A Treasure put in trust: 70
Layd at the Churches doore, Just by the side
Of Saincts, which were his sparkling Crowne, and pride.
That at his death as well as life hee might
Declare the Church to bee his great Delight.
Rest then thy weary bones Thou man of God   75
If ere the Church fall out assume the Rod
Or rather let the Reverence of thy Name
Bee tutelary Angel of the same

And When thy darksom Cell yee saincts pass by
Say there, the Glorie of His Coat doth lie.   80

B.T.
Dignum laude Virum Musa Vetat mori.[11]

TEXT
MS, autograph, Essex Institute, and printed in the *New England Historical and Genealogical Register*, 14 (1860), 141–142. In 1860 S. P. Fowler of Danversport, Massachusetts, forwarded the manuscript of this elegy to the *NEHGR*. Fowler made the following introductory remarks:

> I send to you for publication, if you think proper, what appears to be an elegy on the death of Peter Hobart. You will perceive upon examining it, the initials of the old schoolmaster and poet, Benjamin Thompson. You will also notice upon the back of the poem, the name of Peter Hobart. This undoubtedly is the signature of Dea. Peter Hobart, who was, more than 109 years ago, an inhabitant of Salem Village, now Danvers, and who was, I think, a descendant of Peter Hobart of Hingham, here eulogized. At what time Dea. Peter Hobart came to Danvers, I do not know. He without doubt brought the poem from Braintree, where he may have received it from Benjamin Thompson, the supposed author.

> I find Peter Hobart's name variously spelled by different authors—Josselyn spells it Hubbord; Lechford, Hubbard; in the Hutchinson Papers it is Hubbert; and in Mather, Hobart.

This poem is printed in Hall, pp. 124–127.

EMENDATIONS
title: M^r / Mr.
  8: Aaarons / Aaron's
 14: friends; lowered from above the line in MS
 16: graves.; lowered from l. 15
 20: perfection / Perfection
 23: w^{ch} / which
 24: ffaith / Faith; pray^{rs} / prayers
 29: w^{ch} / which; becom / become
 31: pray^{rs} / prayers
 33: ffrontiers / Frontiers
 34: w^{ch} / which
 40: w^{ch} / which
 48: of sons; lowered from above the line in MS
 51: ffeeles / Feels
 52: ffour / Four
 55: his; lowered from above the line in MS; MS torn and colon added after Cry

COMMENTARY
    1. Peter Hobart (13 Oct. 1604—20 Jan. 1678/79) was ordained at Hingham, Massachusetts, 18 Sept. 1635, as its first minister, and he preached there until his death. For more biographical information see Weis, p. 108; Savage, II, 435; Mather, Bk. III, Ch. XXVII, 153–155; *NEHGR*, 14 (1860), 141.

2. Apotheosis, 23 January 1678. Since Hobart died on 20 January 1678/79, it is reasonable to assume that Tompson believed that "translation" to the glorified state occurred, as with Christ, three days after death.

3. See Exodus 28:4ff. Priests, such as Aaron, were required to wear an ephod, an undergarment of white linen, on the grounds of modesty and the sanctity of their office.

4. Mather, in the *Magnalia*, Bk. III, Ch. XXVII, 155, explains that certain zealots for church discipline in Hobart's church (Hingham, Mass.) were "very pragmatical in *Controversies*, and furiously set upon having all things carried their way . . . . "

5. Lines 15–16 and 60 allude to the physical and psychological difficulties Hobart experienced in later life. Mather, Bk. III, Ch. XXVII, 155, supports Tompson's position that Hobart was relieved of his psychological afflictions; in fact, Mather uses the same biblical expression, "the end of this man was peace," for both Hobart and William Tompson, Benjamin's father, who suffered similarly.

6. Currant: genuine.

7. In lines 47–54 Tompson is referring to four of Peter Hobart's sons who entered the ministry: Joshua (1628—1716/17) was ordained at Sothold, New York, 7 Oct. 1647; Jeremiah (1631–1715) was ordained at Topsfield, Massachusetts, 2 Oct. 1672; Gershom (1645–1707) was ordained at Groton, Massachusetts, 26 Nov. 1679; Nehemiah (1648–1712) was ordained at Newton, Massachusetts, 23 Dec. 1674. In lines 47 and 48 Tompson understands Levites in their original function; that is, the Levites were said to have been given to Aaron and his sons (the priests) as servants.

8. Tompson means here that Hobart generated sons for the priesthood. This complimentary use of the Hydra allusion is very unusual in Puritan poetry and history. Most writers used this image of monstrosity to refer to the Pope, the hierarchy of the Catholic Church, or New England's controversial (heretical) figures; for example, see Mather, *Magnalia*, Bk. VII, Ch. III, "Hydra Decapitata."

9. For a thorough analysis of such emblematic and funerary imagery in New England culture, see Allan I. Ludwig, *Graven Images: New England Stonecarving and Its Symbols, 1650–1815* (Middletown, Conn.: Wesleyan University Press, 1966).

10. Song of Simeon: see Luke 2:29–32; and see Mather, Bk. III, Ch. XXVII, 155.

11. The Muse forbids the man worthy of praise to die. Mather, Bk. III, Ch. XXVII, 155.

New-Englands grand Eclips by the withdrawing of
that vast body, or Trium-virate of Politick, Ec-
clesiastick, Military Light John Leverett[1]
Governour of the Massathuset, and Moder-
atour of the Confederate Colonies In New England,
who disbanded the 16th: of the lst: 1678/9
AEtatis suae: 63.

'Tis not a vulgar straine the Learned know
Can speake the Homage which all fancies ow
To this State-Giant. Had I ne're before
Seen Monarchs in their Ermins rold in Gore,
Had I not read on tombs, where publique trust   5
Assures us lies the most Couragious Dust:
I should have deem'd, twixt us and him this odds
That Wormes like me might die But such turn Gods.
I place not this Grand Heroe in their Spheare
But own by such he wore his title here.   10
Thanks first to Heaven, next to Caesar's beams
Which still gives Light to pen these dolefull Theams.
Hee's something worse then Monster in defect
Who covers such a piece with disrespect.
Heaven did not winke and chuse. Nor did the voice   15
Of an whole Countrey once repent this Choice
Form'd to this very end; sent as a Gift
To help this province at a deadly lift.
Lesse Active spirits might serve turn at helme
While th'Vulgar like the sea is still and Calme,   20
But for a boysterous spell, needs such an one,
Who with his Countenance could quell alone.
Goodness of extract happyly Conjoyn'd
By heavenly Marriage to an Heroe's mind:
In which if anywhere might be confest   25
The Lion with the Lamb did feed and rest.
Abràm in armes, well might th'acute Divine
Make application at this wine of thine.
Tall Cedars[2] in our forrest, In whose shade
Those Sympathizeing twine so long have laid   30
Of State and Church. His valour set a spell
And snib'd[3] the outrage of the Infidell.
This Holy Land was preposest before

131

But Joshua turnd the Heathen out of Dore.
And by the Soul of valour bolted out   35
Whole Nations of the tawny barbarous rout[4]
Hee clos'd the Churches wounds and kept the peace
When secret undermines did Increase.
When some delv'd deep their enterprize to hide
He trumpeted away their envious pride,   40
And Cut that Gordian knot which many thought
Would our Assemblys to Confusion brought.[5]
Tis more then Common vertue must stand here
No vulgar Art could such a vessel steer,
Whose passengers were saincts and Cabins hold   45
Such heavenly treasure as transcendeth Gold.
To keep the Arke so stedy yet not smitten.
In such great Earthquakes may be truly written
Among the Choicest Records: Twas a thing
Whereof from Age to Age our World may ring.   50
Next to that unseen hand which cannot Erre
We may the Crown of praise on him transfer.
Great were his parts, Sublimer much his grace
Some beams of Majesty had toucht his face[6]
Sufficient to enforme a Countrey whence   55
He borrow'd his Magestick Influence.
A Generall of such a noble sphear
His person and his purse both scorn'd the Reare.
So amiable both in Court and Field
His hand could Conquer while his spirits yield.   60
Come fellow souldiers: Chere all hearts amain
The Countreys cordiall is Soveraigne
He Honourably cry'd up all the Joy
When Boston Eccho'd loud *Vive le Roy*
Tis plaine without him we had had no sence   65
What meant the things call'd Royall Influence.
Twas not pure Custome but an anuall debt
Which caus'd our Alma Mater humbly set
Great Leveretts name, maine patron of her rights
In publique acts after their studious nights   70
A Thesis of it self so full of light
All disputations were decided by't.
He left that Marble which before was Stone
Or rather that Created which was none.
A great worke built on ruines former fame   75
Yet but an urne compar'd with his great name.

132

Next that Grand matron, creep the Infant schools[7]
Which save some naturall wits from greatest fools
Drest in the weeds of grief: And well they may
Since their Maecaenas is divorc'd away. 80
The Regiments, professours of the time
Lament in Ranke and file though not in Rhime.
All quarters startled at the suddaine end
Of this brave Joshua their publique friend.
Bring floods of tears, yet some returnd as though 85
The numerous already would not off.
Whose big swoln Clouds are ready to disperse
Their Amber tears upon the Sable herse
This Providence hath baffled all that Art
Which to the World did heav'n's concerns impart. 90
Such who the most by starrs and tide did know
Could not portend this full sea of our woe.
By this prodigious stroke of Cruell fate
Which our Eclypses Scheme doth Antidate,[8]
Who setting in our Clime has great Remarke 95
And proves Star-prophets sometimes in the darke.
Good Reason too Wise men are patent free
And ruld great Starrs themselves and thus did hee.
When angells made a muster in the Skie
And their stupendous ordinance let flie, 100
Ers while what could their Loud report portend
But preparations for this Generals end.
That spacious field was cleard of that black Guard
To Convoy this up to his high reward.
Such as New Englands Annalls mind to sift 105
Will find him by quotation. John the fifth: alias sixth[9]
But I recede from this Illustrious Throne
Whither my phancy roves to make my moane
Poor broken Boston, shall thy bleared eyes
And dolefull sighs which dayly stab the Skies 110
Griefs Hurricanes, what shall they never o're
And force their entry at some other dore?
Must this darke Climate be the onely stage
For Nemesis to act her various rage?
This the Aceldama for wounds and gore 115
The publick hospitall for pox and poor?
And must that man of sin who plots our woe
And Heav'ns dishonour, always Scotfree goe?
Shall the Laviathan who feasts on states

And quaffs the blood of Kings escape the fates?   120
Lord cast some Angry sparke into the nest
Of that blood sucking Anti Christian beast.
What yet remains New England's out of view
To pilate in such storms adventure few.
All Caesars subjects with a Common voyce   125
Cry God save Charles and help you in next choyce.
His diadem which now is soild with tears
So that her Lustre something disappears.
Sole Cordiall in his paines, which by his limbs
In a deep Gulf of tears before you swims   130
Whilst this small province in its freedome stands
Honour the dead by lending liveing hands
This will be omen of your future peace
Heaven will Create or rayse up more of these.

B.T.

TEXT

MS contemporaneous copy, in the commonplace book of John Leverett II, the Massachusetts Historical Society, pp. 1–4; printed in Jantz, pp. 157–161. In order to compress Tompson's longer couplets, Leverett resorted to frequent abbreviation of "the," "that," and "which." He also employed symbols or numerals to indicate the proper order of words. He does seem to have been interested in the accuracy of his transcription and therefore often inserted words or letters above the line.

EMENDATIONS

title: by y^e/ by the; of y^t/ of that; Jno/ John; of y^e/ of the; of ye Confederate/ of the
    Confederate; NE,/ New England,; of y^{e}16th/of the 16th: ; of y^{e}1 st/ of the lst.
  1: y^e/ the
  2: y^e/ the; w^{ch}/ which
  6: y^e/ the
  9: y^r/ their
14: wth/ with
15: y^e/ the
16: one/ once
20: y^e/ the
25: w^{ch}/ which
26: wth y^e/ with the
32: ye outrage/ the outrage
35: y^e/ the
37: ye Churchs/ the Churches; ye peace/ the peace
43: Comon/ Common; Leverett used the symbol ᴍ to indicate double m
48: t^{r}uely/ truly; r raised above the line
51: w^{ch}/ which
54: Majcesty/ Majesty

58: y^e/ the
63: y^e/ the
65: wthout/ without
66: m^t y^e/ meant the
69: her rights; lowered from above the line in MS
73: y^t/ that
74: y^t/ that
75: former ruines/ ruines former; Leverett placed 1 above ruines and 2 above former in MS
76: wth/ with
77: y^t/ that
78: Capital W supplied where MS torn
82: thô/ though
88: y^e/ the
89: y^t/ that
90: ye Wo^{r}ld/ the World; r in World raised above the line
91: y^e/ the
96: y^e/ the
99: y^e/ the; final s in Skies deleted by Leverett
103: y^t/ that
106: Jno y^e/ John the
110: sighs added on the basis of l. 45 in "A short memoriall . . . of Mary Tompson," the following poem in this edition; w^{ch}/ which
111: Greifs/ Griefs; w^t/ what
114: ffor/ For
115: y^e/ the
120: ye blood/ the blood; ye fates/ the fates
125: Coṁon/ Common
127: w^{ch}/ which
128: y^t/ that; disappears written after Lustre, then placed properly at the end of the line
132: y^e/ the

COMMENTARY

1. John Leverett (1616–16 March 1678/ 79) came to New England in 1633, became a freeman on 13 May 1640, married Sarah Sedgwick in 1641, received a command in the Parliamentary Army in 1644, was a member of the General Court in 1651–1653 and 1663–1665, served as deputy governor 1671–1673 and as governor from 1673 until his death. For more biographical information, see Samuel Eliot Morison on John Leverett in *The Dictionary of American Biography*, XI (1933); *NEHGR*, 4 (1850), 121–135; "The Leverett Papers," in *Massachusetts Historical Society Collections*, 4th ser., 2 (1854), 228–233; and Jantz, p. 157.

2. Cedar trees are frequently used in the Bible as symbols of strength (Ps. 29:5 and 37:35), of splendor (Song of Songs 1:17 and Jer. 22:14), and of glory (Ps. 80:10 and Jer. 22:7).

3. snib'd: rebuffed.

4. Lines 31–36 refer to Leverett's military service. He joined the Ancient and Honorable Artillery Company in 1639, was promoted to lieutenant in 1648, captain in 1652, 1663, and 1670, and major general on 27 May 1663 and every year thereafter, until his election as governor in 1673. With Edward Hutchinson,

in 1640, he was sent on a mission to the Indian chief, Miantonomo. In 1654 he led the forces which expelled the French from the Penobscot. And, finally, as governor of Massachusetts during King Philip's War (1675–1676), he was often consulted for military advice.

5. The "deep enterprise," the Gordian knot of confusion, which Tompson describes in lines 39–42, is difficult to identify. Beginning in 1662 New England, particularly Massachusetts Bay, experienced a number of divisive controversies. The Half-Way Covenant threatened to destroy New England's special relationship with God and history; in 1664 the colony's relationship with England was strained to such an extent that Leverett was one of only four men who were entrusted with the colony's charter; in 1668/69 John Davenport's ordination at Boston's First Church caused Thomas Thatcher and Increase Mather to organize the Old South Church; and in 1679 Edward Randolph was sent from England to enforce the laws of trade, and Leverett refused to take the oath to administer them. Leverett was such a popular diplomat that he was appointed in 1665 as the colony's representative to the Lord Protector and the Honorable Council in England, and his election to the governorship was never contested. Perry Miller, in *From Colony to Province* (Cambridge: Harvard University Press, 1962), pp. 93–149, discusses this troubled period in New England's history.

6. According to Savage, III, 83, Leverett was knighted in August 1676 by a special grant from the king. Lines 53–56 of Tompson's poem bear a striking resemblance to the opening passage of John Saffin's poem on Leverett; see Jantz, p. 250, no. 25; and see Alyce E. Sands, "John Saffin: Seventeenth-Century American Citizen and Poet," Thesis, Pennsylvania State University, 1965, pp. 190–191.

7. The Grand Matron was probably Sarah Sedgwick Leverett, wife of John Leverett, and mother of twelve children, six of whom were living in 1679. According to Jantz, p. 157, Harvard students and boys of the grammar schools probably marched in the funeral procession.

8. John Foster's *Almanack* (Boston, 1679) records an eclipse of the sun on 31 March 1679. It also lists 25 March as the date of the governor's burial.

9. Jantz, p. 157, explains line 106 in this way: "By 'John the fifth' 'alias sixth,' Tompson meant that four (or five) of Leverett's predecessors in the colonies had borne the name of John: Governors John Carver, Winthrop, Haynes, Endecott, Webster, and the younger Winthrop (Carver probably having been omitted on the first count, and Webster altogether)."

Upon the very Reverend
SAMUEL WHITING.[1]

MOunt *Fame*, the glorious Chariot of the *Sun*;
Through the *World's Cirque*, all you, her Herald's, run:
And let this Great Saint's *Merits* be reveal'd,
Which, during Life, he studiously conceal'd.
Cite all the *Levites*, fetch the Sons of *Art*,   5
In these our Dolours to sustain a part.
Warn all that value *Worth*, and every one
Within their Eyes to bring an *Helicon*.
For in this *single Person* we have lost
More Riches, than an *India* has engrost.   10

   When *Wilson*,[2] that Plerophory of *Love*,
Did from our *Banks*, up to his *Center* move,
Rare *Whiting* quotes *Columbus* on this Coast,
Producing *Gems*, of which a *King* might boast.
More splendid far than ever *Aaron* wore,   15
Within his Breast, *this* Sacred *Father* bore.
Sound Doctrine *Urim*,[3] in his Holy Cell,
And all Perfections *Thummim* there did dwell.
His *Holy Vesture* was his *Innocence*,
His *Speech*, *Embroideries* of curious *Sence*.   20
Such awful *Gravity* this Doctor us'd,
As if an *Angel* every Word infus'd.
No Turgent Stile, but *Asiatic* Store;
Conduits were almost full, seldom run o're
The *Banks* of *Time:* Come Visit when you will,   25
The Streams of *Nectar* were descending still:
Much like Septemfluous *Nilus*, rising so,
He watered Christians round, and made them grow.
His modest *Whispers* could the *Conscience* reach,
As well as *Whirlwinds*, which some others preach;   30
No *Boanerges*, yet could touch the Heart,
And clench his *Doctrine* by the *meekest Art*.
His *Learning* and his *Language*, might become
A *Province* not inferiour to *Rome*.
Glorious was *Europe's* Heaven, when such as these   35
Stars of his Size, shone in each *Diocess*.

   Who writ'st the *Fathers Lives*,[4] either make Room,
Or with his Name begin your *Second Tome*.

Ag'd *Polycarp*, Deep *Origen*, and such
Whose *Worth* your *Quills;* your *Wits* not *them*, enrich;   40
Lactantius, *Cyprian*, *Basil* too the Great,
Quaint *Jerom*, *Austin* of the foremost Seat,
With *Ambrose*, and more of the Highest Class,
In CHRIST's great *School*, with Honour, I let pass;
And humbly pay my Debt to *Whiting*'s Ghost,   45
Of whom both *Englands*, may with Reason boast.
Nations for Men of Lesser Worth have strove,
To have the *Fame*, and, in Transports of Love,
Built *Temples*, or fix'd *Statues* of pure Gold,
And their vast Worth to After-Ages told.   50
His Modesty forbad so fair a *Tomb*,
Who in Ten Thousand *Hearts* obtain'd a Room.

What sweet *Composures* in his *Angels Face!*
What soft Affections, Melting Gleams of Grace!
How mildly pleasant! By his closed Lips,   55
Rhetoricks Bright Body suffers an *Eclipse.*
Should half his *Sentences* be truly *Numbred*,
And *weigh'd* in Wisdom's Scales, 'twould spoil a *Lombard:*
And Churches *Homilies*, but *Homily* be,
If Venerable WHITING, set by thee.   60
Profoundest *Judgment*, with a *Meekness* rare,
Preferr'd him to the *Moderator*'s Chair;
Where like *Truth's Champion*, with his piercing Eye,
He silenc'd *Errors*, and made *Hectors* fly.
Soft Answers quell *hot Passions;* ne'er too soft   65
Where *solid Judgment* is enthron'd aloft.
Church Doctors are my Witnesses, that here
Affections always kept their *proper Sphere*,
Without those Wilder *Eccentricities*,
Which spot the fairest Fields of Men most Wise.   70
In *pleasant Places* fall that Peoples *Line*,
Who have but *Shadows* of Men thus Divine.
Much more their *Presence*, and Heaven pierceing *Prayers*,
Thus many Years, to mind our Soul-Affairs.
A *poorest Soil* oft has the *Richest Mine;*   75
This Weighty Oar, poor *Lyn* was lately thine.
O Wondrous Mercy! But this Glorious Light
Hath left thee in the Terrors of the Night.
New England, didst thou know this Mighty *One.*
His Weight and Worth, thou'dst think thy self *undone*:   80

One of thy Golden Chariots, which among
The *Clergy*, render'd thee a *Thousand* strong:
One, who for Learning, Wisdom, Grace, and Years,
Among the *Levites* hath not many Peers:
One, yet with God a Kind of *Heavenly Band*,   85
Who did whole *Regiments* of *Woes* withstand:
One, that prevail'd with *Heaven; One* greatly mist
On *Earth;* he gain'd of Christ whate'er he list:
One of a World; who was both born and bred
At *Wisdom*'s *Feet*, hard by the *Fountain*'s *Head*.   90
The *Loss* of such an *One*, would fetch a Tear,
From *Niobe* her self if she were here.

What qualifies our *Grief*, centers in *This*,
Be our *Loss* near so Great, the *Gain* is *his*.

B. Thompson.

TEXT

From Cotton Mather, *Magnalia Christi Americana* (London, 1702), Bk. III, Ch. XXVIII, 160–161; printed in Hall, pp. 131–134. Collation of the *Magnalia* copies at PSt, MH, CtY, MHi, MBAt, and CSmH against the Essex Institute copy showed no substantive variants.

EMENDATIONS

  1: *Sun;*; raised from below the line in copy-text. The printer of the *Magnalia* set the final word or words of Tompson's couplets on a separate, lower line and indented two to three spaces from the left-hand margin.
  2: Herald's hyphenated He-rald's; rald's, run:; raised from below the line in the copy-text
18: Pefections/ Perfections
28: grow.; raised from below the line
30: preach;; raised from below the line
35: these; raised from below the line
37: Room,; raised from below the line
40: enrich;; raised from below the line
44: pass;; raised from below the line
46: boast.; raised from below the line
54: the printer set this line with an extra space after every word or mark of punctuation; Grace!; raised from below the line
58: *Lombard:*; raised from below the line
63: Eye,; raised from below the line
70: Wise.; raised from below the line
73: pierceing hyphenated pierce-ing; ing *Prayers,;* raised from below the line
79: *One.;* raised from below the line
80: *undone:*; raised from below the line
83: Years,; raised from below the line
87: mist; raised from below the line

COMMENTARY

1. Samuel Whiting (1597–1679) B.A. Emmanuel College, Cambridge (1616–1617), and M.A. (1620). He emigrated to New England in 1636 and organized a church at Lynn, Massachusetts, where he was Overseer of Harvard College, and he published *Abraham's Humble Intercession* (Cambridge, 1666) and *A Discourse on the Last Judgment* (Cambridge, 1664). For more biographical information, see Mather, *Magnalia*, Bk. III, Ch. XVIII, 156–161; Morison, *The Founding of Harvard College*, pp. 406–407; Savage, IV, 420; and Weis, p. 223.

2. John Wilson (c. 1591–7 August 1667) was ordained 22 November 1632 as the first minister of Boston's First Church. Wilson wrote the preface to Whiting's *A Discourse on the Last Judgment* (Cambridge, Mass., 1664). Lines 11–14 of Tompson's elegy indicate that Whiting may have delivered a funeral sermon on Wilson, although this cannot be confirmed.

3. Urim and Thummin are the two essential parts of the sacred oracle by which the Hebrews of the Old Testament sought to ascertain the will of God. See Exodus 28:30 where Urim and Thummin are rendered "Light" and "Perfection."

4. For an analysis of the influence of the church fathers on Puritan culture, see Perry Miller, *The New England Mind: The Seventeenth Century* (1939; rpt. Cambridge: Harvard University Press, 1963), Bk. I, Chs. IV and V.

A short memoriall and Revew of sum
Vertues in that examplary Christian,
Mary Tompson,[1]
who Dyed in march 22: 1679.
penned for the imitation of the liveing.

Of all the treasure which this world doth hould
Tru saints are best whose price transendeth gould
And of all Comforts which Concern this life,
None to be found like to a Vertuous wife.
Our proto parent was environd round   5
With Rarest things yet no Content he found
Till such an one was formed by his side
With whom he might Convers, in whom Confide
With out which Comfort all our sweets are sowers
And familyes bear thissels with out floures.   10
And here if any whear it may be said
Lyes the Content of her lamenting head,[2]
His Dearest Choice his Credit and his Crown,
A sweet example to a Christian Town,
Whose life was made of innocence and love,   15
Whose Death doth all to great Compasion move.
Tis hard to tell where love did beare such sway,
Who twas Commanded or who did obey.
The swetest titles ever past betwene,
A Christian paire and Deeds might here be seen.   20
A Choicer spirit hardly Could be found
For Universall virtue on the ground.
One who betimes gave Up her virgin heart,
To Christ with solemn vows never to part,
And when she Changd her state she did attend   25
Such Dutyes as Concernd the maryage end.
With lovely Clusters Round on every side,
The house of god and hers she butified.
Zeal to whose worship in her Constant ways
Makes her an object of transendant prays.   30
What entercourse twixt heav'n and her I guess,
Besides what others did to me Confess,
Makes me Enrole her Reall saint indeed
For whom her turtle[3] may both weep and bleed.
Ask but the neighbour hood and they will tell,   35

141

She was a Dorcas[4] in our israell,
Ready on every hand to run or spend
To sick and pore to minister and lend.
So amiable in her whole Convers,
The least we Can is to lament her hearse.   40
But twas a stock in hand only on trust
Which to Returne upon Demand is just.
Our intrest houlds no longer, heavens decree,
Must give a supersedeas unto the.
Her wedded Consort from those bitter sighs   45
She is above a mortall that ner dyes.
Tis tru she might have lived many a year,
And still have shone in her Domestick sphear.
She might have made your lovely number up,
And you a while adjournd that bitter Cup.[5]   50
You might have livd both long and sweet as ever,
Yet in the end the sword of Death must sever.
The faster love is twisted in the heart
With Roots Confirmd the harder tis to part.
She might have pind a way with tedious mone   55
But her Dispatch is quick, shees quickly gone.
Two lives in one panting foe, Double breath
She yeilds up both in to the arms of Death.
Well may our teares at such a loss run ore
When such as love most Dear must se no more.   60
Well may her Consort Call this marys Day,[6]
Deaths bitterness hath swept his joys a way,
But lett in hers at once or lett her in
Such Chambers where never entered sin.
No Tears or pains, nor what brings Cross or wo   65
The Climate where she is shall ever know.
Should soule and body both posess one grave,
Relations then Could small Refreshment have,
While we discharg poore dutys to the Dust,
Her soule triumphant is among the just.   70
Could heven one glimps of passion once retaine,
Sheed Chide those teares off, and make you refrain.
Now all her prayers and hopes are spedd,
Her memory survives her body Dead.
Let her example as a Coppy stand   75
To Childrens Children upon every hand.
Talk of her sayings, one to another tell,
What in her life you have observed well.

Follow her steps and imitate her life,
Who was a Virtuous virgin mother wife.   80
So when Deaths summons treats you in such wise,
You may with greatest Comfort, Close your eys.

B.T.

TEXT

MS contemporaneous copy, in the Joseph Tompson Journal, Houghton Library, Harvard University; printed in Murdock, pp. 3–5. This manuscript copy-text is the most difficult of all of Tompson's works to transcribe with accuracy and reliability. Joseph Tompson's spelling, punctuation, and capitalization are highly irregular and inconsistent. Further, the ink has begun to bleed through the fragile pages of his commonplace book. The manuscript does clearly indicate that Joseph Tompson's transcription of this poem differs in accidentals from the two extant autograph poems in the Tompson corpus. Yet, having only two autograph poems, emendation here is restricted chiefly to instances where the clarity and sense of the passage are at stake. I have also capitalized the initial letter in the following lines: 1, 4, 5, 6, 8, 9, 10, 12, 15, 16, 18, 20, 22, 23, 26, 27, 30, 31, 33, 36, 38, 39, 40, 42, 43, 44, 46, 49, 52, 54, 55, 56, 58, 59, 60, 61, 63, 64, 65, 66, 67, 69, 70, 72, 73, 74, 78, 80, 81, 82.

EMENDATIONS

    1: treasure is written above the word "Comforts," which has a single line drawn through it
  31: enterCourse/ entercourse
  34: bleed/ bleed.
  36: DorCas/ Dorcas
  38: lend/ lend.
  40: hears./ hearse.
  45: widded/ wedded; Cyes/ sighs
  46: dyes/ dyes.
  72: of/ off
  76: hand/ hand.

COMMENTARY

    1. Mary Tompson, Joseph Tompson's first wife, was the daughter of Deacon Richard Bracket of Braintree. She was born in Braintree on 1 February 1642, married Joseph on 24 July 1662, and died on 23 March 1679. For more biographical information on the Tompson family, see Murdock, pp. xv–lxiii; and *NEHGR*, 15 (1861), 113–118.

    2. husband.

    3. turtle: turtledove, noted for the affection that mates show one another; conventional poetic term.

    4. Dorcas was a woman from Joppa known for her good works and alms-deeds. (See Mark 5:41.)

    5. Tompson is alluding in lines 49–50 to the circumstances of Mary's death. Mary gave birth to five children—Mary, Joseph, Abigail, William, and Deborah—but two others were stillborn, and a third died with Mary on 23 March 1679. Thus, line 49 may be interpreted "she might have given you more children," and line 50 may be read "you might have been spared the grief of losing another child." (See also, ll. 57–58.)

    6. According to Murdock, p. 115, Tompson puns in this line on "Mary and Marah, which in Hebrew means 'bitterness.' Cf. l. 62, and Exodus, 15:23."

A Short
but Sorrowfull memoriall
of my dear Sister Sarah Tompson[1]
who entered into glory 15th: 11th. 1679:
AEtatis Suae 43:
Penned plainly for the bereaved child-
rens use and relations Comfort.

If ever Soule found glorios Land I'll venture
To Say her Soule most cleere and pure did enter
Which though by natures filthyness once stain'd
It hath more than its former beauty gain'd
Being rinsed in that fount whereby Saints bee   5
From filth and Guilt, from fault and charg made free
Tis more than meere Relation that Invites
This testimony of her worth who writes
Twice seven years knowledge bids mee speak the truth
She serv'd her Jesus from her tender youth   10
When others were on bed and dropt asleep
She to her Saviour oft sate up to weep
She heard, she read, confest, she fasted, pray'd
In public and secret and what els is said
Beseeming real Saints shee said and did   15
But still with a design of being hid
An hid one during life of rarest worth
And now or never's time to blaze it forth
For others pattern: Well it may be said
He that obtains a wife like this is made.   20
Speak of her virgin mother maid or wife
She Acted Christian always to the life.
She was a beautious precious crown indeed
Whose soules translation makes her consort bleed
The sweetest fittest Consort could be found   25
For his Affection on New-Englands ground
One that knew when to Spend and when to Spare
One that knew how to Speake when to forbeare
One in whose heart chast modestie did reighn
That could be angry yet in time refraine   30
What diligence and prudent ways she had

To make her Chickens round about her glad
By feeding cloathing giving each theyr part
And ordering her household by an Art
Not common: But in her Example true   35
And imitable but by very few.
An houswife mostly to be found at home
While others from the tents doe ride and rome
A pleasant help to him with whom she joynd
Not meerly for his body but his mind.   40
How often did her teachings like the dew
Her Children deer daily distill on you
Her tender love and prayrs bespeak your tears
With whome She labourd in her tender years.
For your repentance and your birth anew   45
Who from her loyns had sins infection drew
Experience sad hath taught mee to confess
It's dolefull to bee left so Motherless
Mothers advantages are very great
The policies of Satan to defeat   50
Ev'n from the Cradle up their babes to train
In wisdom which to old age may remaine
And hopes I have what of this kind Shee did
When her young hopes spring up will not be hid
Tread in her steps her Christian ways remind   55
Talk of her words you babes shee left behind,
And you her Solitary mate be sure
May out of this poor Carcas sweet procure
View it o're well, Its but an empty Cage
Where shee was chain'd under a feavors Rage   60
The Larke at length hath broke its fretting snare
And sings above your head Surpassing fair
While you Lament Shee Smiles: shall her good hour
The Solace of your life at once devoure
Shee has gaind the Start by far: shold she come back   65
Again to pace her wildernesses track,
Shee From Canaans sweetness: To the bloody Sea
Could this with your desires (her love) agree
Surceas those pitteous heart consuming groans
Intomb them with her sickness wither'd bones   70
YOU and your babes are sadly all depriv'd
But ther's no Sighs nor tears where shee's ariv'd
          for Blessed are the dead
          that die in the Lord[2]

145

TEXT
MS contemporaneous copy, in the Sarah Tompson manuscript, the Connecticut Historical Society; printed in the *Connecticut Historical Society Bulletin*, 36 (July 1971), 72–76. The Sarah Tompson manuscript is divided into four sections: "The Relation of Sarah Tompson, the Wife of Samuel Tompson"; this 72–line elegy by Benjamin Tompson, her brother-in-law; an elegy—listed in Jantz, No. 32, Anonymous Poetry—entitled "To the Memory of his Deceased Friend Sarah Tompson"; and a portion of "Mr. Joseph Allen's Useful Questions." In the *Connecticut Historical Society Bulletin*, 36 (July 1971), 74, Neil T. Eckstein explains that either John Pierce or Benjamin Allen, sons-in-law of Sarah Tompson, wishing "to preserve a private family memorial to their long deceased mother," may have copied or compiled the extant manuscript. "The hand is remarkably legible and consistent, suggesting that all four parts were copied at once, probably in the first or second decade of the Eighteenth Century."

EMENDATIONS
title: 11.th/ 11th.
  1: I,ll/ I'll
  5: St^s./ Saints
  6: ffrom/ From; free; raised from below the line
  9: ye truth/ the truth; truth; raised from below the line
 10: serv, d/ serv'd
 18: never,s/ never's
 22: alwais/ always
 26: ffor/ For
 34: "hold" in household rewritten
 43: yor/ your
 45: ffor/ For; yor/ your
 55: "mind" in remind raised from below the line
 62: yor/ your
 63: hour; raised from below the line
 64: yor/ your
 65: Shee'/ Shee; back; lowered from above the line
 67: Shee; lowered from above the line; ffrom/ From
 68: Cold/ Could
 70: wither,d/ wither'd
 71: yor/ your; depriv,d/ depriv'd
 72: ther,s/ ther's; shee,s ariv,d/ shee's ariv'd

COMMENTARY
   1. Sarah Tompson (1636–15 Jan. 1679/80) was the daugher of Edward Shepard of Braintree, Massachusetts. On 25 April 1656, she married Samuel Tompson, elder brother of Benjamin, the poet. She was the mother of ten children, but three died in infancy. From the first three parts of the Sarah Tompson manuscript, it is evident that Sarah was an extremely devoted Christian, wife, and mother. (See also Tompson's elegy on Samuel Tompson, Sarah's husband.)
   2. Following the final lines of the poem, it appears that the copyist has written the word "dead" and "Anagr. Ah! son, Sam, port" as well as three Christian symbols incorporating the letters of the names Sarah and Samuel Tompson.

EDMUND DAVIE[1] 1682.
anagram
AD Deum veni

To God, the Center of all Souls, I'm flown,
Having been from all eternity his own.

I'm now arriv'd the Soul desired Port
More pleasing far then glories of the Court:
My Saviour is my only Caesar: Here's
Instead of Nobles, Angels hosts, bright Peers,
Great Princes thronging round, thicker then swains   5
Below at publicke votes: Here each one Reigns.
Our streets are pav'd with Saphires, and we pass
Or'e streams of Christial like to fusil Glass
Heres Treasuries, the like weve never seen;
All guesses at the worth have fool'ries been.   10
Mountains of Rubies safe from privateers
Within the Ramphiers of these lofty Spheres.
Here's piles of Scepters, Diadems of Gold
More then the worlds vast space at once will hold.
But that which butifies this boundless room   15
Is great JEHOVAH, unto whom I'm come.
Eternity's the highest link of Bliss;
Its sunshine never sets, nor clouded is.
I've hitt the very Place I wisht at heart,
I'm fixt for ever: Never thence to part.   20
His heart was erst inamourd with delights
In studious Solitudes, in Attick Nights
To prove the greatest avarice of his minde
After the Gems of Skill his Body pin'd.
Hating the sluggards bed, and flattering sloth,   25
Nocturnal Wakes had brought him to vast growth.
His tender years were seasoned with a Juice,
Which might have provd, if spar'd, of gen'ral use.
He clim'd the Shrowds of Science: Now hees dead,
Hees got above the verry topmost head,   30
Hearing that word which set his Soul on fire
With blazing zeal of Love: Brite Soul, come higher,
All that thou see'st is thine, myself to boot;
Heres an Eternal feast of Love: fall to it.

High, we believe, this welcome Guest was seated,   35
And in an instant all his joys compleated.

EPITAPH.

THE World was once in danger to drop out
Sidney's Remains, Wits universe about.
Here in Death's gripes a gemme of Art so rare
New-England's Poverty claimeth her share;   40
Since here she nurst him with a silvane teat
Untill hee's fledgd to seek a distant seat:
Gaining the naked Substance, his Intent's
From statelier Halls to gain Embellishments
Of sciences profound: Twas well essayd;   45
But by that means this gallant Spark hath paid
What England, Honours Throne, his place of Birth,
Did rightly claime, his soul deserted Earth.
Hee lies among that precious Dust unknown
Which with most friendly silence huggs its own.   50
Great Gransiers of most venerable race,
Yield this their Nephew a retiring Place
In their dark Conclave, where there hands and brains,
Under the umbrage of the grave remains.

Hace Genitoris amor, Matris reverentia possit
    Carmina, Tutoris pauperis obsequio.[2]

B.T.

TEXT
MS contemporaneous copy, in the commonplace book of Samuel Sewall, The
New-York Historical Society; printed in Jantz, pp. 161–63; and Meserole, pp.
223–24.

EMENDATIONS
title: anaagram/ anagram
  5: swains; raised from below the line
 10: geuesses/ guesses; corrected by Sewall
 13: pilses/ piles
 14: at once; inserted from above the line
 25: second "g" in sluggards; inserted from above the line
 26: This line originally written: Nocturnal Wakes had brought him to great
     growth. Sewall drew a line through that version, changing great to vast.
 32: "er" in higher; lowered from above the line
 45: essa'yd;/ essayd;
 48: claimg/ claime; corrected by Sewall
 52: their; inserted from above the line
 55: reverētia/ reverentia

COMMENTARY

1. Edmund Davie (d. 1681) was the son of Humphrey Davie and the elder brother of Sir John Davie. Until the publication of Jantz's *The First Century of New England Verse* (1943–44), Edmund Davie was thought to have been the brother of Humphrey Davie. In discovering this poem and the following poem on Humphrey Davie, Jantz clarified one of the most enduring biographical mysteries in early American culture. Genealogists, historians, and antiquarians had searched diligently but fruitlessly to identify Edmund Davie. Cotton Mather, *Magnalia*, Bk. IV, 136–139, "A History of Harvard College," lists Edmund Davie (H.C. 1674) as M.D. Padua University, deceased sometime before 1698. Savage, II, 14–15, says, "Unsatisfactory conjecture may suppose he was the younger brother of Humphrey Davie." Sibley, II, 442, quotes Mather and Savage, and conjectures that Edmund Davie may have been a kinsman of another Edmund Davie who died in January 1692. While there are still many uncertainties about the life of Edmund Davie, Tompson's poem does solve some of the basic biographical problems. See Chapter II, note 37, of this edition.

2. This love of one's parent, this reverence for one's mother, requires a song, with the indulgence of one's guardian.

To my Honoured Patron
HUMPHERY Davie[1]
A renewing the Memory of Dr Edmund Davie.
Who expired at London; Anno 1681

Bereav'd Sir

Delug'd with tears, by what you heard before,
Here Unexpected meets you one stroke more.
Wave upon wave; Blows fall so thicke, so fast,
Arterial blood, I fear, will come at last
Instead of tears; Methinks I feel the smart,   5
Which in this hour of tryal cramps your heart.
A spouses Death, so wise, so Chast, so fair,
Would bring a Job himselfe next Door Despair:
Soon after that, the First fruits of your strength;
I fear your patience will you fail at length.   10
But I recall that word, though hard no doubt
Who tends the Furnace, sure will helpe you out.
Had I an intrest where this Pair are gone,
The Vertuous Mother, with the Learned Son;
I'd beg a Balsom for your bleeding wound,   15
No where below this Climate to be found
Distance cannot be salv'd: let S'impathize
A very little space your heart suffice.

Amplitudini tuae devinctus[2]
Benjamin Tompson.
Braintry; 29 4 1682.
Samuel Sewall His Book written

July 31. 1695.

TEXT
MS contemporaneous copy, in the commonplace book of Samuel Sewall, The New-York Historical Society; printed in Jantz, p. 163; and Meserole, p. 225.

EMENDATION
title: my; inserted from above the line

COMMENTARY
1. Humphrey Davie (bapt. 24 Aug. 1625–18 Feb. 1688/89), a London merchant, emigrated to Boston in 1662; organized the county of Devon, Massachu-

setts, in 1664; joined the Ancient and Honorable Artillery Company in 1665; as Deputy to the General Court, represented Billerica and Woburn in 1666–1679; commissioned as captain in the Boston Militia in 1675; and was appointed assistant to the General Court and *ex officio* overseer of Harvard College, 1679–1686. In England, before 1665, he married Mary White, daughter of Edmund White of London. Mary, who was the mother of nine children by Humphrey, died in Boston, 30 December 1681.

2. Overwhelmed by your greatness.

[Reverend Mr. Mather:]

My Loyalty is still the same
Whither I win or loose the game
True as a Dial to the Sun
Although It bee not shin'd upon

TEXT
MS autograph letter signed to Increase Mather, 25 Nov. 1683, in the Boston
Public Library; printed in *M.H.S.C.*, 4th ser., 8 (1860), 635; printed with a
facsimile in Hall, p. 16 and facing 16. For the entire text of this letter, see
Appendix B. (See also the introduction to this book for an explanation of Tompson's efforts to secure "full imployment, and its comfortable attendants.")

EMENDATION
4:    Althô/ Although

A Character of the most Exemplary
Christian, Mr. Samuel Tompson.[1]
Deacon of the Church in Braintree
who Deceased June 18. 1695. AEtatis. 64.

'Tis not bare custom which provokes my Pen
To lisp the praises of this Man of men
Nor can it in the least advantage him
Whose Soul in Rivers of Delight doth Swim
But such Examples set before this Age   5
And me in special wel deserv'd a Page
Plainness and Purity were his delight
Least I offend his Ghost, plainly I write
I write no Hero's, or Terrestrial Peers
Let them be flatter'd by more learned tears   10
But the translation of one to his place
Who in Gods fear and favour ran his race
An Entercourse with Heav'n mannag'd by Art
And tedious pains of most he did by heart
The morning of his Life's aspireing years   15
Commenc'd in prayers, and Penitential tears
When but a Child and Mates had led to play
His Spirit prompted him to Read and Pray
His Youth so spotless in such Years transpir'd
As rendred him improv'd, belov'd, admir'd   20
Whome fitter for the Church, the Court the Field
Of a more upright Life, did Braintree yeild
It boasted Once of a most worthy Store
Blest Tompson,[2] Flynt,[3] the rare presiding Hoare[4]
Rich Jewels: thou of such hast been possest   25
Whose Weary heads are all layd down to Rest
Make room Renowned's who our Crowns have been
In the same Page to let this Christian in
Whome you all knew, and lov'd, wer't in a fitt
Of Melancholy when these lines were writt   30
Grave Tompson, were clouds ever in that place
Thy sons arrival sure would clear thy Face
He liv'd under the Umbrage of a Wing[5]
Whose great delight to preach, to pray, to Sing
Thousands in Lancashire 'yond Sea did know   35
Who in darke times did to such torches flow

153

And now the Precious Father, and Blest Son
Know whither, and for what they fought and run
Were ever Heav'ns by fair endeavors won
If Prayers could storm it, sure 'twas by this man   40
But when his hand of Faith those doors had bounced
And wrestled stoutly, yet he all renounc'd
His house was Morn, Noon, Night perfum'd with Prayers[6]
And seconded with Heav'ns Melodious Aires
The sacred Text was Read and Opened so   45
As sundry stil'd Divines could hardly do
In conferences with his holy Friends
Assistance from sweet Manuscripts he lends
Such as would Old and Modern Preachers heare
Might find the Kernel and the marrow there   50
With great Affections urged on the hearts
And Balsom poured in after sharp Darts
His Charity was General and Vast
With so small a stock how could it last
By Prayer his secret Key the Heav'ns unlock't   55
And when most Empty, seldom better stockt
Assistances to poor he ne're denie'd
And few such places where it might be try'd
His soundness in the Faith Divines did Own
Who hath abridg'd their labours One by One   60
And Ancient Nectarists whose mouths are stopt
Extending fruitfull boughs by him were cropt
Theyr fruit more choice then Pearls with him even
His Manuscripts I call their Magazeen.
Where Honey dropt this painfull Bee was found   65
Loading his thighs for all his Neighbours round
How many weekly did with him rejoyce
Loveing to see his face, and hear his voice
To Lamentations now our harps are sett
And chearfull Anthems we almost forgett   70
We can as hardly sing with hiarty thanks
As Israel on the Babilonish Banks
So much of God is from poor Braintree fled
As may be sighed for, more free then sed
His Empty place in Church in Court, in field   75
By many teares have every day been fill'd
And poor distressed I, O where, O where!
Shall I find friendly hand, or faithfull Eare
Whome shall the poor seek to in pinching grief

Whome the distressed to Obtain reliefe   80
Whome shall the Widow make her trusty friend
And hand a Prayer at a dead lift to lend,
Here was of Charity a liveing Spring
Whose motives round the Greater wheels did bring
His presence, parts, and Prayers are dearly mist   85
Who could like Luther have what'ere he list
How would he screw into each hearers brest
When he with fervency Our sins confest
What melting streams of Arguments there flew
From his own heart, as if he others knew.   90
Such Instruments, so qualifie'd are rare
And very few fall to one Churches share
Predictions I affect not, though I dread
The places publick peace now he is dead
Who lov'd and studied Unity so well   95
The peace is threatened where this prop is fell
Lord grant us Succour to our sinking hearts
Drop in thy Balsom while we feel thy Darts
Answer the prayers this Blessed Saint hath made
Our Soules let Rest with his when we are laid.   100

B.T.

TEXT
MS contemporaneous copy, in the Massachusetts Historical Society, Edward
Tompson manuscript; printed in *Proc. M.H.S.*, 2nd ser., 10 (1889–1890), 275–
278; and Hall, pp. 137–140.

EMENDATIONS
title: M:/ Mr.
  10: t[ears]
  11: pl[ace]
  19: [transpir'd]
  20: a[dmir' d]
  21: Cour[t the]
  27: been; lowered from above the line
  39: wan/ won
  44: [A]nd
  45: [Th]e
  51: [gre]at
  53: H[is]
  54: [With]
  55: B[y]
  87: he[ar]ers
  90: knew/ knew.
  93: thô/ though

COMMENTARY

1. Samuel Tompson (1631–18 June 1695), Benjamin's elder brother, was chosen deacon of the First Church at Braintree (1679) and representative to the General Court in the years 1676–1686 and 1691. He did not hold this position in the years 1681–1682 because of the death of his first wife, Sarah, in 1680. His second wife, Elizabeth Billings, daughter of Robert Billings of Dorchester, died 5 Nov. 1706. For more biographical information, see *NEHGR*, 15 (1861), 112–116; and see Savage, IV, 288.

2. William Tompson, Samuel's father.

3. Henry Flynt (c. 1613–1668), B.A. 1634/35, M.A. 1638, Jesus College, Cambridge, was ordained at the First Church at Braintree, 13 March 1640, where he continued to preach until his death on 27 April 1668.

4. Leonard Hoar (c. 1630–28 Nov. 1675) emigrated with his family to Braintree, Massachusetts, in 1640; B.A. 1650, Harvard College; M.A. 1653, Cambridge; M.D. 1654, Cambridge; and was inaugurated Third President of Harvard College, 10 Dec. 1672.

5. Psalm 91.

6. Rev. 5:8.

To Lord Bellamont[1] when entering
Governour of the Massachusetts. by Ben. Thompson.

Were I sole sov'reign of rare Fancies now,
All to your Merits Should with Rev'rence bow.

Transcendent Sir,

Your Stamp is royal; Your Commissions Rays
From loyal Hearts demand loud Thanks, high Praise.   5
Our Senators with publick Cares so tir'd,
With chearfullness resign to you desird.
Accept a poor Mans Thanks, a rural Bitt,
E're you arrive the Festivalls of Witt.
The Traveller where Wine's not to be had,   10
With a Cup of cold Water's often glad.
Since Harvards Libertys we fear are lost,
And Hasty-Pudding's Servd in stead of roast.
I've seen some feasted and placd in the Chair
And treated as I thought with Treatment rare: 15
But what was in the Pot he who this writ,
Tasting not once thereof, Still turnd the Spit.
We hope your Grandeur, for whom all have prayd,
Shall never lack our Love, our Purse, our Aid.
We bless our King; we thank the Waves and Wind,   20
That to our Sinking State have been So kind:
To land your Person, Ship'd by Grace of God.
Our loyal Hearts bespeak your long Abode.

Had you arriv'd Some hundred Years agoe,[2]
The naked Tribes with knotty Clubbs and Bow   25
Storming your canvas'd Whale, with spears Head tryd
Whether your Timber had been Soul-ifyd.
An antient Chicataubuts[3] Smoaky Ghost,
Once Lord of all this Soil and dreary Coast
Awakend by the Triumph of this Day   30
Hearing your Lordship was to come this Way,
Beggd Pluto's Leave, but that it would affright
To testifie his Joy at this fair Sight.
Here's running, riding, pressing hard to See
A blazing Beam darting from Majesty.   35
And who among whole thousands can do less,

157

Than for this Voi'ge thank you and Heav'n bless?
Whilst to your Lordship we our Gratias render,
Poor Emmett[4] I tremble as an Offender.
But gen'rous Souls o'er look a World of Faults.   40
The Heart well trimd, the Pen more rarely halts.

    Fam'd Agawam, who once drew salem Fair[5]
Sure prophecyd this Interview so rare.
So what in jest with his Sharp Awl he wrote
Is in good Earnest to our Quarters brought.   45

    Mountains bare-headed Stand; Each fertile Field,
When washd with Showers will rich presents yield.
Adopt this People as we ready be;
An Eden So long hid you'll quickly See.
Deep Mines their Riches tender; Gardens Flowers;   50
Their Sprawling Vines Stretch out to make you Bowers.
Charles River Swoln with Joys, o'er flows with Thanks:
And Sends his golden <u>Trouts</u> up winding Banks.
Old Merimack was ne'er So glad before:
And casts up <u>Salmon</u> free cost on the Shore.   55
Deep Conges[6] drop the <u>Elm</u>; tall <u>Cedars</u> bow-
And Corydon to gaze deserts the Plough.
Damoetas his Nown Self, had hither rid,
But that he's run with Speed to fetch a Kid.[7]
To make this Country Treat more Solemn up   60
Brisk Thesiylis comes panting with a Cup
Of dainty Syllabub: Sweet Amaryllis
Her Flask replete with Rose and Daffodyl.
Down at your Ladys Feet her self she flings;
Whilst Daphne, in her Strains, your Welcome sings.   65
And not one Face in all this Grand Convent
But Smiles forth Tokens of their full Content.
Brisk sons of Mars, Valours right Heirs, all round,
Your modest Arms this Day are richly crownd.
A General you have from Europe blown   70
Whose very Sight might make <u>Quebeck</u> your own
Although With Wrinkled Age my Colours furld,
Under his Conduct we'd soon storm that World.

    Pardon, fair Sir, that many Thousand Meet
To lay a Province' Welcomes at your Feet.   75
A City Treaty for your Worth remains

By Potent Purses and more Powerfull Brains.
I'll to my Coblers Den, with Leave retire:
And if your Grandeur Frowns, there I'll expire.

TEXT

MS later copy, in the commonplace book of Ebenezer Parkman, the Massachusetts Historical Society; printed in Jantz, pp. 165–167. Jantz quotes a letter (27 Aug. 1760) from Parkman to Mather Byles, written just after the arrival of Governor Sir Francis Bernard: Parkman says,

> Now you have all run thro the Ritual a la Mode, and the Congratulations and Addresses to his Excellency for his safe Arrival, are over; sit down and rest you; and I pray you heark to what Ben. Thompson sung when a former Governour came. He is suppos'd in Quality of a shooe-Maker to run out from his stall to pay his homely Complements to his Lordship as he passed through Dedham toward Boston. There break out, now and then, incomparable Strokes—and the 22 pastoral Lines beginning with "Maountains bare-headed stand" etc. give me great pleasure.

EMENDATIONS
title: y^e/ the
2: y^r/ your
3: Sr,/ Sir,
14: y^e/ the
16: y^e/ the
17: y^e/ the
20: o^r/ our; y^e/ the
21: o^r/ our
22: y^r/ your
29: the word "desart" written above the word "dreary," but Parkman did not excise dreary. I have therefore retained dreary.
30: y^e/ the
38: y^r Ldship/ your Lordship; o^r/ our
41: y^e/ the
52: wth Joys,/ with Joys,; wth Thanks:/ with Thanks:
56: y^e/ the
58: Dametas/ Damoetas
61: Thesylis/ Thesiylis; w^th/ with
62: Amaryl/ Amaryllis
63: replets/ replete
64: y^r/ your
65: y^r/ your
71: y^r/ your
72: Altho/ Although
74: Sr,/ Sir,
75: y^r/ your
76: y^r/ your
79: y^r/ your

COMMENTARY

1. Richard Coote (1636–1701), the first earl of Bellamont, governor of New York and New England, was a popular, intelligent, but rather crafty individual. He had been commissioned governor of New England in June 1697, but according to Samuel Eliot Morison, in *Harvard College in the Seventeenth Century* (Cambridge: Harvard University Press, 1936), II, 517, Lord Bellamont "appeared to be in no hurry to visit his Province of the Massachusetts Bay, where the Mather family was so eagerly expecting him. Magnificently received on April 2 at New York, over which he also had a Governor's commission, His Excellency tarried there week after week, and month after month." Near the end of May 1699, Lord Bellamont arrived in Massachusetts Bay, preceded by the news that Harvard College's Charter of 1697 had been disavowed by the Lords of Trade and the King in Council. In 1700 the Council and House of Representatives drafted a charter to their specifications, but Bellamont "like the good fellow he was, decided to urge Whitehall to accept their draft and make a Royal Charter of it" (Morison, *Harvard College in the Seventeenth Century*, II, 528), leaving the College once again disorganized and subservient to English administration.

2. Lines 24 through 29 are probably based on Edward Johnson's account of Captain John Smith's arrival in Massachusetts Bay in 1614. See Edward Johnson, *Wonder-Working Providence of Sions Saviour in New England* (London, 1654), ed. J. Franklin Jameson (1910; rpt. New York: Barnes and Noble, 1959), pp. 39–40.

3. Chickataubut ("house afire") was a sachem of the region about Weymouth, Massachusetts. An Indian of great power and influence, he confronted the Puritans about their intrusions into the Indians' cornfields and burial grounds. He met with Winthrop in 1631 at Boston, "behaving like an Englishman." He died of smallpox in 1632.

4. Emmett: archaic word for "ant."

5. As Jantz notes, p. 164, Tompson probably confused Aggawam (Ipswich) with Salem. Evidently Tompson was dressed as "The Simple Cobbler of Aggawam" after the inspiration of Nathaniel Ward's satirical essay printed in London in 1644. Ward announced himself "Willing to help 'mend his Native Country,' lamentably tattered, both in the upper-Leather and sole, with all the honest stiches he can take."

6. conge: to bow.

7. While the pastoral intention here is clear, there is perhaps a brief reference to Lord Bellamont's special mission in America. He had been commissioned to put down piracy and unlawful trade on the American coast, and therefore he fitted out Captain Kidd and gave him special powers to arrest pirates. However, in 1697 the East India Company complained that Kidd was the most audacious pirate of them all. To protect his honor, Bellamont went to Boston in 1699 and immediately arrested Kidd, who had come to clear himself of the charges.

Celeberrimi
COTTONI MATHERI,
Celebratio;
Qui Heroum Vitas, in sui-ipsius et illorum Memoriam
sempiternam, revocavit.

Quod Patrios Manes revocasti a Sedibus altis,
Sylvestres Musae grates, Mathere, *rependunt.*
Haec nova Progenies, veterum sub Imagine, coelo
Arte Tua Terram visitans, demissa, salutat.
Grata Deo Pietas; Grates persolvimus omnes: 5
Semper Honos, Nomenque Tuum, Mathere, *manebunt.*[1]

Is the bless'd *MATHER Necromancer* turn'd,
To raise his Countries Father's Ashes Urn'd?
Elisha's Dust, Life to the Dead imparts;[2]
This Prophet, by his more *Familiar Arts*,[3]   10
Unseals our *Hero*'s Tombs, and gives them Air;
They Rise, they Walk, they Talk, Look wond'rous Fair;
Each of them in an Orb of *Light* doth shine,
In Liveries of *Glory* most Divine.

When ancient Names I in thy Pages met,   15
Like Gems on *Aaron*'s costly Breast-plate set;[4]
Methinks Heaven's open, while Great *Saints* descend,
To wreathe the Brows, by which their *Acts* were penn'd.

B. Thompson.

TEXT
From Cotton Mather, *Magnalia Christi Americana* (London, 1702), preface.
Printed in Hall, p. 143 and Kenneth Murdock, ed., *Magnalia Christi Americana*,
Bks. I and II (Cambridge: Harvard University Press, 1977), pp. 79–80. Colla-
tion of the *Magnalia* copies at PSt, MH, CtY, MHi, MBAt, and CSmH against
the Essex Institute copy showed no substantive variants.

COMMENTARY
1. The Celebration of the most renowned Cotton
   Mather; who recalled the lives of heroes,
   for his very own and their everlasting memory.

   Because you have called back the ancestral
   spirits from their ancient seats,
   The woodland Muses are repaying you.

161

This new offspring, under the image of old men,
Having been sent down from heaven, visiting the
    earth by means of your art, greets you.
Piety pleasing to God; we all render our thanks:
Your honor and name, Mather, will always remain.

2. See 2 Kings 13:21: "And it came to pass, as they were burying a man, that, behold, they spied a band of men; and they cast the man into the sepulchre of Elisha: and when the man was let down, and touched the bones of Elisha, he revived, and stood upon his feet."

3. *Familiar Arts:* the more ordinary, academic arts but also a spirit or devil, often in the form of a bird or cat, associated with or under the power of man for evil purposes. Tompson here gently satirizes his former pupil, Cotton Mather, who was an authoritative but relatively impartial figure in the witchcraft trials of 1692. For more on Mather's role in the trials, see Chadwick Hansen, *Witchcraft at Salem* (New York: Braziller, 1969).

4. See Exodus 28: 4–43, wherein the priests' vestments are described.

The Illustrious Fitz-John Winthrop Esquire[1]—
Governor of Quinecticott Colony in New England
Memorized and lamented by an aged Sylvan
of the Massathusets

Anno Dom: 1708.

Winthrop this day repos'd his weary bones
Leaving his Province filld with equall groans
To those which by the wrack hee under-went
Ere his brave soul was from its binding rent.
Being the third of a Renowned line   5
Which wee Americans deemd next Divine
The last Gazet which from New-England came
Might ha' been crowned with GREAT WINTHROPs name.
Advertisment Enough to fill a page
And deluge with its tears the present age.   10
His grandsire by direction of a starre
Conducted all our Tribes hither, thus farr
And many thousands of most precious Ore
And SAINTS more precious landed here on shoare
Laying the Platforme of his State so firme   15
No underminers in his life did harme.
Winthrop, the second, of renowned fame
Hath filld this climate with his perfumd name.
CHARLES that hee might his grand Arcanas[2] know
While hee prepard them would the bellows blow.   20
Were there a Balsom, which all wounds could cure
Twas in this Asculapian[3] hand be sure.
WINTHROP, the third with palsied hand I write
His Province pillar, and this lands delight.
His auncient Patent while hee livd was free   25
From all intrusions on their libertie.[4]
While all the neighbourhood was set on fire
Hee kept his Paradisian hearts desire,
Being garrisond with GOD, all fencd about
With living walls, and hearts of Marble stout.   30
New-England Histories so much have said
In WINTHROPS praise, poor I do but degrade.
Europe knows better than wee natives tell
How in thy Parentage thou didst excell.

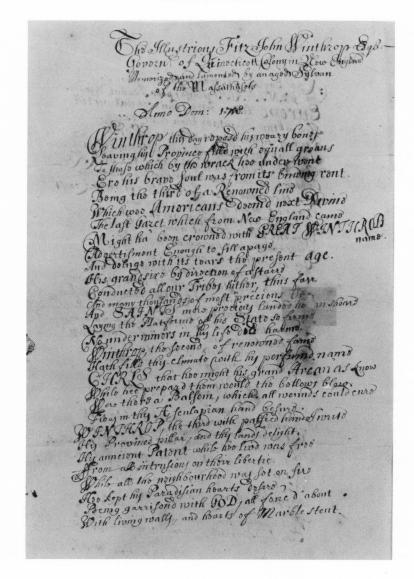

The Illustrious Fitz-John Winthrop Esquire

This autograph manuscript in the Winthrop Deeds, The Massachusetts Historical Society, is the second of the two surviving manuscripts in Benjamin Tompson's own hand. The "aged Sylvan" at 66 years still had perfect control of his beautifully elaborate yet clear handwriting style; for Tompson the production of an elegy was a matter of both literary and visually artistic importance. (*Courtesy of the Massachusetts Historical Society.*)

Vertues sufficient to oblige a World   35
Have at thy Exit all their streamers furld.
In Boston lies the timber of the ARKe
On which before hees borne hee did imbarque
Winthrop the first Lord of the Americk coast
Opning his bosom of his sons may boast   40
In lethall agonies, this, prays for rest
Upon the pillow of that auncient breast.
Lands every where hee had wheron to lie
Yet hee must see his grandsires tomb and die.[5]
By a great favorite hees upward handed   45
Sin and Temptations all at once disbanded
Hee at the Innes of Court such treaty finds
As fully can content ingenuous minds
Heers three great Winthrops under whom wee thrivd
Wee hope the fourth will prove far longer lived.   50
And such as are invested with great power
May bee preparing for a parting hour.

Epilogi vice[6]—

Thus naked Sylvans, guiltless as to Art
Yet in our sorrows need not learne our part,
Since wee can mourn, with all our Vitals black   55
When those are rent from us wee chiefly lack.
Not to renew your sorrows this I write
Not to prevent your surfeits in delight
Accept this offering of a countrey teare
From clouded eys that soon must disappeare   60
Might I with such kind Enterteinment have
Take lands who will, I would request a Grave.

Morti vivemus[7]   B.T.

[endorsed]: 1708 on the Death of Governor Fitz-John Winthrop

TEXT
MS autograph in the Winthrop Deeds, the Massachusetts Historical Society;
printed in *Proc. M.H.S.*, 2nd ser., 10, 369–371; and Hall, pp. 147–149. Dr.
Samuel A. Green, in the *Proceedings*, p. 369, says,

> At a stated meeting of this Society held on December 13, 1877, Mr. Win-
> throp, the President, spoke of five early Elegies—three of them printed as
> broadsides, and the other two in manuscript—which were preserved among
> his family papers. One of the manuscript Elegies was composed on the death of

the third Governor Winthrop, commonly called Fitz-John Winthrop, to distinguish him from his father. It was written soon after the event, and was signed with the initials, "B.T.," which stand for the name of Benjamin Tompson, the earliest native American poet. As these productions were not considered worth printing in the Proceedings, Mr. Winthrop referred to them only to show how in former days the griefs of our fathers strove and struggled to express themselves in metrical and rhythmical form.

Through the courtesy of Mr. Winthrop, Jr., I have been enabled to make a copy of Tompson's lines, which are without doubt in the handwriting of the author.

EMENDATIONS

title: Esqr/ Esquire; Govern^r/ Governor
 8: name.; raised from below the line
 14: he[re]
 18: name/ name.
 19: CHRLS/ CHARLES
 26: ffrom/ From
 60: from/ From
 63: Mortiviemus/ Morti vivemus

COMMENTARY

1. John Winthrop (14 March 1638–27 Nov. 1707), the third governor of that name in America, continued the Winthrop tradition of excellence in military, political, and scientific pursuits. He was a member of the Parliamentary Army in England, a soldier of distinction in King Philip's War, active in the General Assembly of both Massachusetts and Connecticut, and governor of Connecticut from 1698 to 1707. (See also Tompson's elegies on John Winthrop, Jr., "Upon the setting of that Occidental Star John Winthrop" and "A Funeral Tribute to . . . John Winthrop.") Richard S. Dunn's *Puritans and Yankees: The Winthrop Dynasty of New England 1630-1717* (Princeton, N.J.: Princeton University Press, 1962), pp. 191–192, takes a different view of Wait and Fitz-John Winthrop. In Dunn's opinion both men represent their generation of New Englanders by "expressing the tensions and fumblings of a society in flux and epitomizing the final secularization of the New England conscience, the completed evolution from Puritan to Yankee." Fitz's underlying interests were in no way comparable to those of his esteemed ancestors. Dunn describes him as "selfish, petty, confused," and "susceptible to flattery and manipulation," besides nourishing grudges, making enemies over trivia, and holding the accumulation of real estate and his own stylish living as the motivating goals for his life.

2. The Arcanum in alchemy, according to Waite, II, 353, is "understood by Paracelsus to signify an incorporeal, immortal substance which in its nature is far above the understanding and experience of man. Its incorporeal quality is, however, only relative and by comparison with our own bodies. From the medicinal standpoint its excellence far exceeds that of any element which enters into our own constitution. The term is applied also to every species of tincture, whether metallic, vegetable, or animal. In general Hermetic science it signifies viscous mercurial matter, or mercury animated by reunion with philosophic sulphur."

3. Asclepius, the son of Apollo, god of healing; in the *Iliad*, the "blameless physician."

4. In 1693 Fitz-John Winthrop was sent to London to plead for the confirmation by King William of the Connecticut charter. The Connecticut General Assembly granted him £300 as a reward for his diplomatic success.

5. Fitz-John was buried with his father and grandfather in the family tomb in Boston.

6. Epilogues in turn.

7. We will live for death.

A Neighbours Tears dropt on the grave of an
Amiable Virgin a pleasant plant cut downe in
the blooming of her Spring Viz Mrs.[1] Rebecka Sewal.
Anno AEtatis 6. August the 4th. 1710.

O heighth! o Depthe! upon my bended knees
Who dare Expound these Wondrous Mysteries:
That this rare plant is cropt before mine Eyes
(Meer Shadow) left to write her Elegies.
Pray what brave Artist here can Understand   5
What one intends that takes a pen in hand?
Twas t'other day a place I visited
Where stands a palme, one limb where of is dead.[2]
A bow'r which many years Thousands have shaded
By whome one Church was built: and Willard aided[3]   10
Seeking the plat of Immortality
I saw no place secure but some must die
Treading that way their Ancient fathers did
Whose faces are, but Vertues can't be hid.
I saw this pretty Lamb, but t'other day,   15
With a small flock of Doves, Just in my Way.
What New made Creature's this so bright 'thought I
Ah! pitty tis such prettiness should die.
With rare alliances on Every side
Had old physitians liv'd She ne're had died.   20
Must then the Rulers of this Worlds Affairs
By Providence be brought to us in tears.
Lord keep their Eyes from such smart Judgments free
Such mournfull Sights are more becoming mee.
Pleasant Rebecka, heres to thee a Tear   25
Hugg my sweet Mary if you chance to see her[4]
Had you giv'n warning ere you pleasd to Die,
You might have had a neater Elegy.

Ben: Thompson.

TEXT
MS contemporaneous copy, in the Winthrop Papers, the Massachusetts Histori-
cal Society; printed in *Proc. M.H.S.*, 2nd ser., 8 (1892–1893), 387–389; and
Hall, pp. 156–157. The manuscript in the Winthrop Papers is in the handwrit-
ing of John Winthrop, Fellow of the Royal Society, son of Wait Winthrop, and
nephew of Fitz-John Winthrop. The manuscript was given to the Massachusetts

Historical Society on 6 April 1864, by one of Fitz-John Winthrop's descendants. This same manuscript includes Tompson's second elegy on Rebekah Sewall, "A Clowde of Tears, sprinkled on the Dust of the Amiable Virgin, Mrs. Rebeka Sewel." Rebekah was the daughter of Samuel Sewall, Jr., and Rebekah Dudley, and the granddaughter of Judge Samuel Sewall. The diary of Samuel Sewall, Jr., in *M.H.S.C.*, 5th ser., 5 (1878), xxvii, gives the following account of the circumstances of her death: "Aug. 2, 1710. In the afternoon she was taken ill at the Governors. Sent for Doctor Noyes and Mrs. Baily; so continued ill; in the morning after, her mother and myself were sent for: gott there about 6 of the clock . . . . My daughter Rebeckah dyed Aug. 3, 1710, . . . My wife and I went into deep mourning. Gave gloves to several relations, Governors servants and mine. Gave Mr. Tompson a pair; he made two coppies of verses on her." (See also the diary of Judge Samuel Sewall, *M.H.S.C.*, 5th ser., 6 [1879], 285.)

EMENDATIONS

title: ye grave/ the grave; M^rs./ Mrs.; ye 4th./ the 4th.
  5: pray/ Pray
  6: y^t/ that
  7: 'tother/ t'other
 10: the word "kept" appears after the word "one." Winthrop has drawn a single line through kept and written above: "Church was built:"
 11: y^e/ the
 15: to'ther/ t'other

COMMENTARY

1. As noted by Samuel A. Green, in *Proc. M.H.S.*, 2nd ser., 8 (1892–1893), 388, in the seventeenth century it was not uncommon to address young ladies of high position as Mistress or Mrs., whether married or not. Dr. Green, however, records this as the only instance of a little girl six years old addressed as Mrs.

2. The imagery throughout this poem—the palm, multitudes, bowers, Lambs, Doves—is, of course, biblical; for example, see Rev. 7:9: "After this I beheld, and, lo, a great multitude, which no man could number, of all nations, and kindreds, and people, and tongues, stood before the throne, and before the Lamb, clothed with white robes, and palms in their hands." Such images as the palm and the dove were funerary symbols frequently carved into New England tombstones. See Ludwig, *Graven Images*, for a complete analysis of such imagery in New England's aesthetic tradition.

3. Samuel Willard (31 Jan. 1639/40–12 Sept. 1707) aided Thomas Thatcher (1620–1678) in instituting the Boston Old South Church in 1669/70. See Note 4 to Tompson's elegy on Mr. James Allen.

4. Benjamin Tompson's daughter, Mary, died on 28 March 1700, at the age of seven.

A Clowde of Tears, sprinkled on the Dust of the
Amiable Virgin Mrs. Rebecka Sewel who Suddenly died
August. 3 1710. AEtatis suae 6.

Heav'ns only, in dark hours Succours can send
And Shew a fountaine where the streams do End.
Behold the Lamb of God (mourners) for there's
Your pretty Lamb which you bewaile in tears.
She is Enfolded, in her Shepards Armes   5
Hugg'd in a Bosom, full of Heavenly Charmes.
Nothing could Ravish her from your Embrace
But the trancendancy of her Saviours face.
She was so lovely in her Makers Sight
Sweet Virgins may wee Stile his hearts Delight.   10
The Wisest King in his Magnificence[1]
Kept Virgins Numberless without Offence
Shining like Starrs, his faire pavillion round
With heavenly rays of fairest graces crown'd.
The honours he conferd were pitteous things   15
Set by the favours of the King of Kings
The least Donations by him to be told
Are Kings with Carbuncles and Chains of Gold.
Purples and Sattins there are all cast by
And all are clad with Little Majesty.   20
Great Jesus claimd his owne, Never begrutch[2]
Your Jewels rare into the hands of Such.
He with his Righteousness hath finer drest
Your Babe than ere you did, when at your Breast.
Madam, 'tis not your case alone, for thousands have   25
Follow'd their sweetest comforts to the Grave.
Theres no Withstanding fixed Destiny
Which will prevaile who ever live or Die.
Death that Stern Officer takes no Denyall
I'm grievd he found your Door to make a Tryall: 30
And bee it on the Shoar or swelling Seas
His boundless Sovereignty doth what he please.
It is a lesson hard (I must confess)
For our proud Wills with heav'ns to Acquiesce.
But when Death goes before; Unseen behind   35
Theres Such an one as may compose the mind
Pray Madam, wipe those tears from your fair Eyes

170

And with your New made Virgin Sympathize.
Could she from her new School obtain but leave
Shee'd tell you what would make you cease to grieve   40
And Wipe those Briny Streams all off your face
Leaving your loving smiles upon the place.
This Suddain Providence my hand did move
To two great familys[3] to show my love
Like a poor mason to prepare a Room   45
On Earth for one, who finds in Heaven a home.

B:T:

[endorsed] 1710 Mr. Thompson's Verses
on Mr. Sewals Childe.

TEXT

For textual, biographical, and historical information, see the notes to the preceding poem, "A Neighbour's Tears dropt on the grave of an Amiable Virgin . . . . "
This poem is also printed in Hall, pp. 157–159.

EMENDATIONS
title: M^{rs}/ Mrs.; AEtatis suae./ AEtatis suae 6.
  1: Heav'ens/ Heav'ns
  3: theires/ there's
  7: yor/ your
  8: "y" in trancendancy written over an "e"
 12: wth.out/ without
 16: favo^{rs}/ favours
 18: wth with
 20: wth^{y} with
 22: yor/ Your; ye hands/ the hands
 24: yor/ Your; yor Breast./ your Breast.
 25: yor/ your
 26: follow'd/ Follow'd
 30: yor/ your
 34: wth heav'ens/ with heav'ns
 37: yor/ your
 38: yor/ your
 41: of yor/ off your
 42: yor/ your

COMMENTARY
  1. Lines 11–19 allude to the wisdom, magnificence, and generosity of King Solomon; see I Kings 1–14. Carbuncles are fiery red, precious stones specifically referred to in Ezekiel 28:13. Chains of Gold are necklaces given as a sign of royal favor; see Genesis 41–42; and Daniel 5:29.
  2. begrutch: begrudge, a common form in the seventeenth century; see Mather, *Magnalia*, Bk. III, Ch. XXXII, 187, "To begrutch the Cost . . . of a school. . . ."
  3. The Sewalls and the Dudleys.

A Neighbour's TEARS
Sprinkled on the Dust of the Amiable Virgin,
Mrs. Rebekah Sewall,
Who was born December 30. 1704. and dyed
suddenly, August 3. 1710. AEtatis 6.

HEav'ns only, in dark hours, can Succour send;
And shew a Fountain, where the cisterns end.
I saw this little One but t'other day
With a small flock of Doves, just in my way:
What New-made Creature's this so bright? thought I   5
Ah! Pity 'tis such Prettiness should die.
Madam, behold the Lamb of GOD; for there's
Your Pretty Lamb, while you dissolve in Tears;
She lies infolded in her Shepherd's Arms,
Whose Bosom's always full of gracious Charms.   10
Great JESUS claim'd his own; never begrutch
Your Jewels rare into the Hands of Such.
He, with His Righteousness, has better dress'd
Your Babe, than e're you did, when at your breast.
'Tis not your case alone: for thousands have   15
Follow'd their sweetest Comforts to the Grave.
Seeking the Plat of Immortality,
I saw no Place Secure; but all must dy.
Death, that stern Officer, takes no denial;
I'm griev'd he found your door, to make a trial.   20
Thus, be it on the Land, or Swelling Seas,
His Sov'raignty doth what His Wisdom please.
Must then the Rulers of this World's affairs,
By Providence be brought thus into Tears?
It is a Lesson hard, I must confess,   25
For our Proud Wills with Heav'ns to acquiesce.
But when Death goes before; Unseen, behind
There's such a One, as may compose the Mind.
Pray, *Madam*, wipe the tears off your fair eyes;
With your translated Damsel Sympathise: 30
Could She, from her New School, obtain the leave,
She'd tell you Things would make you cease to grieve.

B.T.

A Neighbour's TEARS

This 1710 Broadside elegy for Rebekah Sewall incorporates all of the funerary emblems or images found in Puritan elegiac poetry and on gravestone carvings of the period. For more on this broadside and its importance see Allen Ludwig's remarks in the accompanying textual notes.
(*Courtesy of the Massachusetts Historical Society*)

TEXT

Broadside verse in the Massachusetts Historical Society. This MHS copy was collated against the Boston Public Library copy on the Lindstrand comparator at Harvard University and failed to show any accidental or substantive variants. Both broadsides are 8½ by 13 inches, and the printer and the exact date of the printing are unknown. This poem is printed, with a facsimile, in Hall, pp. 155–156. Facsimiles also appear in *American Broadside Verse*, ed. Ola Winslow (New Haven: Yale University Press, 1930), p. 27; and Evans (E. 1489).

Hall, p. 154, speculates on the composition of this broadside:

> Scrutiny of the three versions shows that the broadside version is made up wholly of couplets from the other two versions. It is not certain that Tompson himself did the compiling of the broadside; indeed, since allusions to the author's age and infirmities, and to the benefactions of the Dudley and Sewall families are omitted from the broadside, it seems likely that the condensing was the work of another person, very likely Judge Sewall, who was himself something of a versifier. In any case, taste was shown in both selection and omission of material from the other two versions.

Hall's scrutiny of the poem is not entirely accurate. While all thirty-two lines of the broadside have their origin in the two manuscript versions, nineteen of those lines vary in either the choice or arrangement of words. Nor does the poet remove all allusions to the Dudleys and Sewalls; lines 23 and 24 are deliberate compliments. Tompson himself may have decided to focus the broadside on the virtues of Rebekah and the consolation of the family. Perhaps he removed references to his own misfortunes, his artistic limitations, biblical events and characters, and colonial ministers because he felt they destroyed the unity of the poem or that some allusions were inappropriate in a broadside, a public medium.

In any case, I included all three versions, the two manuscripts in the handwriting of John Winthrop, FRS, and the printed broadside, so that readers may more easily examine the three stages in the evolution of this poem. For the reader's convenience, the following table provides a cross-reference of lines in the printed version with original lines in the manuscript versions identified as NT ("A Neighbours Tears") and CT ("A Clowde of Tears").

Broadside: 1–2: CT: 1–2
  3–6: NT: 15–18
  7–10: CT: 3–6
  11–16: CT: 21–26
  17–18: NT: 11–12
  19–22: CT: 29–32
  23–24: NT: 21–22
  25–32: CT: 33–40

This particular printed broadside is unique, says Allan Ludwig (pp. 277 and 283), in that

> Most borrowed themes can be traced back only to 18th century sources, because earlier broadsides and engravings have not survived. The only American broadside which looks as if it might have been a "source" for 17th century stonecarving in Greater Boston was cut in 1710 for Rebekah Sewall (plate 156). This later date does not rule out the possibility that the format may be much older. Both surviving broadsides and the gravestones of the period framed the inscriptions with bands of mortality emblems topped with

a skull or death's head. All the emblems found in the Sewall broadside are to be found on New England gravestones. The John Watson stone, 1678, Cambridge, Massachusetts (plate 165 A), made use of similar crossed picks, shovels, and bones, the death's head, and the Latin motto *Memento Mori*. The winged hourglass set upon a skull on the Sewall broadside may be seen on the Kendel stone cut about 1678 in Wakefield, Massachusetts (plate 164 B). Twin flanking skeletons may be seen in more refined form on the Ruth Carter stone of 1697–1698 in King's Chapel, Boston, Massachusetts (plates 168 and 169), suggesting a common source for both . . . . There is no stone in New England which used all the emblems on the Sewall woodcut, but at one time or another every theme was incorporated into the vocabulary of Greater Boston stonecarving.

The Translation by death, of that Holy Man of God,
Reverend Mr. JAMES ALLEN,[1] a very Learned,
Faithful, Painful Pastor of the First Church of
Christ in Boston. *Who Expired*, September 22d,
1710. Aged 78.

FAme, trim thy Wings, call nimble Mercury
To *Arimathaea*[2] hence in haste both fly;
Enquire there for a dextrous Lapicide.
Josephs Acquaintance,[3] by him known and try'd.
Who fram'd our Saviours Sepulchre tell him   5
He should unlock the same: for here's a Lamb
Which to that Blessed Body appertains,
That in the Mount of Highest Glory reigns.
Or from pure Alabaster, hew a Tomb,
And for this PURITAN, polish a Room.   10
Fetch Spices from the Aromatic East,
Fill up the vacant corners of the Nest
Of this rare Phoenix, whose disease was Age,
Who merited a most transcendent Page.
Having Perfum'd the Church with precious Pray'r   15
And by sound Doctrine Clarify'd the Air.
Avoiding florid strains, he dived deep,
One Eye to Heaven, one on the Text he'd keep.
Altho' his Meditations were profound,
His Hearers never saw him run a-ground.   20
Our Living Orthodox[4] with *Allen* joyn'd
Brighter than Gemini in *Boston* shin'd.
When first it was my lot his face to see,
I fancied *PAUL* talking with *TIMOTHY*.
Grave *Cotton*[5] had he been that day commanded   25
Into his Pulpit would them both have handed.
I dare not give the World his Character,
Who am my self too incident to Err.
It's Angels work to write Seraphims praise,
Vertues Divine should be pourtray'd with Rays.   30
But if the Pictures of our Saviour might
Be worshiped, here's one laid out of sight.
Ah could I like him pray, and get my will,
I would have wrote with a Seraphick Quill.
Such is the end of a Laborious Bee,   35

And glad am I such rare Successors see.
Jesus to *Allen* was his All in All,
He never on that Name did vainly call.
Jesus in all his Sermons he proclaim'd,
Who rarely is in many Volumns Nam'd.   40
The Hearts of Thousands have his Name engrav'd
Who by him as Christ's Instrument are sav'd.
The ancient Saints hearing their Pastor's come,
Old *Anthony*[6] his friend, cries pray make room.
But when his faithful Master he found out,   45
No less than JESUS Claspeth him about.
And for his Faithfulness brings him a Crown,
That would all Earthly Diadems weigh down.
Let all my Angels witness what I do,
My faithful Labourers in my Service too.   50
He's not the first, pray mind your work below,
I can and will on you such Honour show.
    October. 2d. 1710

B.T.

TEXT
From Benjamin Wadsworth, *DEATH is Certain, the TIME when Uncertain, A SERMON Occasioned by the Death of the Reverend Mr. JAMES ALLEN* (Boston, 1710), in the Massachusetts Historical Society; printed in Hall, pp. 163–164; and Evans (E. 1492).

EMENDATIONS
  2: *Arimahtea/ Arimathaea*
 13: Phaenix/ Phoenix
 21: Orthodox*/ Orthodox[4]
 42: Christ's; apostrophe reversed
 53: *Otob./ October.*

COMMENTARY
  1., James Allen (24 June 1632–22 Sept. 1710), A.B. (1652) and A.M. (1654), New College, Oxford, was ejected from England in 1662 for nonconformity. He was instituted at the First Church at Boston, 1668, and preached there until his death in 1710. For more biographical information, see Weis, p. 19; Savage, I, 31–32; William Allen, *An American Biographical Dictionary* (Boston: William Hyde Co., 1832), pp. 19–20.
  2. Joseph of Arimathaea obtained the body of Jesus and interred it in his own unused rock tomb; see Matthew 27:57; Mark 15:43; Luke 23:50; and John 19:38.
  3. Nicodemus assisted Joseph of Arimathaea in the burial of Christ; see also John 3:1; 7:50; 19:38.
  4. In Wadsworth's *DEATH is Certain*, the copy-text for this poem, "Living

Orthodox," is noted "Norton." John Norton was Pastor of the First Church of Boston from 1656 until his death in 1663, and he was the author of *The Orthodox Evangelist* (Boston, 1654). Tompson's use of the word "living" to refer to a deceased man is not an unusual puritan usage; they often used the terms "Living under the Lord" to characterize the saints. Moreover, Wadsworth's sermon on James Allen contains the following passage:

> The Grave is the House appointed *for all Living*, Job 30:23. Some possibly while here on earth, can scarce get an house to abide in; but there is a house appointed for them, even the Grave, the State of the Dead. They must enter into that house, and abide there, whether they will or not; 'Tis called their *long home*, Eccles. 12:5. 'Tis the *house* that all living must go to; and their *long home*, because they never more return to live as they now do in this World.

Nevertheless, the passage (ll. 21–26) is still ambiguous because it seems to indicate that Norton and Allen served together at the First Church in Boston, which they did not. Allen became the teacher there in 1668, five years after Norton had died. Perhaps Wadsworth (or the printer) supplied an inaccurate note. Tompson could have had in mind John Davenport, who was ordained the pastor of the First Church 9 Dec. 1668, the same day that Allen was ordained teacher. This ordination ceremony initiated one of the hottest controversies in New England's church history. In 1669 seventeen ministers published testimony against the conduct of Allen and Davenport, who were charged with communicating only parts of letters from the Church of New Haven, Davenport's former parish. The seventeen ministers believed they had been deceived in choosing Davenport as pastor. Subsequently, many of these ministers on 12 May 1669 organized the Old South Church of Boston. For a more complete account of the controversy, see Miller, *From Colony to Province*, pp. 118–120; and Allen, *ABD*, pp. 19–20.

5. John Cotton (1585–1652) served at the First Church in Boston from 1633 until his death in 1652. Lines 25–26 suggest that Cotton would have sanctioned the ordination of Allen and Davenport.

6. I have not been able to identify Old *Anthony*. Perhaps Tompson had in mind Anthony Tompson, who came to New Haven in 1639, was the brother of William Tompson (Benjamin's father), and died in 1647. This Anthony Tompson had a son, Anthony, who was born in England and died in 1654 in Milford, Connecticut. I can find no relatives of James Allen named Anthony. However, Tompson might have been referring to Anthony Tuckney, theologian, Master of Emmanuel College, and friend of many of the American Puritans.

The Amiable virgin memorized Elizabeth Tompson[1] who deceased in Boston at Mr. Leggs[2] august 22 1712

Anagram. o i am blest on top.

The height of heavenly love no soule can know
Till Death disects the knots of flesh below.
Above the sunn, beyond the orbs of light
Is built a Cyty filld with all delight
Where no less person then the son of god   5
Our light, our life, Saints king makes his abode
Here in a pallace heavens fair nunnerye
Chast virgins have faire entertainment free
And such as sought his favour upon earth:
Enjoy their purest love in sacred mirth.   10
Great Jesus daily steps off his bright throne
And gives them hart embraces every one
He lovd me, me, when I was but very young
And seated me his virgin tribes among.
I Dare not tell what here in hart i find   15
All tho i left most Christian friends behind.
Christ lovd me in my short morning dawn,
With Cords of love he hath me upward drawn.
All wedding ornaments he for me hath made
And me unworthy in his bosom laid.   20
Dear parents for your prayers i Dayly prais
Who nurtured me so well in early days
Religious tutors give a blessed lift
To infant souls while millions Run adrift.
Clouded with teares where mourning Clouds I see   25
I made short use in this apostrophe.
A lovely Cluster on a vine i saw,
So faire it did my admiracion draw,
Climbing the sun side of an house of prayer,
And solaceing it selfe in heavenly aire   30
Yet sudenly upon an eastward blast
The beuty of his boughs was over cast
The fairest grapes were pickt off one by one.
The Dresser[3] looking like one half undone
Thers no undoing while a saviour lives   35
Who takes no more then what he lends or gives.
Three manly sons grown up to Comly size,

Two Daughters apples in theire parents eyes,
Pickt out by envious Death, with us remains
Their precious Dust abhorring sin or staine.   40
What importunity in prayer could reach,
Was handed down in showers from heaven on each
Proximity of blood makes me for beare
All Round her prais her while i Drop this tear.
All Comendations Could befall a maid   45
A tribute to her memory might be paid
      A solitary sigh.
So many lashes from a fathers hand
Make providences hard to understand
Why this befalls the Righteus man, but the   50
Great sinner left to wright her Elegy.
While you in biternes of soule thuss mourn
Pray for youre sinking onely brothers turn.
I hope you've learned the art of selfe deniall
When faith is active pacients beares the triall.   55
Keep in the use of such Angellic graces,
Twill make you Cherefull, till you se their faces.
Your streams of grief when you are perchd above
Will all be swallowed up in th' abyss of love
Amazing love o what a sight is here   60
Where jesus raigns and every saint appear.
Such as on earth their virgin love exprest
With hyest potentates Com here abreast
How ever there i was but mean and low.
My love hath Clothed mee from top to toe   65
My hart had faild me in the milkie way
Had i not his right hand where on to stay;
Who led me to the mount of pleasures top
Where i all flowers of paradice do Crop.
Pray in this lodgeing where i find sweet Rest,   70
Let not your sighs nor groans mine ears molest.
Sweet mother close mine eys and turn aside
My Jesus sends for me, Thus said she dyed.
    By my Dearest Brother Benjamin Tompson.

TEXT

MS contemporaneous copy from the Joseph Tompson Journal, Houghton Library, Harvard University; printed in Murdock, pp. 9–11. For textual commentary see Tompson's poem on Mary Tompson in this book. The problems outlined in the notes to that poem, also copied by Joseph Tompson, are here compounded by his age and infirmity. It is almost impossible to distinguish between a comma and a period, but it appears that Tompson placed commas slightly above the last letter, and periods several spaces to the right of the last letter.

I have capitalized the initial letter in the following lines: 2, 3, 4, 5, 6, 7, 9, 12, 13, 16, 18, 19, 20, 22, 24, 26, 28, 31, 32, 33, 35, 36, 37, 38, 39, 40, 41, 42, 43, 44, 45, 46, 47, 48, 49, 50, 51, 52, 53, 54, 55, 57, 58, 59, 60, 61, 62, 63, 64, 65, 66, 67, 68, 69, 70, 71, 72, 73.

EMENDATIONS

title: Mr leggs/ Mr. Leggs
  3: a bove/ Above
  6: maks/ makes; a bode/ abode
  7: hear/ Here
 10: mirth/ mirth.
 13: me, me when i/ me, me, when I
 14: a mong/ among
 15: hear/ here
 16: behind/ behind.
 19: the word "garments" is written after wedding; two lines drawn through garments. The word "hath" has been inserted from above the line.
 20: laid/ laid.
 22: nurtered/ nurtured
 24: adrift/ adrift.
 25: Clowded/ Clouded
 26: apostrophe/ apostrophe.
 27: copyist corrected in to on
 29: the word "shine" is written after sun; two lines are drawn through shine
 33: of/ off; one/ one.
 34: MS illegible; The supplied; loocking/ looking
 39: the word "their" is written after us; several lines drawn through their; remains corrected by copyist
 43: proxinity/ Proximity; maks/ makes
 50: but yᵉ/ but the
 51: Elogie/ Elegy
 54: you-ve leand/ you've learned
 56: yᵉ/ the
 58: a bove/ above
 60: hear/ here; a mazeing/ Amazing
 63: hear a brest/ here abreast
 67: his; inserted from above the line
 69: Crop/ Crop.
 71: molest/ molest.
 72: the words "turn aside" are written after close; several lines are drawn through turn aside, and they are properly placed at the end of the line

COMMENTARY

1. Elizabeth Tompson (29 June 1688–24 Aug. 1712) was the daughter of Joseph Tompson, the compiler of the journal in which this poem appears. Elizabeth was the niece of Benjamin Tompson.

2. Mr. Legg: probably Samuel Legg, a Boston mariner and son of John Legg of Marblehead, Massachusetts.

3. Dresser: vinedresser, one who cultivates or prunes vines.

The following Verses were made by
Mr. Benjamin Tompson
Roxbury June 20th. 1713.
being some of his last lines.

I feel this World too mean, and low.
Patron's a lie: Friendship a Show
Preferment trouble: Grandure Vaine
Law a pretence: a Bubble Gaine
Merit a flash: a Blaze Esteem   5
Promise a Rush: and Hope a Dream
Faith a Disguise: a Truth Deceit
Wealth but a Trap: and Health a Cheat
These dangerous Rocks, Lord help me Shun
Age tells me my Days work is done.   10

TEXT
MS contemporaneous copy, in the Massachusetts Historical Society, Edward
Tompson manuscript; printed in *Proc. M.H.S.*, 2nd ser., 10 (1895–1896), 277–
278; and Hall, p. 167. Tompson's last lines resemble the "Verses found in
[Thomas Dudley's] pocket after his death," printed in the *Magnalia*, ed. Kenneth
Murdock, p. 232 and Meserole, p. 365.

EMENDATIONS
title: Mʳ/ Mr.; 20ᵗʰ/ 20th.

Poems Probably by Tompson

[Samuel Arnold]

1

Independents precise[1] of late did devise
  Of a <u>Boatman</u>† to make a Divine   †Mr. Arnold[2]
A <u>Smith</u>≠ and a <u>Planter</u>≠ did make an Adventure   ≠Ordinery lay-
  Their Wits and their Call to refine.[3]   Brethren.

2

I wish he steer well his new Boat out of Hell
  And that he Mistake not his port:
Or he will steer thither, or I know not whither,
  If instead of Starboard, he port.

3

Our reverend Dea'n≠ with his hands washed clean,   ≠Farmer
  Laid them on our Pastors Head;
And gave him a Charge, which was so very large
  That it struck him almost dead.

4

The other Dea'n† was very whist   †Blacksmith
And on his Head he laid his Fist
But did not express either Word or Letter
And being in a Maze, put his hand out of place
Which indeed became the Anvil better.

5

. . . .
  Blind Zeal they had for their pretencment
Their Doctor they made and were not afraid,
  By a strange and new fashioned Commencement.

TEXT

MS later copy from Ezra Stiles's Miscellanies, 1752–1762, Yale University Library; printed in *Extracts of the Itineraries and other Miscellanies of Ezra Stiles, D.D., LL. D., 1755–1794, with a Selection from His Correspondence*, ed. Franklin Bowditch Dexter (New Haven: Yale University Press, 1916), p. 55. We cannot be absolutely certain that Tompson wrote this poem, but Stiles remarks at the conclusion of the poem, "Supposed to be made by one Mr. Thompson." Harold S. Jantz, in *The First Century of New England Verse* (1943–44; rpt. New York: Russell and Russell, 1962), pp. 264–265, argues that "Since Samuel Arnold was ordained in 1658, this poem, if it is by Benjamin Tompson, was written by him at the age of 16, a possibility which the immaturity of the poem does not contradict. The satiric vein is typically Tompsonian." I have retained the marginalia in the Stiles text and have expanded "Coṁencement" in the final line of the text.

COMMENTARY

1. Tompson's use of the term "Independents precise" was deliberate. Even at age sixteen, Tompson would have understood many of the ecclesiastical distinctions between the nonseparating Congregationalists and the Independents. Following John Cotton and Thomas Hooker, the Congregationalists disavowed the separatism of Plymouth Colony. John Cotton in *The Way of Congregational Churches Cleared* (London, 1648), p. 10, declared his way "neither justly called a sect, nor fitly called Independency . . . . For in some respects it [independency] is too strait, in that it confineth us with our selves, and holdeth us forth as Independent from all others: whereas indeed we doe professe dependence upon Magistrates for Civil Government and protection . . . Dependence upon Christ . . . upon the counsell of other Churches and Synods." John Winthrop, in *The History of New England from 1630 to 1648*, ed. J. K. Hosmer, 2 vols. (1908; rpt. New York: Barnes and Noble, 1959), I, 51–52, and II, 88, illustrates the significance of the ordination or election ceremony:

> We, of the congregation, kept a fast, and chose Mr. Wilson our teacher, and Mr. Nowell an elder, and Mr. Gager and Mr. Aspinwall, deacons. We used imposition of hands, but with this protestation by all, that it was only as a sign of election and confirmation, not of any intent that Mr. Wilson should renounce his ministry he received in England (pp. 51–52).

> The village at the end of Charlestown bounds was called Woburn, where they had gathered a church, and this day Mr. Carter was ordained their pastor, with the assistance of the elders of other churches. Some difference there was about his ordination; some advised, in regard they had no elder of their own, nor any members very fit to solemnize such an ordinance, they would desire some of the elders of other churches to have performed it; but others supposing it might be an occasion of introducing a dependency of churches, etc., and so a presbytery, would not allow it. So it was performed by one of their own members, but not so well and orderly as it ought (p. 88).

2. In his miscellanies, under the heading 26 March 1762, Stiles supplies the following introduction to this poem: "Mr. Samuel Arnold, Pastor of Church of Marshfield, was ordained by the imposition of hands of two lay Brothers, himself having not had a Liberal Education. He was minister there [Marshfield] A.D. 1679 when he assisted in an Ordination Council at Plymouth. Sometime after his

own Ordination and Settlement the following verses were set up on his Meeting-house door." Following the poem Stiles adds, "This Mr. Arnold was in good Repute and acknowledged by the Ministers. Mr. Maxfield Aet. above 70 says he has seen a printed Sermon of Mr. Arnold's which he thinks was an Election Sermon. I have otherwise been informed that this Mr. Arnold was a man of Knowledge and Reading and well qualified for the Ministry and devoted himself to it as learned Ministers did." Arnold did preach an election day sermon in 1674 entitled *DAVID serving his Generation, or A DISCOURSE Wherein is shewed that the great Care and Endeavor of Every Christian ought to be, that he may be Serviceable unto God and to the present GENERATION, Delivered in a SERMON Preached to the GENERAL COURT of the COLONY of NEW-PLIMOUTH in NEW-ENGLAND on the 3d. Day of JUNE 1674. Being the Day of ELECTION there* (Cambridge, Mass.: Samuel Green, 1674). For more on the life of Samuel Arnold see James Savage, *A Genealogical Dictionary of the First Settlers of New England*, 4 vols. (Boston: Little, Brown and Co., 1862) and Fredrick Lewis Weis, *The Colonial Clergy and the Colonial Churches of New England* (Lancaster, Mass.: Society of the Descendants of the Colonial Clergy, 1936); see also Jantz (p. 179) for bibliography of poetry by and about Samuel Arnold.

3. Frances Baylies, in *An Historical Memoir of the Colony of New Plymouth*, 2 vols. (Boston: Wiggin and Lunt, 1866), I, Pt. 2, 25–26, describes the clerical situation at the time of Arnold's ordination:

Mr. Reyner left Plymouth in 1654. Mr. Partridge remained at Duxbury, but died in 1658. Dr. Chauncy left Scituate in 1656. Mr. Street left Taunton for New Haven. Mr. Leveredge, Sandwich for Long Island. Mr. Bulkley Marsh-field, for Concord. Mr. Lothrop of Barnstable died in 1653. The places of these distinguished men were not supplied, and in the younger settlements of Eastham, Bridgewater, etc., no ministers had been settled. Yarmouth was destitute.

The religious zeal of Massachusetts had not been cooled, and they viewed the destitute situation of their neighboring colony with sorrow and alarm; their fears were heightened from the intrusion of the Quakers into the colonies, a sect which they abhorred.

Thus, it is no wonder that Marshfield ordained a boatman and chose a farmer and blacksmith as deacons.

Some OFFERS
To Embalm the MEMORY of the
Truly
Reverend and Renowned,
JOHN WILSON;[1]
The First Pastor of *Boston*, in *New England;*
Interr'd (and a Great Part of his Countries
Glory with him) *August.* 11. 1667. Aged, 79.

MIght *Aarons* Rod (such *Funerals* mayn't be *Dry*)
But broach the *Rock*, t'would gush pure *Elegy*,[2]
To round the Wilderness with purling *Layes*,
And tell the *World*, the Great Saint WILSONS Praise.

Here's ONE, (*Pearls* are not in great clusters found)   5
Here's ONE, the *Skill* of *Tongues* and *Arts* had Crown'd;
Here's ONE (by frequent *Martyrdome* t'was Try'd)
That could forego *Skill*, *Pelf*, and *Life* beside,
For CHRIST: Both ENGLANDS *Darling*, whom in Swarms
They Press'd to See, and Hear, and felt his *Charms*.   10

Tis ONE, (when will it Rise to Number *Two*?)
The World at once can but ONE *Phoenix* Show:)
For *Truth*, a PAUL; CEPHAS, for *Zeal;* for *Love*,
A JOHN; inspir'd by the Celestial *Dove*.
ABRA'MS true Son for *Faith;* and in his *Tent*   15
Angels oft had their *Table* and *Content*.

So *Humble*, that alike on's *Charity*,
Wrought *Extract Gent:* with *Extract Rudi*.[3]
Pardon this *Fault;* his Great Excess lay *there*,
He'd Trade for *Heaven*, with all he came anear;   20
His *Meat*, *Clothes*, *Cash*, heed still for *Ventures* send,
Consign'd, *Per* Brother *Lazarus*, his *Friend*.[4]

Mighty in Prayer; his Hands Uplifted reach'd
Mercies High Throne, and thence strange Bounties fetch'd,
Once and again, and oft: So felt by all,   25
Who *Weep* his Death, as a Departing *Paul*.
All; Yea, *Baptis'd* with Tears, Lo, *Children* come,
(*Their* Baptism *he* maintain'd!) unto his *Tomb*.

'Twixt an *Apostle*, and *Evangelist*,
Let stand his Order in the Heavenly *List*.   30

Had we the Costly *Alabaster Box*,
What's Left, wee'd spend on this *New-English* KNOX;[5]
True *Knox*, fill'd with that Great *Reformers* Grace,
In *Truths* Just cause, *fearing no Mortals Face.*

Christ's Word, it was his *Life*, *Christs Church*, his *Care;*   35
And so *Great* with him his *Least* Brethren were,
Not Heat, nor Cold, not Rain, or Frost, or Snow
Could hinder, but he'd to their *Sermons* go:
Aarons Bells chim'd from far, he'd Run, and then
His Ravish'd Soul *Echo'd, AMEN, AMEN!*   40

He traverst oft the fierce *Atlantic Sea*,
But, *Patmos* of *Confessors*,[6] t'was for THEE.
This Voyage Lands him on the Wished shore,
From Whence this *Father* will return no more,
To fit[7] the *Moderator* of thy Sages.   45
But, Tell his *Zeal* for thee, to After-Ages,
His Care to Guide his *Flock*, and feed his *Lambs*,
By *Words*, *Works*, *Prayers*, *Psalms*, *Alms*, and ANAGRAMS:[8]
Those *Anagrams*, in which he made to Start
Out of meer *Nothings*, by *Creating Art*,   50
Whole *Worlds* of Counsil; did to *Motes* Unfold
Names, till they Lessons gave Richer than *Gold*,
And Every *Angle*[9] so Exactly say,
It should out-shine the brightest *Solar Ray.*

Sacred his *Verse*, Writ with a *Cherubs* Quill;   55
But those Wing'd Choristers of *Zion*-Hill,
Pleas'd with the *Notes*, call'd him a part to bear, ⎫
With *Them*, where he his *Anagram* did hear, ⎬
I Pray Come in, Heartily Welcome; Sir.[10] ⎭

TEXT
Cotton Mather, *Johannes in Eremo: Memoirs* (Boston, 1695), pp. 42–46; rpt. in
Magnalia, Bk. III, Ch. III (London, 1702), pp. 50–51. The *Magnalia* version
contains three substantive variants: 1.7: was try'd; 1.49: no start; and 1.51:
Words.
   Collation of the Boston edition copies at MHi and MBAt against the Essex
Institute copy showed no substantive variants. Collation of the *Magnalia* copies
at MHi, MBAt, PSt, CSmH, and MH against the Essex Institute *Magnalia* copy
showed no substantive variants.
   In *The First Century of New England Verse* Harold Jantz lists this poem under
the heading of anonymous poetry and refers the reader to item 10 under the
Cotton Mather bibliography. There, Jantz says:

There is less excuse for attributing the long elegy on John Wilson . . . to Mather, for the preceding matter makes it quite clear that he is not the author. He states that the shortcomings of his prose account "might be made up with several expressive passages, which I find in elegies written and printed upon his death . . . . But waving [sic] the rest, let the following poem, never before printed, offer some odours"; i.e., this was one of the elegies which had not been printed but had remained in manuscript, perhaps in the large Mather collection of New England material.

Jantz suggested that possible authors are Benjamin Tompson or Nicholas Noyes, but I believe, from both internal and external evidence, that Tompson is the author of this elegy on John Wilson. First, John Wilson was a neighbour and friend of William Tompson. In fact, Wilson was one of Braintree's first land-holders, along with William Coddington, Edmund Quincy, and William Hutch-inson, husband of Anne Hutchinson. Second, William Tompson probably at-tended the Synod of 1637, in which John Wilson's battle with Anne Hutchinson and the Antinomians was a major controversial issue. As the Pastor of the First Church of Braintree, William Tompson would have supported, at least publicly, Wilson's faction of the First Church of Boston. Third, Wilson wrote one anagram on Abigail Tompson and two on William Tompson, all of which are printed in Murdock's *Handkerchiefs from Paul*. Wilson's anagrams demonstrate a personal sense of sorrow and loss; the poems are not generalized exercises written for moral exempla.

The argument for Tompson's authorship is even stronger when internal evi-dence is weighed. First, the meter and diction are typically Tompsonian. In many of Tompson's elegies on public figures of either political or religious re-nown, the same phrases appear; for example, "Embalm," "Skill of Tongues and Arts," "Crown'd," "Phoenix," "Throne," "Tears," "Alabaster Box," "Ravish'd Soul." Of course, these terms are conventional in the seventeenth-century elegy, but their use in context gives them a Tompsonian slant. For example, Tompson often likes to include the last words of the elegized person, as he did here and in the elegy on his father, William Tompson. In both poems, written only one year apart, congregations press to see and hear the wise divines, both divines are types of Old Testament figures, both ministers are persecuted (in England and Amer-ica, to some extent), both are holy, evangelical, and now sainted. Lines 21–22 of the Wilson elegy are perhaps the strongest piece of evidence for Tompson's authorship. In that passage Tompson is referring to Wilson's role in recommend-ing William Tompson for the missionary voyage to Virginia in 1642. Although Tompson does not mention his father by name, he calls him Lazarus, the friend of Wilson. In the elegy on William Tompson, Benjamin calls his father "Lazarus new rais'd from death" (1. 61).

At the conclusion of this 59-line elegy on Wilson, Mather writes: "Thinking, what EPITAPH, I should Offer unto the *Grave* of this Worthy Man, I call'd unto Mind, the fittest in the World, which was directed for him, immediately upon his *Death*, by an Honorable Person, who still continues the same *Lover*, as well as *Instance*, of Learning and Vertue, that he was, wherin he *Then* advised them to give Mr. *Wilson* this EPITAPH.

And now Abides FAITH, HOPE, & CHARITY,
But CHARITIE'S *the Greatest of the Three.*

To which this might be added, from another Hand,

188

Aurea, quae (obstupeo referens!) Primaeva Vetustas
Condidit Arcano, Saecula Apostolica,
Officiis, Donisque itidem Sanctissimus Heros,
WILSONUS, *tacitis Protulit Ex Tenebris*."

EMENDATIONS

I have reversed every apostrophe in this poem
  4: Praise.; raised from below the center of the line
  6: Crown'd; raised from below the center of the line
  9: in Swarms; raised from below the center of the line
 12: *Phaenix*/ *Phoenix*
 18: *Rudij*/ *Rudi*
 24: fetch'd,; raised from below the center of the line
 31: *Alablaster*/ *Alabaster*
 32: KNOX;; raised from below the center of the line
 48: ANAGRAMS:; raised from below the center of the line
 59: I Pray Come in, Heartily Welcome; set in Dutch Gothic type

COMMENTARY

1. John Wilson (c. 1591–7 Aug. 1677) was one of the seventeenth century's most influential and respected ministers. Wilson received a B.A. (1610) and an M.A. (1613) from King's College, Cambridge, and in 1610 he read law at the Inner Temple. By 1618, however, Wilson was a lecturer at Sudbury in Suffolk, where he was continually harassed for his nonconformity. In 1630 he made his first voyage to the Massachusetts Bay Colony and accepted the position of teacher of the First Church of Boston. The following year he sailed back to England, rejoined his wife, and returned to America, this time as pastor of the First Church. In 1634–1635 he made his last voyage to England, and upon his return to Massachusetts he became, with his assistant John Cotton, a chief spokesman for the New England Way. Wilson was vigorously opposed to the Society of Friends (Quakers), fiercely antagonistic to Anne Hutchinson and the Antinomians who "infected" his church, and, paradoxically, was a man beloved for his hospitality and graciousness. For more on Wilson, see Mather's *Johannes in Eremo: Memoirs*, the source of the copy-text for this poem; Mather's *Magnalia*, Bk. III, Ch. III; Kenneth B. Murdock on John Wilson in *DAB*, vol. 20; and Morison, *The Founding of Harvard College*, Appendix B, p. 408. See also Benjamin Tompson's poem on Samuel Whiting in this book for another reference to Wilson.

2. Tompson's typological use of Aaron is both deliberate and historically-biblically appropriate. Aaron was the elder brother of Moses, a liberator of the Israelites from Egyptian bondage, the first high priest, and the ancestor of all lawful priests. In Exodus 7:8 and 9:8, God reveals to Moses and Aaron His plans for deliverance of the Israelites from Egyptian bondage. The two patriarchs perform miracles with rods, or staffs, as commanded by God. In Numbers 20:2–13 Aaron and Moses are faced with dissension and possible revolution among the Israelites. But God averts rebellion by again granting Moses and Aaron miraculous powers in order to secure water from a rock in the desert wilderness. Thereafter, Aaron's rod was to be taken as a sign against rebellion. Wilson, like Aaron, was the first high priest of New England, the liberator from English "captivity," and the author of a poem entitled "A Song of Deliverance." Moreover, Wilson was, like Aaron and Moses, faced with possible rebellion in his

church when the Antinomian forces doubted his leadership in the American wilderness.

3. This is a playful allusion to Wilson's learning and his generosity. Tompson says that in Wilson were joined the qualities of the polished gentleman and the rude (from the Latin *rudus, rudi*, unsophisticated fellow); that is, Wilson was so hospitable and self-effacing that he would willingly allow himself to be "cheated."

4. Tompson seems to be saying that Wilson was so devoted to the Christian cause in America that he would not hesitate to send his best friend, William Tompson, on a missionary voyage to a remote colony such as Virginia. Both here and in Tompson's elegy on his father, "Remarks on the Bright, and dark side of that American Pillar Mr. William Tompson [,]" Benjamin's father is referred to as Lazarus because he regained his spiritual life after a long period of "Ember weeks of grief," a type of spiritual death.

5. John Knox (1505–1572) was a Scottish reformer and historian about whom Morton, the Scottish Regent, said at his grave, "Here lies one who never feared the face of man." Although I cannot prove that Tompson was familiar with this epitaph, it seems possible that line 34 is a deliberate paraphrase. See Aeneas MacKay, "John Knox," *DNB*, XI, 308–328.

6. Patmos is one of the Sporades Islands in the Icarian Sea to which those who confessed their religion, that is, those who witnessed or testified before the Romans for their Christianity, were banished. Thus, Tompson praises Wilson for his willingness to cross the Atlantic, to be banished, for God's cause. For more on Patmos as a place of banishment, see Rev. 1:9.

7. fit: to become, to be suited for.

8. Wilson was renowned for his skill in anagrammatizing. He contributed eight anagrams to Thomas Shepard's *The Church Membership of Children* (1663) and John Norton's *Three Choice and Profitable Sermons* (1664). Three of his anagrams on the Tompsons are reprinted in Murdock, *Handkerchiefs from Paul*. Nathaniel Ward, a friend of Wilson, wrote the following poem on his pastor's skill:

We poor Agawams
are so stiff in the hams
that we cannot make Anagrams,
But Mr John Wilson
the great Epigrammatist
Can let out an Anagram
even as he list.

9. *Angle*: Angel?

10. On page 39 of Cotton Mather's *Johannes in Eremo: Memoirs*, Mather says, "There was a Little more of Humour, in the Fancy of Mr. *Ward*, the Well-known *Simple Cobler* of Agawam, as that *Witty Writer* Styled himself, who observing the Great *Hospitality* of Mr. *Wilson*, in Conjunction with his *Meta-grammatizing* Temper, said, *That the Anagram* of JOHN WILSON *was*, I PRAY, COME IN, YOU ARE HEARTILY WELCOME."

[On the arrival of Urian Oakes,[1] 1671.]

Welcome, *Great Prophet*, *to* New-England *Shore*,
The Fam'd Utopia, *of more Famous* MORE,[2]
Unfabled, *for* New-England *is by thee*,
Now Twisse's[3] *Guess too must Accomplisht be;*
That for the New-Jerusalem, *there may*
A Seat *be found in Wide* America.

TEXT
Cotton Mather, *Magnalia Christi Americana* (London, 1702), Bk. IV, Ch. V, p.
187. Collation of the *Magnalia* copies at PSt, MH, CtY, MHi, MBAt, and
CSmH against the Essex Institute copy showed no substantive variants.

Jantz also lists this poem under the heading of anonymous poetry and refers
the reader once again to item 10 in the Cotton Mather bibliography where he
says:

> Most puzzling is the fine excerpt from a poem hailing Urian Oakes' return to
> America in 1671. Morison attributes this to Mather (*Harvard College in the
> Seventeenth Century*, p. 419), saying "on his arrival he was thus greeted with
> an ode by Cotton Mather." Here again a chronological check would have
> revealed that Mather was only seven years old at the time. Eleven years later,
> however, Mather did write an elegy on the death of Oakes in which a loose
> paraphrase of these lines occurs. Whether Mather, as so often, here tinkered
> with another man's lines, or later in the *Magnalia* pushed his own lines
> farther back into the past, we do not know. If they are by another, Samuel
> Sewall or Benjamin Tompson appears as the most likely authors.

Mather's poem of 1682, entitled "A Poem Dedicated to the Memory of the
Reverend and Excellent Mr. Urian Oakes" (Boston, 1682, Evans no. 319),
contains the following passage:

> Welcome! great Prophet! to *New-England* shore!
> Thy *feet* are *beautiful!* A number more
> Of Men like thee with us would make us say,
> The *Moral* of *More's* fam'd *Utopia*
> Is in *New-England*! yea, (far greater!) wee
> Should think wee *Twisse's guess* accomplisht see,
> *When New Jerusalem comes down, the Seat*
> *Of it, the vast* America *will bee't.*

The excerpt from the *Magnalia* appears to be earlier than the 1682 version of
those lines; that is, the *Magnalia* excerpt is probably a more accurate version of
the original 1671 celebratory poem. The 1682 elegy by Mather has been length-
ened to make it easier to understand at a funeral ceremony or for the consolation
of the immediate family. Too, there is a sense that Urian Oakes has accomplished
what the first poem had hoped for upon his return to America. The 1682 elegy is
more characteristic of Mather's poetry: there are puns, several exclamations,
parenthetical remarks, and a little more colonial bravado and confidence. The
Magnalia poem, however, is more characteristic of Benjamin Tompson's verse: it
celebrates a colonial event of immediate importance but leaves some room for

doubt about America's future greatness, the meter is more regular and smooth, and the exclamatory asides are less frequent. Two other poems in the Tompson corpus resemble this poem in its colonial and occasional import: the address on the arrival of Lord Bellamont, and the prefatorial poem on Hubbard's *A Narrative of the Troubles with the Indians in New-England*. In the final estimate, however, there is not sufficient evidence to identify Tompson positively as the author of this poem. Perhaps some external evidence will be discovered to support my belief that Tompson did write this welcoming address to Urian Oakes.

COMMENTARY

1. Urian Oakes (c. 1631–25 July 1681) was a clergyman, a poet, and President of Harvard College. In 1671 the church at Cambridge recalled Oakes from England where he had organized a Congregational church at Tichfield. Oakes had received the degree of B.A. from Harvard in 1649, had prepared the 1650 Cambridge Almanac, and had tutored students at Harvard until 1653, but it is not clear why he left New England or why he returned. We do know, however, that Oakes was an accomplished poet and preacher; his elegy on Thomas Shepard, Jr., and his Jeremiad sermons are to this day regarded as great achievements in American literature. For more on the biography of Urian Oakes, see Morison, *Harvard College in the Seventeenth Century*, II, 418–439; also see Meserole, pp. 207–220, for a brief biography and two of Oakes's poems.

2. Sir Thomas More (1479–1535) was Lord Chancellor of England and author of numerous English and Latin works, including *Utopia*, which was written in 1515–1516. For more biographical information, see Sidney Lee, "Sir Thomas More," *DNB*, XIII, 876–896.

3. William Twisse, D.D. (1578–1646), was a strict and brilliant English Puritan divine who resisted any attempts to liberalize Calvinism. In 1646 Twisse published *A Treatise of Mr. Cotton's . . . Concerning Presdestination . . . with an Examination thereof*. Twisse objected mildly to Cotton's view of predestination and stated that "God's conditionate will maye faile of accomplishment" (pp. 97–98). Twisse's treatise also contains an extended discussion of the New Jerusalem and speculation about the nature of that state, pp. 296 ff. See also Alexander Gordon, "William Twisse," *DNB*, XIX, 1324–1325.

[Edward Tompson: Epitaph]

HERE IN A TYRANTS HAND DOTH CAPTIVE LYE
A RARE SYNOPSIS OF DIVINITY
OLD PATRIARCHS PROPHETS GOSPEL BISHOPS MEET
UNDER DEEP SILENCE IN THIS WINDING SHEET
HERE REST A WHILE IN HOPES AND FULL INTENT
WHEN THEIR KING CALLS TO SIT IN PARLIAMENT.

TEXT

From the inscription on the broken footstone of Edward Tompson's grave, Marshfield, Massachusetts; variant printed in Harriette M. Forbes, *Gravestones of Early New England* (Boston: Houghton Mifflin, 1927), p. 35. Forbes says, "In Marshfield we find a beautiful stone over the grave of the Reverend Edward Tompson. It is cut with the same originality and freedom as the Peacock stone, and like that bears at the top of the curve the letters 'J.N.' It, too, is unique with its vase of flowers and borders made of large lilies." A detail of the Tompson stone and an analysis of the work of "J.N." are provided in Ludwig, *Graven Images*, pp. 296–300. Edward Tompson (1665–1705) was the son of Deacon Samuel Tompson of Braintree, and thus a nephew of Benjamin Tompson. He graduated B.A. 1684, Harvard College, and was ordained at the First Church of Marshfield, 14 Oct. 1696. For more information on the biography of Edward Tompson, see Weis, p. 205; Sibley, III, 306–310; *NEHGR*, 15 (1861), 112–116; and for a bibliography of his poetry, see Jantz, p. 269.

[Moses Fiske: Epitaph]

Braintrey! thy Prophet's gone. This tomb interrs
The Reverend Moses Fisk his Sacred herse,
Adore Heav'ns praise-ful art that form'd the man,
Who souls, not to himself, but Christ oft won,
Sail'd thro' the straits with Peter's family,
Renownd, and Gaius' hospitality
Paules patience, James his prudence, Johns sweet love
Is landed, enter'd, clear'd, and crown'd Above.

TEXT
From the faded inscription on the tombstone of Moses Fiske, Quincy, Massachu-
setts; variant printed in *NEHGR*, 9 (1855), 151. This poem is attributed to
Tompson by Jantz, p. 268, "on the basis of its style and location." Moses Fiske
(12 April 1642–10 Aug. 1708) graduated B.A. 1662, Harvard College, and was
ordained at the First Church, Braintree, Massachusetts, 11 Sept. 1672, where he
preached until his death in 1708. Moses Fiske was, therefore, a neighbor and a
classmate of Benjamin Tompson. For more biographical information on Fiske,
see Weis, p. 84; and see Sibley, II, 122–127.

EMENDATIONS
1: gone this/ gone. This
7: prudence/ prudence,

The Letters of Benjamin Tompson

To the Reverend Mr. Increase Mather at Boston. D.D.

Rever^d Mr Mather/
Most humble and kind salutations premised to yourselfe
and yours.

It is not so much an ambition of Honour, as of full imployment, and its
comfortable attendants, which have moved mee to try what interest a
branch of an auncient Lancashire Christian and your most precious and
Renowned friend and fellow sufferer may find, with your Christian selfe,
whom influence so many others. I had by my brother a copie of New
Laws, one whereof being for multiplying Schooles, in observance
whereof I thought you would not bee backward, or in any other designe
of publiq^{ue} good. My yeare being up in the place where I am I am bold to
present my service to you, as your parishioner & Schoolemaster. It being
the first time of offering myselfe in like case. Whether the place bee open
for me or not, I begge that no forreigner or stranger may have it, if those
of our owne Countrey and acquaintance may fitt the same. And though I
sit unimployed,

> My Loyalty is still the same
> Whither I win or loose the game
> True as a Dial to the Sun
> Althô It bee not shin'd upon

If you have an hora vaciva in the long winter nights vouchsafe a
minute in a line to, and rest in prayers for

S^r, your hearty and humble friend & serv^t,
Benj. Thompson

25. 9. 83
S^r, the Cold apologizeth for the scrawles.

TEXT
MS autograph letter signed; Prince Collection, Boston Public Library, Mather
Papers, Letter 45, vol. 5. This letter is also printed in Hall, p. 16; *The Proceedings of the Massachusetts Historical Society*, 57 (1923–24), 68; *Collections of the Massachusetts Historical Society*, 4th ser., 8 (1860), 635.

[To Sir Edmund Andros]

To his Excellency,
Sr Edmund Andros Knight Govern^r
Capt Generall of all his Majesties territories
in New England.

The most humble Petition of Benjamin Tompson Physician and Schoole Maister of the towne of Braintrey, Shewing that Your poore Suppliants father, a divine of good note, declaring it was not lands hee came for, lived and died with his heart always above worldly things, his not begging as others did, others of far inferiour note being vastly accomodated, puts mee who have a numerous race upon this essay, not having found y^r Excellency averse therunto. I therefore humbly Begge part of the lands to mee demised by the towne, viz. twenty acres of upland fit for pasturage only, lying between Mr Shepards Farme and the towne, As also twelve Acres of Salt Marish by mee this yeare demised to Capt. Saml White, Also one or two hundred Acres of Wilderness land, bounded Southerly with land Petitioned by Saml Niles, the Roade Running thorow the same. I know not any other way to gaine a lasting acknowledgment of my fathers and his orphans service in the towne. I am also hereby willing to shroud my person, my children, and my estate under the umbrage of o^r gracious Sovereigne, and shall seasonably bring in an account of the small shreds of land I have that I may obtaine a patent thereof. WHICH granted, I shall owne y^r EXCELLENCY the GREATE MAECENAS and rebuilder of my decaying family. And as it is my duty myself, teaching my children for ever to pray o^r dread Sovereigns subject.

9 Junis Calendas
1688

^{yor} Excellencys faithful serv^t.
BENJAMIN TOMPSON.

Annoq Regni Regis Jacobi Secundi tertio. Mag. Brit. Angl. Scot. Franc. & Hib. Fidei defensoris, &c.

TEXT
From a microfilm of the MS autograph letter signed; *Massachusetts Archives*, *Book 128*, p. 247. This letter is also printed in Hall, p. 17; and *The New England Historical and Genealogical Register*, 15 (1861), 116.

[To an unknown addressee]

Honoured Sr,

I cannot unlesse I relinquish my imploy which is meane and Incouragements meaner, prosecute my petition as I ought to doe: But it would bee the highest incivility and ingratitude not to owne his Excl^{lc} Indulgency therein. If my petition bee arrived y^r hands. I begge of you, a writt to the Survey^r, and I hope to obtaine the desireable hand usual to soulifie it and In all other things intend a full and Customary prosecution as far as purse and my small interests amounts unto: Meane time I most humbly kisse y^r hand.

His Maj^s faithfull Subject &
Y^r Hon^{rs} frd. & serv^t.

April 4th:
1689

BENJ: TOMPSON.

The petition I hereby intend is my last petition:—

TEXT

From a microfilm of the MS autograph letter signed; *Massachusetts Archives, Book 129*, p. 357. This letter is also printed in Hall, p. 18; and *The New England Historical and Genealogical Register*, 15 (1861), 116.

APPENDIX C

A Latin Salutatory Oration of 1662

Honorandi et ter illustres viri, penes quos jus et imperium est, quibus salus populi, summa lex est: in Rep⟨ublicâ⟩ administrandâ, vobis jure primatum tribuimus, et salutem in salutari illo summam apprecamur.

Reverendi Ecclesiastae et Oeconomi Mysterioru⟨m⟩ Dei, praecones salutiferae doctrinae, vobis, ut par est, e suggesto salutem plurimam annunciamus.

Viri Mae[ce]nates Benignissimi qui mercaturam aut mi[lit]iam exercetis, qui in cumulandis beneficiis [l]argi et effusi, utinam cu⟨m⟩ foenore gratiarum et salutum vicem vobis rependere valeamus.

Denique vos Hospites pientiss⟨imi⟩ viri desideriorum qui estis εὐγενέστεροι quiq; terras et maria tantis cum sumptibus et vitae discrimin[e] transivistis, ut nobiscum crucem atq⟨ue⟩ unà jugu⟨m⟩ suave Jesu Christi subeatis et instituta divina observetis, jungimus putate vobis hospitio dextras, et in amplexus vestros effundimur. Quid obsecro, nobis gratiùs aut exoptatiùs potuit accidere, quàm adventus et aspectus vester qu[i] praesto estis, vel in praesidiis agentes ἀλεξίκακ[οι] καὶ ἀποτρόπαιοι, vel in subsidiis operam ves[tram] commodantes.

Audivimus quid factum sit Regnante Rehoboa[m] quando sacerdotes et Levitae Israëlitici sua liquerunt suburbana praedia et possessiones et alii [ex] tribubus Israëlis, qui stabili sententiâ in animum induxerunt se Deum Israëlis ex[qui]situros; qui migrarunt Hierosolymas, illi m[u]niverunt et corroborarunt regnum Judae: et consimilis planè vestra transmigratio hodierna quod est pietatis vestrae argumentu⟨m⟩ non vulgare certè non exiguum nobis robur et firmamentum subministrabit.

Vt dicamus igitur vobis, appositè ad rem, oh praeclari advenae, quod Boaz olim illi quae exiit ex arvis[1] servatoris, Dominus remuneretur, opus vestrum, ut plena merces vobis retribuatur a Domino Deo Israelis sub cujus alis accessistis credituri.

Honored and thrice illustrious gentlemen, in whose authority lie right and rule, for whom the well-being of the people is the highest law, we have allotted to you the first place in administering the Republic and we pray for the greatest success in that salutary endeavor.

Reverend ministers and stewards of the mysteries of God, heralds of the doctrine which brings salvation, to you, as is proper, we extend the fullest greeting from the platform.

You gentlemen, our most beneficent patrons, who are engaged in commerce or in the military, and who are most generous and overflowing in the benefits which must be acquired, I pray that we may be able to repay you with interest for your favors and aid.

Finally, you, most gracious guests, greatly beloved gentlemen, who are noble and who have crossed lands and seas at such great expense and hazard of life, so that you might join us in taking up the cross and easy yoke of Jesus Christ and observe the divine ordinances, believe that we join hands with you in hospitality and we extend ourselves into your embraces. What, I ask, more welcome and hoped for thing could have befallen us, than the sight of you having arrived, who are here either providing a defence to protest and ward off evil, or as auxiliaries providing your work.

We have heard what happened while Reheboam was reigning, when the priests and Levites of Israel abandoned their farms and possessions outside the city, as well as others from the tribes of Israel, who with steadfast resolve strengthened themselves with courage seeking the God of Israel. Those who moved to Jerusalem fortified and strengthened the Kingdom of Juda; similarly your transmigration today, which is an exceptional proof of your faithfulness, will surely supply us with no small strength and support.

Therefore, distinguished newcomers, we may say to you, as befits the occasion, the same thing that Boaz said to her who came out from the fields of her deliverer: The Lord recompense thy work, and a full reward be given thee of the Lord God of Israel, under whose wings thou art come to trust.

Dicamus cum psalte Regio aud[ite] mansueti, et collaetamini, magnificate J[eh]ovam nobiscum et extollamus nomen ejus pa[r]iter, cum non tantum mulierem eremicolam hactenus incolumem á faucibus immanis rubri Draconis eripuit, et sartum tectum mirificè á diluvio conservavit nè esset ποταμοφόρητον: sed etiam adhuc alas animumq⟨ue⟩ addit, et plures obstetricantes et auxiliares manus praebentes ultrò suppeditavit[.] ille, ille, nobis haec otia fecit et salutem posuit pro munimentis et propugnaculis.

Oh si omnes sancti conjunctim valeant assequi et compr[ehen]dere et justis ponderibus librari τὸ ὑπερπερὶσσευον μέτρον clementiae divinae.

Oh si de Monte Sionis diceretur quod in vallem subsiderit, et depressa sit, vallem autem non Lachrymarum; sed vallem Berakah, quae nomen sortita est tam á benedictione Dei in Israelem quàm ab Israelis ad Deum Benedicentem reciprocâ benedictione, usque et usque ascendente.

Sed fortè dicat aliquis de statu Reipub. quod libris saepe voluminosis appingi et subscribi assolet, multa desiderantur vel non-nulla desiderantur.

Hoc liberè profitemur neque tamen despondemus animos; sumus adhuc in viâ et exules à patria; sed quae suppetant nobis volumina pervolvamus, quae praesentia sunt animo laeto amplectamur.

sed quia multa desiderantur, multa importunè et ardenter [a] vobis, efflagitamus, et á Deo desideramus. Magnum est et memorabile nomen et au[re]is literis insculpendum semper Nomen omnipotentis foedere et pactione se obstringentis, nomen inquam ⟨Hebrew: Shaddi⟩ quod 70 Interpretes reddiderunt ἱκανός et παντοκράτωρ, quid tandem desit illis bonis quibus Deu[s] ἱκανός, aut quid tandem mali iis accidat quibu[s] Deus est παντοκράτωρ aut παντοδυνάστης, hu[c] si cursum corripiamus tanquam ad unicu⟨m⟩ asylum habemus validam consolationem et fieri no[n] potest ut Deus mentiatur. Hic si anchoram spei figamus intra velum, saevientibus et fe[r]ventibus procellis in portu navigabimus. Neq[ue] nos terrebit ut μορμολυκεῖα pueros mise[rri]ma praesentis seculi facies; cum singulae perio[di] rerum, sicut annorum habeant itidem solstitia bina; vidimus non ita pridem solem culmina[n]tem et quasi in quadrijugo curru gloriosè triumphantem, mox á solstitio aestivo declinantem subito et vergentem ad inferiorem circulu[m] videbimus prope diem, ut verisimile est in Tropico Capricorni in maximâ declinatione, quod Bruma Nivale⟨m⟩ interiore diem gyro trahit horrida cano gelu:

Let us say with the royal psalmist, Hear, gentle people, and rejoice together, magnify Jehovah with us and let us exalt his name together, for he has not only snatched the woman dwelling in the wilderness from the jaws of the great red dragon, and wondrously preserved the well built house from the flood, lest it should have been carried away of the flood, but he has also supplied wings and wind and also furnished many midwives and helping attendant hands. He, he has made this peace for us and has appointed salvation for walls and bulwarks.

Oh, if all the saints joined together were strong enough to understand and to comprehend and with proper weights to weigh the generous measure of divine clemency.

Oh, if it were said of Mount Sion that it had sunk down and subsided into the valley, not the valley of tears, but the valley of Berachah which was allotted that name as much from the blessing of God upon Israel as from Israel's praise to God with reverberating blessing ever and ever ascending.

But by chance someone might say concerning the state of the Republic what is often accustomed to be written and asserted in voluminous books: that many things are desired or that some things are desired.

We freely confess this; nevertheless we do not lose courage. We are as yet on the road and exiles from the homeland; but what books are available to us let us thoroughly consider and those which are present let us embrace with a joyful soul.

But because many things are needed, we troublesomely and ardently request many things from you and desire much from God. Great and memorable is the name, and fit to be carved in golden letters forever is the name of the omnipotent binding himself by treaty and covenant. I mean the name Shaddai [sufficient], which the seventy interpreters render ἱκανός [sufficient] and παντοκράτωρ [all-powerful]. What, in the end, could be lacking to those good men for whom God is sufficient, or what evil, in the end, could befall them for whom God is all-powerful or ruler of all. If we steer our course hither, as if to our only refuge, we have a strong comfort, and it cannot happen that God should lie. Here, if we fix the anchor of hope within the veil, we will sail into port from cruel and raging tempests. Nor will the miserable appearance of the present time terrify us as a goblin terrifies children. For the individual cycles of things have two solstices, just as the years have two solstices. We have seen, not so long ago, the sun rising as if in a four-horse chariot, gloriously triumphant. But soon we will see it suddenly declining from the summer solstice and turning to the smaller circle as it nears the day, as is probable in the greatest decline in the tropic of Capricorn because the winter solstice, bristling with hoar frost, draws a cold day into a narrower circle. Then slowly, without being perceived, the sun returns from

tum sensim sine sensu redit infimus ab hyperno solstitio sol in apertiorem lucendi campum: sic videre est in periodis regnorum et ecclesiarum, vidimus religionem quae per tot annorum centurias sepulta magna ex parte et obruta jacuerat, ex alto lethaeoque somno superstitionis evigilantem et rediviva⟨m⟩ vidimus inquam ingens et stupendum incrementum lucis in novâ παλι[γγ]ενεσίᾳ reformationis, datis quasi in dotem Religionis literis universis. sed solstitium ae[sti]vum praetervecti sumus, hinc fluere et multum retrò sublapsa referri res christi visa, et praeceps ad hybernum solstitium festinat, mundo qui praebet lumina Titan: hinc dies est contractior. Sed pater luminum οὐκ ἔχει παραλλαγήν οὔτε τροπῆς ἀποσκίασμα. Altissima lux nullam patitur parallaxin et qui solus immutabilis suum illud, semper idem, in aeternu⟨m⟩ tenet: ne umbraculum quidem τροπικορu⟨m⟩ aut variationum patitur: licet omnia loco mota huc et illuc transferantur et in cor maris p[r]ae[ci]pitentur. Praeterea jam quasi in crepi[d]ine novi seculi positi sumus, nova lucis αὐγάσματα et incrementa exspectamus, et certè ἀποκαραδοκοῦντες, estq⟨ue⟩ non vespertinum sed matutinum crepusculum, cujus in ipso pene sumus caliginoso articulo, quod fiere amat breve nigricat horrore tenebrarum plusquam cimmeriarum; sed erit honore lucis laetissimum, mox orituri solis aeterni prodromum.

Adhuc sacra capita coelum volvitur;
Non omnium dierum sol occidit.
Durate igitur et rebus vosmet servate secundis.
Et Dicet Ecclesia Christi (date verbo veniam) vasallis Antichristi; ut vitis in Anthologia capro,

κῆν με φ[άγ]ῃς ἐπὶ ῥίζαν ἔτι καρποφορήσω
ὅσσον ἐπισ[πεῖσ]αι σοι τράγε θνομένῳ

i.e. Rode cape[r][v]item tamen hin[c] cu⟨m⟩ stabis ad aras
In tua quo[d] spargi cornua possit erit.

Bono animo esto, dixit Gubernatori meticuloso imperator Magnanimus, intempesto coelo mare procellosum trajecturus, bono animo esto Caesarem vehis et fortunam Caesaris imò Christum vehitis Magnanimi Naucleres, Christum, inquam, cui ventus et m[are] auscultant, Christum qui pro Israele perennes excubias agit suavissimum est illu[d] quod in proverbii consuetudine venit: fluctus insurgunt, potest navicula jactari, sed quia Christus ad clavum sedit, et oratore⟨m⟩ agit, non potest submergi; infracto igitu[r] animo estote Christophori Remiges, circ[um]spicite pericula curiosi, sed suspicite praesidia fideles et magnanimi. Eadem manu[s] quae coelum fecit, et terram sustentat Beli Mah, super non aliquid, ecclesiam fecit omnipotens suam.

below, from the winter solstice, into a broader field of light. The same thing can be seen in the cycles of kingdoms and churches. We have seen religion, which for so many centuries lay for the most part buried and hidden, awakened and revived from the sleep and dream of superstition. We have seen, I say, a great and stupendous increase of light in the new regeneration of reformation, universal learning having been granted as if for a dowry of religion. From this point the kingdom of Christ, the Titan who provides light for the world, has seemed to flow away and to be borne far backwards, and it hastens headlong to the winter solstice. From here the day becomes shorter. But the father of lights has no variableness nor shadow of turning. The highest light suffers no change, and he who is alone immutable holds his own always the same forever. Nor, indeed, does he suffer a small shadow of turns and variations, although all things moved hither and thither are transferred from their place and are ordered into the heart of the sea. Furthermore, now, as if we have been placed at the brink of a new age, we expect a new brilliance and increase of light, and surely we are eagerly awaiting it. And it is not an evening but a morning light, to the darkest point of which we have almost come and which loves to be short and grows black with the horrors of shadows more than the shadows of the Cimmerians; but it will be most joyful with the glory of light, as a herald of the soon to arise eternal sun.

Up to this point the heaven turns the celestial bodies. The sun of all days does not set. Endure, therefore, and save yourselves for better things. And the Church of Christ will say to the vassals (forgive the word) of the Antichrist, as the vine in the Anthology said to the goat:

Even though you devour me to the root, yet I will bear fruit,
So much as to pour over you, goat, while being sacrificed.

[translation of Latin version:

Gnaw, goat, the vine, nevertheless, when you stand here at the altar,
There will be that which can be poured over your horns.]

Be of good cheer, the magnanimous commander, about to cross the sea which was stormy because of the inclement sky, said to the fearful steerman. Be of good cheer, for you carry Caesar and the fortune of Caesar. You, on the other hand, magnanimous ship-masters, carry Christ; Christ, I say, whom the wind and sea obey; Christ, who keeps constant watch for Israel. Most soothing is that which comes in the words of the proverb: the waves rise, the boat can be tossed about, but because Christ sits at the helm and guides it with his voice, it cannot be sunk. Be, therefore, of unbroken spirit, Christ-bearing oarsmen, carefully guard against perils, but faithfully and courageously suspect defences. The same all-pow-

Ridete circumlatrantes impetu fracto gubernaculum vestrum vortices, et serpente[s] abdito capite calcaneu⟨m⟩ vestrum mordentes.

Sed quo feror? oratio forte longius provecta est quam res et ratio proposita postulat. Compendio verborum brevissimo reliqua amplectar in quibus de re nostra pauca dicturus sum: quia Dixit nobis Dominus, ne quaeratis vobis grandia; ecce inducam malmu⟨m⟩ &c. Nolite quaeso, res magnas aut novas in novo orbe exspectare, sive de rebus publicis, sive de Academiâ verba faciam; dicam de utrâque liberè. CALAMITAS NOSTRA MAGNUS EST, nolite ungues [ro]dere aut caput rodere superciliosi [g]ramatiscastri, repeto, non est lapsus lingu[ae]: CALAMITAS NOSTRA MAGNUS EST, dictum olim de pompeio plaudente populo Romano tam eleganti soloecismo: dico consimiliter Faelicitas nostra minutulus est perpusillus, nam pauperes evangelizantur, et cantat vacuus coram latrone viator.

Sed neq⟨ue⟩ omnia exspectate nova, habemus multa nomina urbium et oppidorum veteris Angliae, sed nomina tantum; et vitioru⟨m⟩ nomina non pauca, utinam tantum nomina; sed vereor ne quod quorundam sermone jactatu⟨m⟩ est pro comperto á vobis habeatur, ut dicatis de novo orbe quod sit mundus alter et idem; alter et ex diametro appositus si intervallum spectetur, idem si mores habitumq⟨ue⟩ peregrinum consideretis: Academiam quod spectat, si magna aut nova pollicemur, sanè exspectationi non respondebimus. Celebre est illud Ciceronianu⟨m⟩ Honos alit artes, at è contrà ὅπου οὔτε κτῆσις οὔτε τέχνη. Haud facilè emergunt quorum virtutibus obstat—res angusta domi:

Sunt Maecenates, non deerunt Flacce Marones
Virgilumq⟨ue⟩ tibi vel tua rura dabunt.

Hactenus spes nos aluit, sed spe non saginatur venter, Magister artis ingeniiq⟨ue⟩ largitur rex ut [largia]tur poeta.

Neque nova expectetis licet Athenienses simus, et ut est humana natura sumus novitatis avidi[.] antiquitas, libros, quibus operam impendimus, solet commendare, et lacera si spectetis aedificia, et si quandoq⟨ue⟩ vestimenta, Gabeonitas, nos esse existimabitis; non est novum quod unà

erful hand which made heaven and sustains the earth Beli Mah, over nothing, made his own church.

Laugh at the whirlpools roaring around your helm with broken force and at the serpents biting your heel with hidden head.

But whither have I been carried? My speech, by chance, has been borne further than the subject and plan set before me demands. I will embrace the few remaining things I have to say about the matter at hand with the briefest of words: because the Lord said to us, Do not seek great things for yourself, for behold I will bring evil upon all flesh, etc. Do not, I beg, expect great or new things in the new world, whether I speak about the republic or about the Academy; I will speak of either freely. CALAMITAS NOSTRA MAGNUS EST.[2] [The great man is our disaster.] Do not bite your nails or scratch your heads, you supercilious grammarians. I repeat (it is not a slip of the tongue), CALAMITAS NOSTRA MAGNUS EST. This was once said of Pompey, with the Roman people applauding such an elegant solecism. Similarly, I say, *Felicitas Nostra minutulus est perpusillus.* [Our happiness is the small and insignificant man.] For the gospel is preached to the poor, and the empty-handed traveller sings in the face of a thief.

But do not expect all new things. We have many names of cities and towns of old England, but only the names. We also have not a few names of vices; would that they were only names. But I fear that what has been common talk may be regarded by you as ascertained fact, so that you will say of the new world that it is *mundus alter et idem* [another world and the same]. It is other and diametrically opposed if the distance between them is considered; it is the same if you consider the customs and dress of the foreigners. With regard to the Academy, if we promise new or great things we will not answer fully to expectation. That saying of Cicero, Honor nourishes the arts, is well known. But on the other hand, Where there is no profit there is no art. It is difficult for those to rise up, whose virtues are cramped by narrow means at home:

There is many a Maecenas, many a Maro, Flaccus,
  will not be lacking, even your fields will give you a Virgil.

Up to this point hope has nourished us, but the belly, the master of art and genius, is not fattened by hope. The king is generous, so that the poet may be generous.

Nor should you expect new things, even though we may be Athenians, and, as is human nature, we are eager for novelty. Antiquity usually commends books, to which we apply our labor. If you see dilapidated buildings and sometimes torn clothes, you will judge us to be Gibeonites. It is not new that we—as I hope, along with you—consider impor-

vobiscum, ut spero, magni facimus, et omnibus aliis facile praeponimus, novum nempe Testamentum et Novu⟨m⟩ Cor.

Sed ut summam rationu⟨m⟩ vobis exhibeamus de candidatis bonaru⟨m⟩ artium in hisce comitiis: Abortum fecit mater Academia in pa[r]tu magistroru⟨m⟩, neque in lucem protulit magistros hujus anni; aut quod suspicor, p[as]tores doctores rurales per saltum inaugurati magisterium fastidiosè praetereun[t] et nullo in numero habent, ne sint retrogradi, et in inferiorem conditionem dilabantur, porro ἀδάπανον et εὔωνον σοφ[ί]αν (ut scité vocat Plutarchus) frugi sapientiae adolescentes praeferunt; itaq⟨ue⟩ calidè se subduxerunt, quod ad primi gradus candidatos spectat, sex vobis obtulimus, ad numer⟨um⟩ Hydriarum aquâ repletaru⟨m⟩ in nuptiis canae Galilaeae, de quibus spei non nihil affulsit, fore ut virtute Christi mirificâ, vinum optimum et exhilarans aliquando exhauriendum esse.

Depromamus si placet et desistemus, vos vero viri amplissimi qui a[d] [r]em literariam animu⟨m⟩ habetis propens[um] ac benevolu⟨m⟩ estote propitii interpretes pro candore et clementiâ vestrâ, quale quale fuerit boni consulatis.

tant, and easily prefer to all other things, the New Testament and a new heart.

But now we should show to you the sum of our reckonings concerning the candidates of the good arts in this assembly: Mother Academy has had a miscarriage in giving birth to the Masters, and she has not brought forth into the light any Masters of this year; or what I suspect, these learned country shepherds, having been introduced to the Master's grove, disdainfully pass it by and hold it of no account, that they should be moving backwards and slipping into an inferior condition; moreover, the youths prefer the inexpensive and easy wisdom (as Plutarch wisely calls it), to the proper wisdom; therefore they have quickly withdrawn themselves. With regard to the candidates of the first level, we have offered you six, the same as the number of jars filled with water at the wedding at Cana in Galilee from which some hope shines, that someday there will be, by the wonderful virtue of Christ, the best and most refreshing wine to be taken out.

Let us test it whether it is agreeable, and let us put it away. You generous gentlemen, who are well disposed and favorable to literature, be the propitious judges with your frankness and moderation, and advise us as to the quality it will someday have.

TEXT
From George Lyman Kittredge's edition in the *Transactions of the Colonial Society of Massachusetts*, 28 (1930-33), 1–24. I have retained Kittredge's text, but I have expanded abbreviations ⟨in brackets⟩ and have silently incorporated his corrections of the Greek.

COMMENTARY
1. aviis, wanderings; or arvis, fields.
2. In this phrase, at first reading, the author seems to be modifying the feminine noun *Calamitas* with the masculine adjective *magnus*. In fact the adjective *magnus* is a substantive, the great man, and is predicate nominative.

A List of Works Consulted

Primary Sources

MANUSCRIPTS
The Commonplace Book of Ebenezer Parkman (Bound MS, Massachusetts Historical Society)
The Commonplace Book of John Leverett, II (Bound MS, Massachusetts Historical Society)
The Commonplace Book of Samuel Sewall (Bound MS, New-York Historical Society)
Edward Tompson Manuscript, "elegies of the Tompson family" (Fragment MS, Massachusetts Historical Society)
Ezra Stiles Miscellanies, 1756–1762 (Bound MS, Yale University Library)
Joseph Tompson Journal (Bound MS, Houghton Library, Harvard University)
Massachusetts Archives (Bound MS, Massachusetts State House, Boston)
Massachusetts Historical Society Photostats (MSS, Massachusetts Historical Society)
Prince Collection, Mather Papers (Bound MSS, Boston Public Library)
The Records of Quincy (Braintree), Massachusetts (MS, Quincy Historical Society)
"The Reverend man of God Mr. Peter Hubbard" (MS, Essex Institute, Salem, Mass.)
Sarah Tompson Journal (Bound MS, Connecticut Historical Society)
Suffolk Deeds (Bound MSS, Suffolk County Court House, Boston)
Winthrop Deeds (MSS, Massachusetts Historical Society)
Winthrop Papers (MSS, Massachusetts Historical Society)

PRINTED SOURCES
Hubbard, William. *A Narrative of the Troubles with the Indians in New England.* Boston, 1677.
———. *The Present state of New England.* London, 1677.
Kittredge, George Lyman. "A Latin Salutatory Oration of 1662." *Publications of the Colonial Society of Massachusetts: Transactions*, 28 (1930–33), 1–24.
Mather, Cotton. *Magnalia Christi Americana.* London, 1702.
Tompson, Benjamin. "A FUNERAL TRIBUTE *To the Honourable Dust of that most Charitable* Christian, *Unbiassed* Politician, And *unimitable* Pyrotechnist John Winthrope esq: . . . " Broadside, Boston, 1676. Massachusetts Historical Society.
———. "The Grammarians Funeral OR, An ELEGY composed upon the Death

of Mr. *John Woodmancy*, formerly a School-Master in Boston: But now Published upon the DEATH of the Venerable Mr. Ezekiel Chevers, . . . " Broadside, Boston, 1708. Massachusetts Historical Society.

―――. "A Neighbour's TEARS Sprinkled on the Dust of the Amiable Virgin, Mrs. Rebekah Sewall, . . . " Broadside, Boston, 1710. Massachusetts Historical Society; Boston Public Library.

―――. *New Englands Crisis.* Boston, 1676. H.E. Huntington Library, San Marino, Cal.; Boston Athenaeum.

―――. *New-Englands Tears FOR HER Present Miseries.* London, 1676. John Carter Brown Library, Brown University, Providence, R.I.

―――. *Sad and Deplorable NEWS from NEW ENGLAND.* London, 1676. H.E. Huntington Library, San Marino, Cal.

Wadsworth, Benjamin. *DEATH is Certain, the TIME when Uncertain, A SERMON Occasioned by the Death of the Reverend Mr. JAMES ALLEN.* Boston, 1710. Massachusetts Historical Society.

Secondary Sources

Works marked with an * contain transcriptions or facsimiles of Tompson's poems.

Adams, Charles Francis. *Three Episodes in Massachusetts History.* 3 vols. Boston: Houghton Mifflin, 1894.

Adams, Randolph C. "William Hubbard's 'Narrative,' 1677," *Papers of the Bibliographic Society of America*, 33 (1939), 25–39.

Akers, Charles W. *Called Unto Liberty: The Life of Jonathan Mayhew.* Cambridge: Harvard University Press, 1964.

Allen, William. *An American Biographical Dictionary.* Boston: William Hyde, 1832.

The American Puritan Imagination. Ed. Sacvan Bercovitch. Cambridge: Cambridge University Press, 1974.

American Thought and Writing: The Colonial Period. Ed. Russel B. Nye and Norman Grabo. 2 vols. Boston: Houghton Mifflin, 1965.

Anon. "New England's First Fruits." Ed. Samuel Eliot Morison. *The Founding of Harvard College.* Cambridge: Harvard Univeristy Press, 1935, Appendix D.

An Anthology of American Humor. Ed. Brom Weber. New York: Crowell, 1962.

The Antinomian Controversy, 1636–38: A Documentary History. Ed. David D. Hall. Middletown, Conn.: Wesleyan University Press, 1968.

Arnold, Samuel. *DAVID serving his Generation* . . . . Cambridge, Mass.: Samuel Green, 1674.

Austin, John Osborne. *The Genealogical Dictionary of Rhode Island.* Albany, N.Y., 1887; rpt. Baltimore: Genealogical Publishing Co., 1969.

Banks, Charles Edward. *The History of Martha's Vineyard.* 3 vols. Edgartown, Mass.: Dukes County Historical Society, 1966.

Bates, Frank A., and Edward E. Jackson. "Braintree Pioneers." MS, New England Historical and Genealogical Society, Boston, date unknown.

Bates, Samuel A. *The Early Schools of Braintree.* South Braintree, Mass.: Frank A. Bates, 1899.

―――. *Records of the Town of Braintree: 1640 to 1793.* Randolph, Mass.: Daniel H. Huxford, printer, 1886.

Baylies, Frances. *An Historical Memoir of the Colony of New Plymouth.* 2 vols. Boston: Wiggin and Lunt, 1866.

*Benjamin Tompson . . . His Poems. Ed. Howard Judson Hall. Boston: Houghton Mifflin, 1924.

Bercovitch, Sacvan. *The Puritan Origins of the American Self.* New Haven: Yale University Press, 1975.

————"New England Epic: Cotton Mather's *Magnalia Christi Americana.*" *English Literary History*, 33 (1966), 337–350.

Black, Robert C. *The Younger John Winthrop.* New York: Columbia University Press, 1966.

Bornstein, Diane. "Captain Perse & his coragios Company." *Proceedings of the American Antiquarian Society, 83 (1973)*, 67–102.

Bradford, William. *Of Plymouth Plantation, 1620–1647.* Ed. Samuel Eliot Morison. New York: Alfred A. Knopf, 1976.

————.*Of Plimouth Plantation (1620–1647). The Literature of America: The Colonial Period.* Ed. Larzer Ziff. New York: McGraw-Hill, 1970.

The "Chappel of Ease" and Church of Statesman. Ed. D.M. Wilson. Cambridge, Mass.: John Wilson and Son, 1890.

Cherry, C. Conrad. "New England as Symbol: Ambiguity in the Puritan Vision." *Soundings: An Interdisciplinary Journal*, 58 (1975), 348–362.

*The Club of Odd Volumes. Boston: University Press; Cambridge, Mass.: John Wilson and Son, 1894.

Collections of the Massachusetts Historical Society. 4th ser., 2 (1854), 228–233.

————. 4th ser., 8 (1868), 635.

————. 5th ser., 5 (1878), xxvii.

————. 5th ser., 6 (1879), 285.

*Colonial American Poetry. Ed. Kenneth Silverman. New York: Hafner Publishing Co., 1968.

*Colonial American Writing. Ed. Roy Harvey Pearce. 2nd ed. New York: Holt, Rinehart, and Winston, 1969.

*Connecticut Historical Society Bulletin, 36 (July 1971), 72–76.

Cotton, John. *The Way of Congregational Churches Cleared.* London, 1648.

Cusanus, Cardinal Nicolaus. *The Idiot in Four Books.* 1543; rpt. London, 1650.

Danforth, Samuel. "now i am past ill." Joseph Tompson Journal.

The Diary of Cotton Mather D.D., F.R.S. for the Year 1712. Ed. William R. Manierre II. Charlottesville: University Press of Virginia, 1964.

The Diary of Samuel Sewall, 1674–1729. Ed. M. Halsey Thomas. 2 vols. New York: Farrar, Straus and Giroux, 1973.

Dictionary of American Biography. Ed. Dumas Malone. New York: Scribners, 1928–37.

Dictionary of National Biography. Ed. Sir Leslie Stephen and Sir Sidney Lee. 22 vols. London: Oxford University Press, 1917.

Discoveries and Reconsiderations: Essays on Early American Literature and Aesthetics, Presented to Harold Jantz. Ed. Calvin Israel. Albany: State University of New York Press, 1976.

Duyckinck, Evert A., and George L. Duyckinck. *Cyclopaedia Of American Literature: Embracing Personal and Critical Notices Of Authors. And Selections From Their Writings.* 2 vols. New York: Charles Scribner, 1855.

Eckstein, Neil T. "The Pastoral and the Primitive in Benjamin Tompson's 'Address to Lord Bellamont,'" *Early American Literature*, 8 (Feb. 1973), 111–116.

"Eirenaeus Philoponos Philalethes, *The Marrow of Alchemy* (London: 1654–55)." Ed. Cheryl Z. Oreovicz. Thesis. Pennsylvania State University, 1972.

Elliott, Emory. *Power and the Pulpit in Puritan New England.* Princeton, N.J.: Princeton University Press, 1975.

Extracts of the Itineraries and other Miscellanies of Ezra Stiles, D.D., 1755–1794, with a Selection from His Correspondence. Ed. Franklin Bowditch Dexter. New Haven: Yale University Press, 1916.

Feidelson, Charles, Jr. *Symbolism and American Literature.* Chicago: University of Chicago Press, 1952.

Felt, Joseph B. *The Ecclesiastical History of New England: Comprising Not Only Religious, But Also Moral, And Other Relations.* 2 vols. Boston: Congregational Library Association and The Congregational Board of Publications, 1855.

*Forbes, Harriette M. *Gravestones of Early New England.* Boston: Houghton Mifflin, 1927.

Foster, John. *Almanack.* Boston, 1679.

Fussell, Edwin S. "Benjamin Tompson, Public Poet." *New England Quarterly,* 26 (1953), 494–511.

Goddard, Ives. "Some Early Examples of American Indian Pidgin English from New England," *International Journal of American Linguistics,* 43 (1977), 37–41.

*Green, Samuel A. *Ten Fac-simile Reproductions . . . .* Boston, 1902.

Griswold, Rufus Wilmot. *The Poets and Poetry of America, To the Middle of the Nineteenth Century.* Philadelphia: A. Hart, Late Carey & Hart, 1852.

Handkerchiefs from Paul. Ed. Kenneth B. Murdock. Cambridge: Harvard University Press, 1927.

Hansen, Chadwick. *Witchcraft at Salem.* New York: Braziller, 1969.

Hayden, Anna. Untitled elegy on Benjamin Tompson. Joseph Tompson Journal.

The Hermetic and Alchemical Writings of Aureolus Philippus Theophrastus Bombast, of Hohenheim, Called Paracelsus The Great. Ed. Arthur Edward Waite. 2 vols. New York: University Books, 1967.

Hooker, Thomas. *A Survey of the Summe of Church-Discipline.* London, 1649.

Hubbard, William. *History of New England.* 1680; rpt. Boston: Little, Brown and Co., 1848.

———. *A Narrative of the Troubles with the Indians in New England.* Boston, 1677.

*Jantz, Harold. *The First Century of New England Verse.* Worcester, Mass.: American Antiquarian Society, 1943–44; rpt. New York: Russell and Russell, 1962.

Johnson, Edward. *Wonder-Working Providence of Sion's Savour in New England.* 1654; rpt. New York: Scholars' Facsimiles & Reprints, 1974.

Kettell, Samuel. *Specimens of American Poetry, with Critical and Biographical Notices.* 3 vols. Boston: S.G. Goodrich and Co., 1829.

Lechford, Thomas. *Plain Dealing or News From New England.* Ed. J. Hammond Trumbull. Boston: J.K. Wiggin and William Parsons Lunt, 1867.

Lincoln, Waldo. "The Lincolns of New England." MS, 1926, Worcester, Mass., in the possession of the New England Historical and Genealogical Society, Boston.

The Literature of America: The Colonial Period. Ed. Larzer Ziff. New York: McGraw-Hill, 1970.

Lowance, Mason I., Jr. *Increase Mather.* New York: Twayne Publishers, 1974.

Ludwig, Allan I. *Graven Images: New England Stonecarving and Its Symbols, 1650–1815*. Middletown, Conn: Wesleyan University Press, 1966.

Magnalia Christi Americana. Ed. Kenneth B. Murdock. vol. 1. Cambridge, Harvard University Press, 1977.

Mather, Cotton. *Dr. Mather's Student and Preacher*. London, 1789.

———. *Johannes in Eremo: Memoirs*. Boston, 1695.

———. *Magnalia Christi Americana*. London, 1702.

Mather, Richard. *A Farewel-Exhortation To the Church and People of Dorchester in New-England*. London, 1657.

———, and William Tompson. *An Heart-Melting Exhortation, Together with a Cordiall Consolation, Presented in a Letter from New-England, to their dear Countreymen of Lancashire; Which may as well concern all others in these suffering times*. London: J. Rothwell, 1650.

———. *A Modest and Brotherly Answer to Mr. Charles Herle his Book, against the Independency of Churches . . . .* London: Henry Overton, 1644.

Mather, Samuel. *The Life of the Very Reverend and Learned Cotton Mather*. Boston, 1729.

The Memorial History of Boston, Including Suffolk County, Massachusetts: 1630– 1880. Ed. Justin Winsor. 4 vols. Boston: Ticknor and Co., 1880.

Middlekauf, Robert. *The Mathers: Three Generations of Puritan Intellectuals, 1596–1728*. New York: Oxford University Press, 1971.

Miller, Perry. *Errand Into The Wilderness*. New York: Harper and Row, 1959.

———. *The New England Mind: From Colony to Province*. Cambridge: Harvard University Press, 1962.

———. *The New England Mind: The Seventeenth Century*. 1939; rpt. Cambridge: Harvard University Press, 1963.

Morgan, Edmund S. *The Puritan Dilemma: The Story of John Winthrop*. Boston: Little, Brown and Co., 1958.

Morison, Samuel Eliot. *Builders of the Bay Colony*. 2nd ed. Boston: Houghton Mifflin, 1958.

———. *The Founding of Harvard College*. Cambridge: Harvard University Press, 1935.

———. *Harvard College in the Seventeenth Century*. 2 vols. Cambridge: Harvard University Press, 1936.

Morton, Nathaniel. *New Englands Memorial*. 1669; rpt. Boston: The Club of Odd Volumes, 1903.

Morton, Thomas. *New English Canaan*. Amsterdam, 1637.

Murdock, Kenneth B. *Increase Mather: The Foremost American Puritan*. Cambridge: Harvard University Press, 1925.

The New England Historical and Genealogical Register, 4 (1850), 121–135.

*———. 9 (1855), 151.

———. 13 (1859), 12.

*———. 14 (1860), 141–142.

———. 15 (1861), 112–118.

———. 17 (1863), 156.

———. 23 (1869), 437.

———. 26 (1872), 158.

Norton, John. *The Orthodox Evangelist*. Boston, 1654.

Old South Leaflets. Gen. Ser. Boston: D.C. Heath, n.d., leaflet 177.

Pattee, William S. *A History of Old Braintree and Quincy, with a sketch of Randolph and Holbrook*. Quincy, Mass.: Green and Prescott, 1878.

Pearce, Roy Harvey. *The Continuity of American Poetry.* Princeton, N.J.: Princeton University Press, 1961.

Pope, Robert G. *The Half-Way Covenant.* Princeton, N.J.: Princeton University Press, 1969.

Proceedings of the American Antiquarian Society, 83 (1973), 67–102.

Proceedings of the Massachusetts Historical Society, *2nd ser., 5 (1889–1890), 2–4.

*————. 2nd ser., 8 (1892–1893), 387–389.

*————. 2nd ser., 10 (1895–1896), 275–278; 281–283; 369–371.

————. 3rd ser., 57 (1923–1924), 68.

Publications of the Colonial Society of Massachusetts, Collections, 30 (1933), 904–909.

————. 31 (1935), 82–84; 266; 240.

Publications of the Colonial Society of Massachusetts, Transactions, 27 (1927–1930), 130–156.

————. 28 (1930–1933), 1–24.

————. 32 (1933–1937), 184–185.

————. 34 (1937–1942), 528.

The Puritans: A Sourcebook of Their Writings. Ed. Perry Miller and Thomas H. Johnson. 2 vols. New York: Harper and Row, 1963.

The Registers of St. Martin Outwich, London. Ed. W. Bruce Bannerman. London: Publications of the Harleian Society, 1905.

Report of the Boston Records Commissioners. 39 vols. Boston: Rockwell and Churchill, City Printers, 1876–1909.

Rutman, Darrett B. *Winthrop's Boston.* Chapel Hill: University of North Carolina Press, 1965.

Sands, Alyce E. "John Saffin: Seventeenth Century American Citizen and Poet." Thesis. Pennsylvania State University, 1965.

Savage, James. *A Genealogical Dictionary of the First Settlers of New England.* 4 vols. Boston: Little, Brown and Co., 1862.

Seventeenth-Century American Poetry. Ed. Harrison T. Meserole. New York: Doubleday, 1968.

Sibley, John Langdon. *Biographical Sketches of the Graduates of Harvard University.* 17 vols. Cambridge: Harvard University Press, 1873–1881.

Sprague, Waldo C. "Genealogy of the Families of Braintree, Mass. 1640–1850, including the modern towns of Randolph, and Holbrook and the city of Quincy after their separation from Braintree, 1792–93." MS, Quincy Historical Society, Quincy, Mass.

Thompson, Ralph Newell. "Some Descendants of Rev. William Tompson First Pastor of Braintree, Mass." MS, Quincy Historical Society, Quincy, Mass.

Torrey, Clarence Almon. "New England Marriages Prior to 1700." MS, bound 1962, New England Historical and Genealogical Society, Boston, vol. 11.

Torrey, Samuel. "Upon the Death of Mr. William Tompson . . . ." Joseph Tompson Journal.

Transactions and Collections of the American Antiquarian Society, 3 (1857), 200.

Transactions of the Colonial Society of Massachusetts, 28 (1930–33), 1–24.

Tyler, Moses Coit. *A History of American Literature: 1607–1765.* 2 vols. 1878; rpt. Ithaca, N.Y.: Cornell University Press, 1949.

Ward, Nathaniel. *The Simple Cobler of Aggawam.* London, 1644.

Weis, Frederick Lewis. *The Boston Transcript,* May 1932.

————. *The Colonial Clergy and the Colonial Churches of New England.* Lancaster, Mass.: Society of the Descendants of the Colonial Clergy, 1936.

Wendell, Barrett. *Cotton Mather: The Puritan Priest.* 1891; rpt. New York: Harcourt, Brace and World, 1965.

Whiting, Samuel. *Abraham's Humble Intercession.* Cambridge, Mass., 1666.

——. *A Discourse on the Last Judgment.* Cambridge, Mass., 1664.

Williams, Roger. *A Key Into the Language of America.* London, 1643.

Wilson, John. "Anagram . . . upon the Death of Mrs. Abigail Tompson . . . . " Joseph Tompson Journal.

——. "most holy paule mine." Joseph Tompson Journal.

Winslow, Edward. *Good News from New England: or a true Relation.* London, 1624.

*Winslow, Ola. *American Broadside Verse.* London: Oxford University Press, 1930.

Winthrop, John. *The History of New England, 1630–1649.* Ed. J.K. Hosmer. 2 vols. 1908; rpt. New York: Barnes and Noble, 1959.

——. "A Moddell of Christian Charity." Delivered in Boston, 1630.

Winthrop Papers. Ed. Allyn Bailey Forbes. 5 vols. Boston: Merrymount Press, 1955.

Ziff, Larzer. *Puritanism in America: New Culture in a New World.* New York: Viking Press, 1973.

Index

Morton, Thomas, 5, 6, *53*
Mount Wollaston, 6–7
Moxon, James, 123, 125 n9
Moxon, Joseph, 123, 125 n9
Mystic, Conn., 10
mythology, ix, 16, 38, 39, 44, 50, 116

Newbury, Mass., 57
New Englands Crisis, ix, 19, 25, 36, 37, 45, 46, 49, 50–52, 57–59, 61–63, 67, 115, 116, 121 n5
New-Englands Tears, 25, 41, 44, 51, 59, 67, 99, 102 n25, 103–118, 121 n1, 122 n11
New Haven, Conn., 80 n2, 116 n2, 178 n4
Newman, Noah, 49
Newman, Samuel, 49, 97, 102 n27, 108
New York, 53, 160 n1
Niles, Samuel, 196
Norton, John, 20, 178 n4, 190 n8
Noyes, James, 18
Noyes, Nicholas, 58, 62, 188

Oakes, Urian, 53, 57, 65, 191–192

Paracelsus, 116 n3, 117 n5, 117 n12, 117 n14, 122 n9
Parkman, Ebenezer, 159
Pawkatuck, Rhode Island, 10
Payson, Prudence, 28, 30
Payson, Samuel, 29
Philalethes, Eirenaeus Philoponos, 76 n9
Phipps, Samuel, 24
Phips, Governor, 57
Pierce, John, 65, 146
Plymouth Colony, 5
Providence, doctrine of, 39, 40, 48, 52
Providence, Rhode Island, 96, 102 n26, 103, 106
Purchase, Samuel, 123, 124 n3

Quakers, 46, 74, 108, 185 n3, 189 n1
Quincy, Edmund, 6, 188

Ramus, Petrus, 40
Randolph, Edward, 136 n5
Rationalism, 37
Reforming Synod, 16
Roxbury, Mass., 11, 17, 28–30, 118 n30, 182

Saffin, John, 62, 136 n6
Seekonk (Seaconk or Rehoboth), Mass., 96, 97, 102 n27, 103, 107, 108, 115
Sewall, Rebekah (variant spellings), 41, 42, 47, 59, 65, 67, 168–175

Sewall, Samuel, 24, 25, 148, 150, 169, 174, 191
Sewall, Samuel, Jr., 30, 42, 57, 58, 169
Simons, Samuel, 26
Shepard, Edward, 146 n1
Shepard, Mr., 196
Shepard, Thomas, 190 n8
Shepard, Thomas, Jr., 192 n1
Smith, John, 123, 124 n3, 160 n2
Springfield, Mass., 23
Standish, Miles, 5
Stiles, Ezra, 184, 185 n2
Stoddard, Solomon, 18
Stoughton, Governor, 57
Sudbury, Mass., 103, 111
Swansea, Mass., 100 n7, 101 n10
symbolism, 38, 40

Taylor, Edward, 12, 20, 36, 37, 42, 60
Thatcher, Thomas, 136 n5, 169 n3
Thompson, Ralph Newell, 22, 69
Tompson, Abigail, 17, 18, 188
Tompson, Anna (Hayden), 21, 31–32, 60
Tompson, Anthony (and Anthony Tompson, Jr.), 178 n6
Tompson, Benjamin: (birth) 17; (adopted) 18; (education) 18–21; (oration) 19–20; (marriage) 22, 29; (preaching) 22; (mathematics) 22; (teaching) 22–24, 27–30, 56, 195; (children of) 24–25, 29–30; (medicine) 24–25, 30, 45, 50; (legal affairs) 26–29, 31; (death) 30, 41
Tompson, Edward, 30, 41, 47, 59, 65, 66, 193
Tompson, Edward, II, 41, 57, 59, 65, 66, 74, 77, 155, 182
Tompson, Elinor, 17
Tompson, Elizabeth, 42, 47, 141–143, 180
Tompson, John, 17
Tompson, Joseph, 17, 42, 57, 59, 65, 66, 77, 143, 180, 181 n1
Tompson, Mary, 21, 42, 47, 141–143, 180
Tompson, Samuel, 17, 21, 41, 47, 48, 56, 65, 66, 146, 153–156, 193
Tompson, Samuel (Harvard A.B. 1710), 57, 65, 66
Tompson, Sarah, 42, 47, 48, 57, 62, 65, 144–146, 156 n1
Tompson, Susanna Kirkland, 24, 28, 47
Tompson, William, ix, x, 1–15, 17, 21–23, 38, 41, 43, 45, 46, 66, 73–76, 77, 130 n5, 156 n2, 178 n6, 188, 190 n4